THE PINCH RUNNER MEMORANDUM

"Those who know Ōe will be delighted with this vintage grotesque realism where cosmic laughter lights up his meticulous critical engagement. Those who don't will instantly recognize the sure hand of one of the world's greatest fiction writers today."

—Masao Miyoshi,
University of California, San Diego

"A maelstrom of a novel: haunting, delirious, hypnotic and extremely funny. With devastating contemporary originality, Ōe explodes the nuclear family into bits and reassembles it into a startling new combination—the bizarre odyssey of a Japanese father and son it will be hard to forget."

—Ariel Dorfman,
Author of *Death and the Maiden*

"Ōe Kenzaburo ... maintains his reputation as one of the premier novelists of postwar Japan. ... Thanks to the talents of two gifted translators, ... we have a new and provocative version of a book many Japanese readers consider one of the author's major accomplishments. ... It is about time we knew this book, and we owe the translators real gratitude for finding the fortitude, and the requisite sensitive vocabulary, to allow the many contrasting surfaces and depths of this novel to render themselves to a new audience of English-language readers with such clarity and resonance."

—Thomas Rimer,
University of Pittsburgh

The publication of this book was partially funded by the
Ellen Bayard Weedon East Asian Studies Fund of
the University of Virginia.

Ōe Kenzaburo

THE PINCH RUNNER MEMORANDUM

Translated by
Michiko N. Wilson and **Michael K. Wilson**

An East Gate Book

M. E. Sharpe Inc.
Armonk, New York
London, England

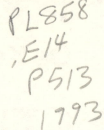

An East Gate Book

Library of Congress Cataloging-in-Publication Data

Oe, Kenzaburō, 1935–
[Pinchi rannā chōsho. English]
The pinch runner memorandum / Oe Kenzaburo; translated by
Michiko N. Wilson and Michael K. Wilson
p.   cm.
"An East gate book"
ISBN 1-56324-183-8. — ISBN 1-56324-184-6 (pbk.)
I. Title.
PL858.E14P513 1993   93-16114
895.6´35—dc20
CIP

Printed in the United States of America

The paper used in this publication meets the minimum requirements of
American National Standard for Information Sciences—
Permanence of Paper for Printed Library Materials,
ANSI Z 39.48-1984.

MV (c) 10   9   8   7   6   5   4   3   2   1
MV (p) 10   9   8   7   6   5   4   3   2

This translation is for
Edie, Kenny,
Mary, Jamie,
Junko, and Michio

Contents

Introduction

Nineteen ninety-three, which started with the changing of the guard at the White House in the United States, also signaled a change for Japan which very few Japanese had foreseen even a year earlier. That summer, when the thirty-eight-year majority rule of the Liberal Democratic Party was replaced by a coalition government which promised a series of social, political, and economic reforms, one of the first things the newly elected Prime Minister Hosokawa Morihiro did was to say what no other Japanese leader, including the Emperor, had dared to say for forty-eight years: he publicly acknowledged that World War II was a "war of aggression, a mistaken war."

In his speech at the August 15 annual war memorial services, Hosokawa said: "Our condolences extend beyond our borders. Reflecting the general sense of the Japanese people, I want to express my deep condolences first of all to the people of our neighboring Asian countries, and then to war victims around the world and their survivors."[1] Speaking after the Prime Minister, Takako Doi, the first Japanese woman to hold the position of Speaker of the House, put the matter more bluntly: "We have still not reached a point of reconciliation with the Asian people who were forced into horrible sacrifices by our misdeeds."[2]

For Ōe Kenzaburo, a representative of the new postwar generation, Prime Minister Hosokawa's public acknowledgment that Japan was responsible for the Pacific War was long overdue. It also marks a signifi-

---

1. *The Washington Post*, Aug. 16, 1993, A12.
2. AP News Service, Aug. 16, 1993.

ix

cant personal vindication that brings a kind of closure to his life-long political stance. This issue of "war responsibility" has been the bone of contention underlining the critical perspective of Ōe's writings, both his fiction and his essays. As recently as 1986, in a speech he gave at "The Challenge of Third World Culture" conference at Duke University, Ōe, playing the role of the "disappointing clown," took issue with a Japanese foreign policy full of discriminatory practices toward neighboring countries, a continual frustration for him as a Japanese citizen:

> . . . Japan appeared on the international scene clearly as a Third World nation from about the time of the Meiji Restoration (1868). In her process of modernization ever since, she has been a nation blatantly hostile to her fellow Third World nations in Asia, as evidenced by her annexation of Korea and by her war of aggression against China. Her hostility toward her neighbors continues even today . . . even now, more than forty years after the end of the war, I do not think that we Japanese have done enough to compensate for what we *can* compensate for—either economically or culturally. . . . We are often aggressors toward nations of the Third World, of which we ourselves are in fact a member. The burden of that image weighs heavily on my back as I stand before you now.[3]

When Japan surrendered unconditionally to the Allied forces on August 15, 1945, Ōe was ten years old, a patriotic boy ready to die at the command of the Emperor. The spontaneous sense of elation and liberation among Japanese at the end of the war was soon replaced by uneasiness about the impending crisis of the Cold War. For the sensitive and precocious Ōe, the Occupation of Japan (1945–1952) turned out to be doubly humiliating. On the one hand, Japanese adults who made an about-face overnight on emperor worship, had betrayed the young patriot and abandoned him; on the other hand, the United States, in the name of fighting the Communist Menace, took away the freedom of speech and the spirit of tolerance and democracy given to the Japanese with such generosity at the beginning of the Occupation. Ōe could forgive neither country for the duplicity of its actions. This double sense of betrayal had an enormous impact on him as it cut deep into his own vulnerability.

In his passionate espousal of progressive issues that range from nuclear disarmament, the environment, A-bomb victims and dissident writers to minorities and the handicapped, Ōe has unleashed enormous energy and imagination in playing, through his writings, the roles of

---

3. *World Literature Today,* vol. 62, no. 3 (Summer 1988):359.

clown and novelistic gadfly. In 1963, at the age of twenty-eight, he was to find a very private voice for his socio-political belief: he became the father of a mentally handicapped baby boy, Hikari, who was born with a defective cranium. This personal tragedy precipitated a series of short stories, novellas, and novels that pursue an alternative view of the world and humankind, and in which Ōe the writer makes dramatic leaps in his experimentation with techniques drawn from French, Russian, and American literary and anthropological theories. The cumulative result of these intellectual exercises is a whole set of multi-voiced and multi-layered texts in which the reader is invited to engage, with the narrators, in a kind of emotionally and psychologically complex detective work.

The cycle of what Ōe affectionately calls the "idiot son" narratives began in 1964 and temporarily closed with the publication of *The Pinch Runner Memorandum* in 1976. Ōe found in Hikari's presence a boundless source of energy for his literary imagination, offering him the opportunity to explore, in addition to the dangers posed to the modern world by nuclear weapons, the socio-cultural implications of being on the margin, being an anomaly—a challenge he has taken to heart ever since his child's birth.

The first story of the "idiot son" cycle, "Agwhee the Sky Monster" (1964) focuses on the guilt of a young father who abandons a dying infant. In the same year, as if to counter that easy-way-out solution, Ōe wrote *A Personal Matter* (translated into English in 1968), the "happy ending" of which many Japanese critics panned as melodramatic and unrealistic. Four years later, Ōe returned to the "idiot son" theme in a short story, "Father, Where Are You Going?" Based on William Blake's poem, "The Little Boy Lost," the story reveals the conundrums of a father whose own father refused to see, hear, and speak with anyone, and whose son is unable to hear and speak because of his autism. In this extremely imaginative narrative, Ōe tackles his own sense of being lost, his quixotic struggle to come to terms with himself, his family, and the world. Here is a father caught between a desire to recapture his childhood and communicate with his father, and a desperate need to be part of his idiot son's mental and emotional world. With neither road open to him, Ōe the writer activates his imagination to create a father's fantasy that would allow him to see the past, the present and the future in one simultaneous moment—a dominant theme developed fully in *The Pinch Runner Memorandum.*

In the 1969 story, "Teach Us to Outgrow Our Madness" (translated into English in 1977), Ōe experimented further with this theme. However, the father is no longer alone in the perilous journey of growing up. This time he finds a perfect companion and ally, his double, in the character of the idiot son Mori, nicknamed Eeyore. Whenever the Ōe-like protagonist hears himself calling the boy Eeyore, the name becomes a source of reassurance which as an anxious, paranoiac father he badly needs. The Japanese pronounciation of Eeyore happens to sound like "Iiyo," meaning *Things are OK, I'm fine, Don't worry,* etc.

In 1973 the apocalyptic *The Waters Are Come in unto My Soul* again picks up the father/son duo, this time holed up in a nuclear-shelter-turned home, where the father discovers the joy of living alone with the boy, called Jin. Ōe again relies on his "muse" Hikari to create a most unforgettable character: the little innocent Jin, like Hikari, possesses an extraordinary ability to discriminate fine differences of musical notes and identify the songs of wild birds. In this work, Ōe seems to bring together all the anti-hero characters he has created in the past to let them mingle with the odd pair in a collective fight for a land of "trees and whales." It is clear that Ōe sees the fate of humankind as inextricably tied to the wholesomeness of the environment.

So it is no accident that the image of the idiot son inevitably develops from that of a simple retarded boy into a complex symbol of unspoiled nature—as well as that of a trickster, a sacrificial lamb for humankind—in *The Pinch Runner Memorandum.* Based on the metaphor of a sandlot baseball pinch runner, the novel centers around the exchange of identities of a father and a son who venture out together to confront the kingpin of the political underworld. Ōe unfolds the adventure through the complex narrative structure of the protagonist's words, which sometimes resonate and sometimes clash with the narrative voice of his ghostwriter, who initiates the tale. These two layers of the text are further enriched by a third voice, that of the idiot son Mori who speaks to his "switch*ed*over" father through the conduit of their clasped hands. Simultaneously, the reader is treated to a smorgasbord of satire, black humor, *manga*-like slapstick, Mikhail Bakhtin's grotesque realism, and various socio-political phenomena such as marginalization, factionalism, and terrorism—all served up on pots and pans *à la* François Rabelais.

Although Ōe retired his imaginary idiot son with *The Pinch Runner Memorandum,* his real life saga with Hikari continued, providing the writer's imagination with a spring that never runs dry. In 1983, Hikari turned twenty. To celebrate his birthday, Ōe penned a moving autobiographical account about the boy, *O, Rouse up, Young Men of the New Age.* The title is taken from William Blake's Prophetic Books. For the first time, Ōe felt secure enough to portray the intimate story of his delicate relationship with Hikari as it is and to show how his family copes with a handicapped child. At the end of the story, Ōe's son, whom everyone in the family affectionately calls Eeyore, is back home for a short visit from a special school. He suddenly seems to withdraw into his own world and fails to respond to invitations to engage in one of his favorite activities, eating:

> . . . I called out to him.
> ——Suppertime, Eeyore. Come on over.
> Eeyore sat still facing the record player, his massive imposing back ramrod straight, and, as if bracing himself to make a long deliberate announcement, said,
> ——**Eeyore will not come! Eeyore does not exist anymore, so Eeyore can never join you!**
> I averted my eyes, staring down at the table as my wife quietly watched me. A deep sense of loss assaulted me with such brutal force that I could not handle the situation under her intent gaze. What in the world happened? Did it actually happen, will it continue to happen? . . .
> ——Eeyore, that's not true, you are back, so Eeyore is home. His little sister spoke coaxingly, but he remained silent.
> His kid brother, who has a tendency to pause a few seconds before he knows what to say, always lagging behind his older sister, took up where she left off,
> ——Since Eeyore will be twenty this June, he probably doesn't want to be called Eeyore anymore. I think he wants to be called by his real name. Everyone at the dorm does, right?
> Once the kid brother knows his opinions can stand the test of logic, he takes action without hesitation. He immediately stood up, went over to squat next to Eeyore and spoke to him.
> ——Let's have supper, Hikari. Mom's made lots of goodies for you.
> ——**Yes, let us do so! Thank you very much!** Eeyore said in a clear, child-like voice, in obvious contrast to the cracking voice of his kid brother, while my wife and Eeyore's sister, in numb relief from the tension, suddenly let out a gale of laughter.[4]

* * *

Ōe's prolific career, launched almost four decades ago during his college days at Tokyo University, shows no sign of slowing down. In addition to the 1978 twelve-volume set of his complete works of fiction and the 1981 ten-volume set of collected critical essays, between 1978 and 1993 he published seventeen new books that include fiction as well

---

4. *Atarashii Hito yo Mezame yo* (Tokyo: Kodansha, 1983), pp. 290–92. The translation is mine.

as social and literary criticism. A recipient of virtually all the major literary prizes in Japan, he has gone on to achieve literary acclaim in Europe. In 1989 the Belgian-based Europelia Arts Festival, which chose Japan as its theme that year, awarded Ōe the prestigous Europelia literary award. He was also nominated for the 1986 Neustadt International Prize for Literature.

A Personal Matter, Ōe's first novel-length work to be translated into English (1968), winning rave reviews from British and American reviewers, has since been translated into Dutch, French, German, Norwegian, Spanish, and Swedish. Of Ōe's other major novels, *Manen-gannen no Fottoboru (The Football Game of the First Year of Manen)*, has been translated into into French, German, Polish and Russian, and English (the 1974 English version is entitled *The Silent Cry*); *M/T to Mori to Hushigi no Monogatari (The Tale of Marvel, M/T and the Forest)* into French; *Pinchi Runna Chosho (The Pinch Runner Memorandum)*, into Russian. A large number of his short stories are also available in many foreign languages. Ōe's works have been the subject of critical studies by several Japanologists in the United States.

In spite of his non-stop writing schedule, Ōe has often found time to travel and lecture in the United States, Europe, and Latin America. He has been a writer-in-residence at the Colegio de Mexico and the University of California at Berkeley. Ōe resides in Tokyo with his wife, their other children, and Hikari, a promising composer of contemporary music.

Michiko Niikuni Wilson
Charlottesville, Virginia

THE PINCH RUNNER MEMORANDUM

1

The Golden Age of Postwar Sandlot Baseball

1

You know for sure they were a Stranger's words because of your clear memory of the circumstances. Yet, you feel convinced that those same words had gushed forth straight from the deepest recesses of your soul. Assuming that words come to life only in the relationship of two human beings, there's no earthly reason why you should not insist that your own existence be the wellspring of the Stranger's words.

One day a *former* nuclear power plant engineer, a man with whom I was always at loggerheads, calculatedly adjusted the volume of his voice, just loud enough for me to hear, and said to himself,

——Nothing quite as terrifying, soul-stirring, as being picked as a pinch runner! Now there lies the "passion" of sandlot baseball. See, these children aren't rooting for the pinch runner, but he must feel as if they are. . . .

——That's it, even when nobody bothers to shout and cheer him on with *Go, Go,* I chimed in.

But it was more than that. The instant I responded to the words the *former* engineer uttered, a hot, burdensome, twisted cord, like the parent-child *bond,* but not anything as simple as empathy, connected us. To

3

be specific, we saw that we were of the same generation, give or take a year or two. We knew very little about each other save that we both had graduated from Tokyo University, he in physics, I in literature, a fact that put us on the collision course to which I referred earlier. How did we know we were contemporaries? Because he instantly understood my response to the voices *Go, Go*, because I had sensed in his words the passion of a pinch runner, that very voice of the soul. We fell silent in the glow of the late spring and took in the voices of *Go, Go, Go*, reverberating through our innards.

Almost at noon, on the field, the *children different from ours* were playing ball, their voices barely audible out of consideration for those in class in the school buildings that surrounded the playground. They were brilliant children climbing the ladder of elitism who regarded phys ed as something outside the curriculum. They would not dare express the pleasure they savored in sports, the pleasure that wells up from carnal depths. Primeval emotions: how could they possibly let loose and not suppress them? Screeching sounds suddenly burst from the classroom of *our children*. The man and I were keeping our eyes on the quiet children on the field with their undeniable intellectual agility and good reflexes, in constant fear that *our children* might start screaming at any minute.

——No choice, I had to participate in the ballgame as a pinch runner. No glove.

——Got you, I replied. In the golden age of postwar sandlot baseball there was a sharp contrast between the rage for the game and the piddling number of country children who owned a glove. We were lucky that there were altogether nine mitts in our settlement, but every single one of them was the private property of a *regular player*. Only those children who got hold of a glove on the black market won the status of a regular. With shame and embarrassment, keeping my home-made cloth glove well out of sight, I scurried around in the outfield to pick up a ball fumbled by a regular. They let me participate in practice sessions in which my only function was not to lose sight of the ball, yet another possession of a regular.

I still remember the excitement and terror I felt at a game against a visiting middle school team, and the resolution I had reached that no matter what, one must live in the real world. I even remember the way a painful shudder erupted in the hollow of my belly. And in the core of my head, *Go, Go, Go*. Besides, a game with an early lead would provide no agony for a pinch runner waiting for his chance. It would be boring as hell; victory or defeat would have no relevance to me on the bench. One run behind in the bottom half of the ninth, or in the bottom of an extra inning, the moment impregnated with crisis, that's the real game, wouldn't you say? So, in the bottom of the ninth we were losing by one run, and a regular ballplayer got a hit, the moment of passion for a pinch runner. Our coach, the Sofus' second son, recently demobilized and loafing around, in his attempt to show what he's got—he called it a theory, ha, ha—immediately put his sleight of hand into action: the installation of a pinch runner. My timely appearance. If I had been a musclebound bruiser, a master of the game, I would have been called in as a pinch hitter, so you'd think. Right? However, I was just an ordinary substitute perched on a two-seater wooden chair which I'd managed behind my teacher's back to manhandle out of a classroom. Well, at least my legs were rested. I dashed toward first base as fast as my legs would carry me, trying to prove to everyone how quick a runner I was. The guy I was about to replace was already glaring at me. Why? Because he had just barely managed to get a hit and was about to make the big time, and here I was, a slow-foot, snatching it away from him. If I failed to steal, he would rub it in for the rest of my life. You loused up my day, he would moan. Aaaah! Aaaag! But supposing it were the other way around and I stole second and scored the tying run on a hit; we would go into extra innings. For a brief period I would be a hero, and during the tenth, the regular would have to lend me his glove. That's why he gave me the dirty look. For the rest of the game I was allowed to stay on as a pinch runner. All my teammates, even the guy in a stew, roared, *Go, Go, Go*! Come on, come on, take a lead, be a man and steal! they shouted. As if the two meters between myself and the base and my watchful eye on the pitcher could hardly win me their confidence, but easily could cost it. Assailed by *Go, Go, Go*, my seething brain buzzed. The moment called for a rational assessment of the situation, my ability to run and coordinate with the pitcher's moves; however, with my head in a whirl, there was no time for such a decision. The pitcher looked crafty, and the burly-shouldered catcher was the spitting image of the boy in the photogravure *The Young Ballplayer*! Under normal circumstances, like a farm brat who regarded himself as more sophisticated than any city kid around, I would have laughed my head off at the way they put on airs. But all I could do was to let them intimidate me. Run or simply hang on? Should I or shouldn't I take a chance? With my head on fire, arms and legs petered out, the thunderous *Go, Go, Go*! urged me on. Totally terror-stricken as I was, I still had the nerve to toy with an ambition, however pathetic, a desire to succeed by stealing. . . .

Did he actually utter all those words? Nothing was as heartrending yet so exhilarating as being a pinch runner. This might have been the only thing he said. However, I can attest that the substance of his anguished soul searching for expression was as I related it. And my soul devoured it in one gulp. That was not all. We fell silent, standing in the corner of a playground whose grandeur surpassed anything we had ever seen in the postwar years, as our scorched heads broiled, embroiled in the still-smoldering traces of a quarter century past, heeding the visionary cries of *Go, Go, Go,* not quite a curse, not quite encouragement.

Besides ourselves at the moment, waiting for *our children,* were several mothers. Some of them worked in bars or cabarets and once in a while smelled of liquor even in the morning: inescapable situations that broke up their marriages and forced them into unseemly professions. As *our children* were more or less the cause of all this, we rarely started conversations, barely exchanged greetings, and with as little eye contact as possible, most of the time in total silence, whiled away the time watching the *children different from ours* on the playground.

Our children finally emerged from the classroom and marched toward us. The rule was that we parents were to wait for them on the other side of the playground. Slow tempo, in single file, *our children* advanced toward us. As they reached the end of the playground where the *children different from ours* were playing ball, they continued the march, holding their hands above their heads. They looked like a bunch of little POWs. The teacher had originally given this instruction to only two children; the child of the *former* engineer with whom I was carrying on a conversation, and my own, both of whom had the defective section of their skull covered with a piece of plastic. However, the instruction was simultaneously perceived as an order by those with Down's syndrome and cerebral palsy. *Our children* continued to plug along, big and small alike, holding their hands upon their heads. By the time they finally reached our waiting place, the *children different from ours* were through with their game and were sweeping the field with bamboo brooms. Engulfed by thick clouds of dust, *our children,* with their weak eyes half open, looking straight ahead, and straining every nerve, took small pigeon-toed steps toward us.

Name tags on their chests, indicating their addresses and telephone numbers, also identified their guardians' names; conversely, we parents relied on the children's names for identifying other parents. For example, I am Hikari-father; the *former* nuclear power plant engineer, Mori-father. Even though from the very beginning I felt somewhat uneasy about the name Mori, I never asked him about its origin. The same went for Mori-father; he never asked me about the origin of my son's name, Hikari.

In one of the roundtable discussions between parents and teachers, however, Mori-father with renewed resentment said to us again and again that at the time of his son's birth a green young intern had pigheadedly proclaimed that a baby with certain cranial defects had no prayer of ever gaining sight. If that were true, he must have detected my psychological state when I named my son, who had precisely that defect of the skull. I remember my moment of regression: how in the commotion between delivery and the emergency operation I had held off registering the new infant, and then finally went with a letter of apology to the ward office, where the Latin word *mori*, which relates both to death and idiocy, passed through my mind. . . .

No sooner did *our children* reach us in the waiting area than they shed comradeship, and we parents likewise immediately lost interest in each other. We reconfigured into inseparable pairs, conscious only of our own child, and departed the waiting station which took up one corner of the playground.

Nothing changed on that day when Mori-father and I witnessed a faint ray of light emanating from our naked souls.

2

Whenever Mori-father spoke to me, it was to demonstrate his blatant hostility, not to open up any avenue for sympathy. One morning in April, the first time he had come to pick up his son himself—I had been faithfully retrieving my own son since the previous semester—Mori-father said to me in a provocative voice,

——I once studied abroad. I've seen people with a bad set of teeth like yours before. It really shows your class, you know. And Mori-father bared his impossibly straight teeth and pulled both corners of his well-shaped but childish lips back tight into a Cheshire cat smile, flashing the superabundant splendors of his teeth.

——You're right. There's history in my teeth; it betrays my class. They tell their own story, don't they, the story of our class, the young boys who lived through the terrible food shortages during and after the war. I think our entire generation falls into that class, don't you agree?

Mori-father mulled this over for a few moments as he cast a sidelong glance at me, his eyes round and moist, too childish for an adult male. Quickly he withdrew his challenge.

——Right, I guess you're right.

The reason he challenged me was this: earlier in the morning I had seen him positioned on the playground like a general issuing orders for a battle; he didn't know where the waiting area was for the parents of the special class, and I had to show him. Now he was clearly trying to even the score. I am not that tolerant, but that morning I managed not to lose my temper.

To take one of *our children* on a bus during rush hour, clamber up and down a pedestrian bridge over a busy thoroughfare, and somehow make it to the primary school, there to entrust the anxiety-ridden child to a stranger—given that Mori-father went through all this for the first time in his life, his belligerence against the entire outside world was a rather natural reaction. How could I, a seasoned veteran who had experienced the same thing time and again, not recognize it?

For no reason at all I began to think of Mori-father as an avant-garde composer. Actually, he bore a striking resemblance to Yuji Takahashi, a top interpreter of Olivier Messiaen's music who created stage sets and directed a stage "happening" in our country. Although I made a conscious distinction between Takahashi and Mori-father, I still fancied Mori-father an avant-garde musician.

The following morning, the mother, in other words, Mori-mother, replaced Mori-father. She was explaining to the teacher—post hoc— why she, instead of the father, had brought Mori. Obliged to wait in line like every other mother to speak with the teacher, Mori-mother—standing there in black, diminutive and stoic like an Indian—got it into her head that what she had to say was absolutely necessary; this was not anything she could forfeit and let pass unspoken, but something she had to say in its entirety, unabridged. That was the attitude of every mother there; however, it was transferred into a thing of beauty through the sheer will power of this smallish woman with the inlaid ebony eyes. My husband was supposed to bring our son here and pick him up later, she said to the teacher, that's what the child expected; it's not that he's avoiding his mother, but the anticipation of being with his father has consumed his mind and he must feel terribly insecure now. Is there anything you can do to transfer his anticipation to me, before I come to pick him up? My husband's undergoing treatment for pyorrhea in his upper gums, and he broke his spare set of false teeth this morning so he refuses to appear in public. . . .

When Mori-father, sporting the makeshift false teeth given to him in the emergency room, ran into me the following morning, he nonchalantly chatted about the treatment.

——When a tooth's pulled, you always become conscious of the palpable progress with which death is advancing. I can taste it when my tongue prods the plastic teeth and gums. Mori's got a piece of plastic sewed into his cranium; he must experience the same sensation, internally that is.

At that point, I realized that the abnormal symptoms manifested by Mori-father's son at birth corresponded exactly to those of my own son.

In my experience, despite Tolstoy's dictum in *Anna Karenina*, all families are alike not only in happiness but in misfortune as well.

—— But once you get used to false teeth, you can't taste death all the time, can you?

——Do you wear dentures, too?

——Nope, my own teeth, every last one, sort of an advertisement of my class.

——When you want to practice capturing that material feel of death, nothing works better than a trip to the dentist's office.

The family dentist who removed the plaque from my teeth was always in a very cheerful mood. There was another side to him, however: the air of a manic-depressive plummeting down, down into the abysmal depths, a man about to smash his skull against a pneumatic drill running at 500,000 rpm. I'll never know whether this high-spirited dentist was trying to cheer himself up as he fell deeper into a bottomless pit of melancholia, or was secretly bracing himself to slap his patient with the exorbitant dental fees he would soon be gleefully extracting. However superficial it might have been, I was very grateful for his staged cheerfulness.

As anesthetics were stabbed into my gums, and the tenacious plaque, a part of my own flesh, was scraped away, I couldn't help contemplating my fate, the slow continual deterioration of my teeth, and the plaque-removing ordeal I had to endure every six months just because I possessed these teeth. At such moments I shed tears with my mouth agape, the fetid shards of my mortality exposed to other eyes. A toothpaste commercial blaring from the television in the waiting room augmented my already low spirits. The voiceover was full of pep and good cheer: SOME PEOPLE SAY, "MY TEETH HAVE STARTED GROWING." BUT ADULTS' TEETH DO NOT GROW. THEIR GUMS ARE ROTTING!

——When I go to my dentist to have my plaque removed, I'm reminded of *Essentials of Salvation*.

——*Essentials of Salvation?*

——That book has a section on several aspects of the body. When I contemplate it in the dentist's office, I can appreciate the whole horror, I said. I couldn't remember the quote offhand then, but I copied the passage later. This is what it says. "Like a dilapidated house, a body consists of 360 bones supported by various joints, and four tiny blood vessels meander through the entire body. The 500 muscles, like walls, are connected with six vessels, and in addition, 700 small veins are intertwined with the muscles, and sixteen additional big vessels are all interlocked with each other. How can it be possible that the human body, made up of such structures, feels no pain? Seven days after birth, worms crawl out of the 80,000 holes inside the infant and start devouring his body."

It is a mystery why the great Buddhist scholar Genshin did not come across a single passage in the scriptures that deals with plaque build-up.

——Since you mention *Essentials of Salvation*, are you the type who believes in life after death?

——I think about it constantly. To me, it's a vision revolving around my son who's surviving in this world independent of me, with only the haziest sense of my existence. If I die, he'll quickly lose even that. With only the tiniest flecks of dim memory floating in his head, he won't be able to conjure up either by himself or with anyone else's help, an image of his dead father. So, after my death, there's no escaping that I'll be nothing but bits of utter nothingness floating around in my son's body and brain. This is the vision I have; it's as real as life itself.

——I've experienced the same sort of thing. I sometimes feel as if that vision of life after death were crushing me. And it's often triggered by a newspaper article. . . . For example, did you read about the man who lived in the hills on the island of Miyakejima?

——I did! I did! Once more I was choked by the emotions that article evoked in my mind the first time, and again we fell silent. Certain newspaper articles never go unnoticed by parents of *our children*. Both Mori-father and I had read the following feature article. A man with hearing and speech disabilities was abandoned for eighteen years at Matsuzawa Mental Hospital, where he was a "gardener." He had contracted polio at the age of three and lived with his family in a cave on Miyakejima until he was twenty-seven, when the family left the island, abandoning him. He stayed behind and lived alone in the hills. Either a forest fire broke out, or those who feared that his cooking might start a fire launched a "manhunt," and he was hunted down and locked in the loony bin, where he sank into oblivion for eighteen years. In the nineteenth year his case came to light, and he was handed over to the National Hearing and Speech Disability Center; after the eighteen-year separation he was reunited with his sister, then living in Kanagawa. There he remained in his room and wept to himself. He gave up caring for a bird he had volunteered to keep, and one day he just suddenly vanished into thin air. "If only we had told him we no longer live on Miyakejima," said his sister. Height 159 centimeters, weight sixty kilograms, left foot crippled by polio, wearing glasses, sneakers and a yellow jacket, forty-eight years old, abdominal scar from a wound incurred while living in the hills. That injury was something so out of the ordinary, it was actually written up in a medical journal. "Extraordinary lower abdominal trauma." Eighteen years of institutional confinement, a forsaken and forgotten being, and the only telling vestige of this cryptic man existing in the larger world: an extraordinary scar on the lower abdomen. Eighteen silent years, then a reunion with his sister, and something suddenly catches fire within the man, a man who's never been in a bad mood during his entire incarceration in an asylum. He bolts, in hopes of returning from whence he came, someplace beyond the "manhunt." . . .

——The vision of my son evoked by that newspaper article was so vivid, so realistic, that I got truly fed up with it, said Mori-father after a long pause. I see my son as that madhouse gardener, a man who never got into a bad mood, not for an entire eighteen years. And suddenly his emotions explode, his secret, intrinsic essence comes alive. Naturally, after my death, aside from my wife's eyes, nothing will be capable of seeing my son's full identity. Anyway, he'll set out for his own Miyakejima, the Miyakejima before the time of the "manhunt." But the day will probably never arrive when my forty-eight-year-old son will recover his objective, following the dictates of his own burning emotions. He'd just be declared "missing," a missing person. Still, wouldn't it be a gallant departure? You know, he's got a severe handicap with his head patched up with a piece of plastic. Whenever I envision life after my death, I burn with a desire to overturn the entire structure of the world. . . .

Holding their hands over their heads, *our children* slowly made a pigeon-toed advance toward us. No matter where we are at, this abruptly terminates our conversations in midsentence.

3

I'd be lying if I said those dialogues didn't disturb me at all. Here I was, minding the flushed body of my son, all fired up to protect his mind turning round and round in its tiny eclipsed space, and by the time we got home, the turbulence within me closed up like early spring buds.

But those wintry buds would blossom forth in my dreams at night. In those days I often had one particular dream that corresponded so closely to real life in its minute details, details merciless in their clarity. Whenever I woke from this dream I would immediately start dwelling on the cruelty of reality. Once out of bed, I felt driven to take charge of this reality with my own hands, or, even as I slept caught in a painful dream, plaque would continue to build up on my teeth like barnacles. Depressing.

This dream—it started after I talked with Mori-father about the man who returned to Miyakejima—was an amorphous, murky one, a dream within a dream, and I barely retained any memory of it after I awoke. However, its disgusting impact stubbornly persisted. Although he reaches Miyakejima, the man—my son, myself—confounded over how to get back to the cave, prowls around a wharf, undoing his pants and trying to peek at the scar on the lower part of his abdomen as though that were his sole reliable map.

Mori-father scrutinizes me with a stinging rudeness—I was still tethered by the dregs of the dream even after I brought my son to the school that next day.

——Hangover? Ha, ha, he laughed.

——Just a stupid dream. I managed not to get miffed, but had no intention of revealing its content to him. I wonder if we've gotten to the point where sleeping is an impediment. I mean, insomnia was different when we were young.

——Sleeping's a nuisance for me, too. Doesn't it affect everyone that way at our age? The sort of abnormality in a dream that sneaks up on us while we sleep is really painful. There's no simple operational pattern to it, and whenever I encounter a new one, it really catches me off guard. When I wake, I'm like a trapped insect sucked dry of all its life fluids by a spider. My spirit's totally stupefied, in perfect accord with my enfeebled body. . . . I sometimes wonder if it's a portent of things to come. I felt the presence of some force pulling us together. Not a joyful sensation, I might add.

——You know something about a disease that attacks middle-aged men and suddenly finishes them off, don't you? At first I thought my dream portended that ominous death, but apparently that's not the case. For a while, I was so terrified of the idea of dying that I had to get dead drunk to sleep. I was already past thirty, ha, ha. Boy, I thought about death every which way possible. That was the sum total of my nocturnal spiritual activities. So believe me, I can tell right off if a stranger dwells on death. Even a schoolboy I pass on the street—I can see right through him. Aha, this kid's thinking about death. It's the same when I'm reading something. Bergson* defined imagination as "a natural defensive counterreaction against the intellect which tells us that death is inevitable." I open my eyes at midnight and imagine a man looking at his veins in the dark, ha, ha. Remember how Hideo Kobayashi† opens his discussion of Bergson with a story about a big firefly buzzing around his ankle on the day his own mother died? That critic has been my idol since I was a kid because he was also familiar

---

*Henri Louis Bergson, French philosopher and author (1859–1941).
†Well-known literary critic (1902–1983).

with nuclear physics. Suppose Kobayashi had blown off his studies of Bergson and started on Motoori Norinaga.* In fact, he actually once began to write about the cherry tree planted next to one of the two tombs Norinaga built, and how that burial mound was the plainer, and therefore the truer tomb. Remember? When I read that, my dream changed to an *idée fixe*. But how can I possibly seek help from Hideo Kobayashi? Unless we're victims in some mass murder, we die alone. Right? Meantime, death retreats into the background; some current problem takes its place in the foreground. I attribute all this, by the way, to some yellow sleeping pills which a colleague of mine at the research center gave me, saying they work better than alcohol. After taking one of those tablets at night, I wake up the following morning with my nose buried in a pillow drenched like a used rag with tears, snot, and slobber. I'm actually smothering to death, but I feel ecstatic; I'm in seventh heaven . . . an infinite gratification . . . an obscene bliss.

Since my weeping, slobbering, and snotting can be taken as sufficient evidence of my madness, although I've got no memories of any of this or the afterglow of that ecstatic bliss, although I've got no memories of any of it, can't I say the experience which the pill induces must be a ferociously powerful one? Aren't my outpourings a futile protest, a revulsion for coming back from the world of ecstasy? Isn't that why I drool and weep? I grappled endlessly with this dream of which I had no memory until I came across a book written by that Latin American Castaneda[†], who recorded the same sort of experiences.

The Yaqui tribe in Mexico initiated him into the hallucinatory pleasures of flowering cactus and he underwent a spiritual enlightenment. The tribesmen encircled him while he dreamed. When he came to, he was violently nauseous with a splitting headache, his heart pounding to burst. The Yaqui made him keep hopping, and only when he wound up crawling into a latrine in front of a house did he come back to himself. For him, that's how deeply disgusting it was to return to the real world from the land of dreams. No one witnesses what I do while asleep, but didn't I have the same kind of dream? Isn't it possible that in the land of dreams I was liberated from the terror of death? This is only a hypothesis; naturally I didn't go back again to ask for more of those yellow pills. In the end, Castaneda ran away from the Yaqui tribe. And I likewise concluded that if I continued to experience that dream I would remain the captive of my colleague.

---

*Eighteenth-century literary scholar (1730–1801) known for his studies of *The Tale of Genji*.
†Carlos Castaneda, Brazilian-born American author, anthropologist (1931–).

Pressing his appealing lips together incongruously, Mori-father gave me the onceover, as though he were testing me. He knew full well that I craved one of those yellow tablets, and he was visibly smug over the way the punchline to his rambling talk—true story or hoax—dashed this hope. Taken aback, I imagined, by the candid look of disappointment on my face, Mori-father relented and gave me this advice:

——You can settle almost all your dream problems by reading Jung's *Autobiography!*

I had already accepted him as a specialist in his own field, a man of wide reading whose opinions were to be trusted. At his suggestion I read Jung's* book and experienced a profound sense of liberation. The book helped me in my effort to reconcile what was rational with what was irrational in me in a communal life. As I continued to read the *Autobiography,* my onerous dream no longer contributed additional misery to real life. I was subsequently able to drive a wedge between dream and real life the instant I awoke. I ceased to superimpose the dream onto waking life as I struggled to drag my body out of bed. I admit, I was still in the clutches of the dream emotionally, but I finally succeeded in planting my feet in firm reality on the floor. What heightened my joy was the idea of the "prenatal wholeness of the unconscious," a view held by a Yoga ascetic whom Jung himself encountered in his own dreams. Wholeness exists within the realm of the unconscious, but on the "other side." Consciousness on "this side" manifests fragmentation and appears devoid of wholeness. Other dream imagery of Jung: a magic lantern, a flying saucer, a box equipped with a lens. "We always think of a flying saucer as our projection. However, we have now become its projection. The magic lantern projects me, a C. G. Jung. But the question is, who is operating the machine?" I did not particularly try to figure out that question because I found it delightful as posed. Jung adamantly said: "The meaning of my existence lies in the fact that life has hurled down the question at me. Or, conversely, I myself am the very question being hurled at the world."

I pictured, with intense pleasure, a flying saucer projecting an image onto the earth, the image of my son and me. I pictured drawing dots and lines tracing that image back to its original light source using a system I learned in high school physics. Tracing the image of my son back to its source shows there would be only a single point of *light.* That wholeness encompassing my son and me is the "prenatal wholeness of the unconscious."

---

*Carl Gustav Jung, Swiss psychiatrist and theorist of the unconscious (1875–1961).

My heart soared, believing in this wholeness—though I can't quite say I entirely believed it. I too was aware that although we originated from a single point of *light* we still formed two separate shadows that branched off by themselves in the world, and that my son and I each would have to die individually, separate from one another.

For the week or so while I was experiencing this new sensation stirred up by Jung, Mori-father did not show up to pick up his son. Instead, Mori-mother, like an Indian, with her slender legs peeking from under her black dress, with a gravely downcast look on her face, came to the school. I exchanged words with her only once, a weird exchange indeed.

——Do you know the TV personality Ōno? She's having an affair with my husband. Bitch! When you see her, tell her not to do a thing like that! she said, looking straight at me, her pupils tawny dots in the expanse of the whites of her eyes.

——I just know the name Ōno, that's all. While I hemmed and hawed, Mori-mother insolently moved on, quickly propelling her small, tough frame into the group waiting for *our children.*

Despite Mori-mother's jet-black hair, swept tightly back into a bun in the style of our mother's generation, something about the way her head jutted forward slightly, with her unblinking downcast eyes set in a dark-skinned face that broke out in goose pimples, something in her was unlike any of the waiting mothers—an odd sense of modernity. What I found most noticeable about her, however, was that quality common to all the mothers of *our children*—a look characteristic of someone who has suffered an unhappy surprise—which the tiny frame of Mori-mother's body had registered to the utmost. She quivered like a little bird from head to toe in an effort to shield herself from other mothers who might want to speak to her.

4

——How was Jung? One morning—after he had resumed the pick-up job—Mori-father asked, fixing me with that customary belligerent, insolent look in his eyes, staring and trying to read my reaction, Wasn't it interesting? Wasn't it just the right thing for you?

——I did find it interesting. One of Jung's dreams really whetted my curiosity. Rather, I should say it lifted my spirits. His dream of a flying saucer.

——Uh-huh, that magic lantern, said Mori-father, his high cheekbones imbued with the glimmer of a slight ornamental smile that was nothing more than a reflection of his arrogance. But then the insolence in his eyes quickly caved in as if collapsing from inside. . . .

——Have you taken courses in psychology or philosophy? I thought you had a physics degree.

——Professionally, I'm an *ex*–nuclear physicist. Or, I should say, just to avoid a misunderstanding, I was an employee at a nuclear power plant. A *former* engineer at a nuclear power plant. I know a lot about you. I even wrote to you. No reply, though. Well, it was a protest letter, so I can't say I resented your silence. Besides, I couldn't just write off my own wretchedness, the mortification of working with my colleagues, by merely dashing off a protest letter.

——What? You wrote me? Come to think of it, I do recall receiving a letter I never responded to, from a researcher at some nuclear power plant. Three, four years ago, wasn't it? I vaguely remember. I don't think it was one of those letters I could answer, though.

——Now I'm not raising Cain over it, you know. Do you often get protest letters of that sort?

——I sure do. They generally come in two types: one to which I can easily respond; the other, like yours, where the author makes sure I can't respond. What really depresses me, though, is something else altogether. I've got to explain it to you.

——What?

——It's really a rotten story. For six years I was harassed by a young man I'd never met in my life. His voice was somehow familiar; he'd call up drunk and breathing hard, and over a poor connection he'd go:

——I'll bump you off! I'm a "dead monkey." Why should I suffer alone for five, six years? I'll fix you. Once he called twelve times in a single day; he hung up every time I picked up the receiver. The thirteenth time, he goes in a feeble voice:

——You go to the loony bin. However, his most damaging weapon was his letters, which hounded me day and night. He'd write with a graphite pencil on a torn piece of paper; I had to hold the letter up against the light to make anything out. "What I've got to tell you is this: you've got an idiot child because both of you have contaminated blood. It probably won't be necessary for me to come over and beat you to death. Once my message sinks into your heads, there'll be no choice left but for the whole family to commit suicide." These were the kinds of words he used.

"This 'dead monkey' has a father," he said with pride, "who, unlike yours, is an elite white-collar worker at the biggest steel company in Japan." Plus, being a "son of a good family," my tormentor went to a psychiatrist every week. His mother, who copied sutras as a pastime, sent us copies of a monthly magazine, *Masaharu Taniguichi,* which she hoped would help ease the nervous breakdown my wife suffered because of the letters. In short, with the exception of my wife and me, not one single soul considered the filthy antics of this "dead monkey" to be antisocial behavior.

He first identified himself as a "dead monkey" over the phone. He seemed very proud of the label, and explained in his letter where he got it. In Nelson Algren's *The Man with the Golden Arm*, "dead monkey" is what a drug addict hallucinates about during withdrawal; the addict feels a dead monkey stuck like glue to the scruff of his neck. The sender of the letter proclaimed himself a "dead monkey" clinging to my neck.

"I'm telling you, the only way to get rid of me is either to kill me or turn me in to the police. I'll be your 'dead monkey' till the day I commit suicide. It's not at all difficult for a determined man to keep on harassing you till you kill yourself. More so, when his scheme is hallucinogenic. I want you to know I've already messed up the life of a young woman. You're my next target; what you've got here is a veteran 'dead monkey.' "

Turn him in to the police? They already knew the young man wrote many letters to a female college student whom he met at a "Travel Club," love letters in which he enclosed Gillette blades among other things, but in the end he pleaded innocent—I had no intention of harming her, he said—and was released. This experience taught the "dead monkey" that a "son of a good family" who was voluntarily seeing a psychiatrist could get away with anything, that the police would look the other way.

But why did this "dead monkey" decide to cling to my neck after he no longer found it worthwhile to hang on the tiny neck of that poor girl? I could never figure it out even though I read and reread the eighty-odd letters that arrived within a year. He did recommend, however, that to "atone for my sin" I should sponsor him, help him get his foot in the door. He somehow found out either from the enrollment list of the special class published by the ward office, or from a bulletin circulated among the parents, that our son was retarded. The "dead monkey" intuitively sniffed things out and concluded that the novelist father of such a child would be the ideal candidate for him to latch on to. I must admit his intuition proved to be quite remarkable, because the "dead monkey" wasn't the only one to suffer for five, six years.

——I don't think the young man lived only for the sake of playing dirty pool with you, did he? It's possible that when he began to write those monstrous letters, he was motivated by a genuine desire you could fulfill, and probably your uncommunicativeness incensed him. And that poor young woman whose life he messed up, isn't it possible he first had a crush on her?

——He claims he wants to be a critic, and that his family expects he will. After the letter that denounced my wife and me, he sent me a copy of some of his work, asking if I would somehow help him get an in with the literati.

——You just hate him, which I'm not blaming you for, but the way you tell it, you're deliberately fuzzy about the validity of his aspiration to be a writer. As far as he's concerned, though, he might consider you a kindred spirit.

——You mean the "dead monkey" and I are also projections from a single UFO light source?

——At least that's what he's thinking. Mori-father cheerfully skewered me while I got more and more angry. He fantasizes, Mori-father continued, that one day a role reversal, a transfiguration, or what have you, will occur, and he'll assume all your literary work; in turn you'll deal him dirty and start writing to him. I bet he's willing to take over not only your job, but your entire family life. That's why he slanders your wife and Hikari, who've got nothing to do with his literary aspirations. Isn't that so? Until the day of the switch, you probably won't be freed from the "dead monkey," ha, ha. But, don't you think it's pointless to hate him, curse him endlessly, all year round? Because if he were not around, you would fixate on another "dead monkey" and hold him in abomination night and day. The "dead monkey" might be the very symbol of your own aversion to the reality projected by that magic lantern, ha, ha. The same goes for the author of the protest letter; I had to project the abhorrence that was festering inside me, and coincidentally selected you as my target. It doesn't bother me at all that you ignored the letter.

——That's not true. I just didn't know how to come up with a reply; it was one of those letters I tend to shove in the corner of my bookshelf and forget.

——Because I didn't come around to threaten you, that's why. If I ever decide to blackmail my enemy—to imitate the "dead monkey"—all I need to say is that I possess the technological know-how to mess up ten million people, ha, ha. Theoretically speaking, I can manufacture a small-scale atomic bomb, ha, ha.

Building a small-scale A-bomb! Middle-aged males shouldn't be discussing such matters standing around on the edge of an elementary-school playground waiting for *our children* under a cloudy May sky. So, I shifted my attention to Mori-father's quasi-neurotic wife, always buried in thought. Does this mean, I wondered aloud, that Mori-father, the pseudo–avant garde composer/nuclear physicist, messed up her life and not the other way around? Although my suspicions were groundless, I had assumed it was Mori-father who was forced to live in the threatening shadow of his Indian-like wife, so self-consciously tense, so physically depleted. Free of that oppression, he surely would have behaved more maturely than to blab threats about a small-scale atomic bomb. Whatever he meant, I realize, when I look back now, he spoke that day for the first time of the "switchover" that was to become central to his way of thinking, his *modus vivendi*.

5

Late in the afternoon on that same day Mori-father paid us a social call, accompanied by the son, Mori. At first Mori-father, checking out our house, paced up and down a few times on the other side of the hedge speckled with young, still-scrawny leaves. I saw a small man wearing something like a Mao cap that almost came down to his eyes; every time he swung around, his frame wobbled up jerkily, then resumed walking. Through the crack of the drawn curtains at the window as I caught sight of him, the reason for that peculiar movement dawned on me: I realized Mori-father was accompanied by his son, Mori. Once *our children* start walking in a certain direction, if you try to change their direction without carefully explaining in words or by gestures, they resist with all the force of inertia of soul and body combined. Holding the child's hand, a parent can sometimes sprain his own wrist by carelessly attempting an about-face. *Our children* were corpulent from their fattening diet and lack of exercise: that inertia drew upon a powerful strength. Just before Mori-father finally resolved to step on the brick walkway leading to our gate, I went out to meet him, rousing my son from the warmth of his favorite spot—the ventilation duct of the refrigerator—and bringing him in tow as though his were the helping hand I would soon need.

No sooner did Mori-father catch sight of me and my son facing him in front of the low wooden gate than he became flustered; however, in keeping with his belligerent eyes and faint smile at the corner of his lips, his utterances betrayed no faintness of heart, only the strong will power to deny it.

——You sure look cowed by the "dead monkey." Did you mistake me for him?

——Cowed is not the word; I just can't stomach him.

——I may have told you already, but that must simply be your way of expressing your aversion to reality. Well, considering I'm barging in on you like this, you must feel some real repugnance, too, ha, ha.

I unlatched the gate, and succeeded in witnessing a drama unfolding between my son and Mori, each discovering the other. Soundlessly, and without looking at each other, they rekindled an intrinsic warmth each felt for the other, a warmth that rose by degrees like a fire carefully stoked. Without realizing it, they began touching the pockets of each other's jackets with their fingertips as their mirrored, expressionless faces slowly brightened with dim-lit smiles.

——Say hello, I said to my son.

——Hulloo.

——Say hello, Mori-father then said to his son.

——Hulloo.

——At any rate, I said after letting *our children* take care of our greetings, Why not come on in.

——No need. We can discuss matters standing here. Have you dug the item out and read it?

——The item? If you mean that stack of letters I told you about, I haven't gone through it yet. I did take it off the shelf, though. I'm put off by the sheer bulk of it all—nasty letters, protests, you name it.

——You've been in publishing for quite a while, I can tell. Well, in the next couple of days you'll look for my letter, reread it, and get sore. I wrote it with a lot of hostility, for sure, ha, ha. Mori-father came to smooth things over, but felt his mediation plan crimped his style. He ran his tongue over his makeshift set of dentures, apparently assessing the degree of awkwardness he felt. Then he shook off indecision and broached a personal matter as though talking about somebody else.

——My wife told me she appealed to you to do something about Ōno. She thinks those who've got anything to do with mass communication are all related like a large extended family. . . . Well, I've thought about it. Suppose you make trouble for Ōno. You know, it'll even make trouble if you mention me and Ōno when you shoot the breeze with editors. I'm nobody, so who cares, but she's famous. I initially contacted her protest group because of an accident I had at the nuclear power plant, and since that was how we met, there's always the possibility of some reactionary weekly magazine doing a write-up on us.

——I don't write gossipy stuff, and I don't chitchat with my editors.

——You lied to my wife about not knowing Ōno personally. You made me suspect a plot was being hatched.

——It's true that I do know Ms. Ōno personally. But did I need to tell that to your wife? Your association with Ōno and my own are on different planes, it seems to me. . . . Why don't you come inside and tell me the rest.

Whereupon Mori-father and I sat facing each other in the study, and *our children*, although not speaking to each other, began to play together and draw figures on pieces of torn paper. My wife, who brought in paper, pencils, and candy for the children, and tea for us, bowed out when Mori-father took no notice of her.

——After I heard from my wife that you said you didn't know Ōno, I began to worry. Because Ōno herself told me about you.

——I would say I'm an admirer of hers. Let me ask you again, I don't have to confide in your wife, do I? Some say Sakurao Ōno threw away the best years of her life by studying in Spain, but she and the majority of her groupies disagree with that assessment; she is a female activist who hasn't yet undertaken any definitive projects, but is well known in journalism circles. Her life's goal is to make films, to follow in the footsteps of Luis Buñuel,* to surpass his work. However, before she could get into movie production, she was set up as something of a manager-housekeeper for the national civil rights movement. As far as she was concerned, her task was to recruit as many young men to the cause as possible, and then spiritually/emotionally/physically prepare them for a movie she intended to shoot. Her civil rights activities neatly facilitated other of her Spanish-directed aspirations: she arranged to host a poet, a defector living in Mexico since the Spanish Civil War, taking him on a lecture tour all over Japan. However, she achieved her greatest fame speaking out on television on behalf of the Women's Liberation Movement, which has nothing to do with filmmaking. She may have wasted the best years of her life, but the combination of her dignity and humor in her massive body gave her a scintillating star quality whether at a rally or on television. One of her TV debates was shot in commemoration of the dramatic discovery and return of a WWII soldier—this is a story everyone knows—who, enlisted in the army during the reign of the absolute emperor, participated in the invasion of Southeast Asia, and, left behind there for twenty-five years, maintained stalwart solitary battle alert at his one-man outpost! After the television camera panned the small pit where he bivouacked and the nationwide welcoming celebrations, the debate opened. Ōno looked positively ill, and in fact when she spoke the only thing she could say was that she was unwell. Later when she recounted the soldier's story to the Spanish poet (who had been persevering in his own quixotic political struggle ever since his defection—longer than it took the Japanese soldier to learn about the end of the war), I saw her again visibly sicker and pale.

——I think she's quite a woman. My observation is that she comes across as a very unusual person on television as well as in public.

---

*Luis Buñel (1900–1983), Spanish-born French film director of avant-garde political works.

——Only an observation? I hear you even washed her feet.

——But, that was. . . .

——Sure, all you did was wash her feet, Mori-father said, obviously gratified that he had succeeded a second time in rattling me.

It all started on the night of the party we held for the Spanish poet to celebrate the completion of his lecture tour. After the official party—all of us were on the organizing committee—we threw another small bash to thank the young people who did the actual work. During the first party the sky thundered with a downpour. It was the height of summer. I still can feel the 100-percent humidity, the 102-degree heat, that drenched and clogged all our pores, every duct and pipe from our oral cavities to our lungs, including even our very emotions. To get to the second gathering we took the subway and exited onto flooded streets. By the time we reached the address the women's sandaled feet were completely muddy. That's how it happened that, in a cramped toilet equipped with a commode and sink set, I rinsed off the strapping feet that went with the hefty body of one scriptwriter-to-be crammed into that cubicle. It was just happenstance, and both of us bombed.

——I'll tell you how I know that you washed Ōno's feet and that's all you did. Because after that party at the crack of dawn Ōno and I made love for the first time. I was very conscious of you through the whole shebang; you didn't even know I was there, did you? Anyway, you were really gone goods, although I shouldn't talk.

——Why not? I think you belong to the class of people who keep a sober eye on drunks like me. I went home so dead-drunk I couldn't remember a thing except the feet-washing, but you, you were even able to make love.

——I was soused, too. And in that state made rather unsatisfactory love, so my relationship with Ōno soured afterward. As I told you before, I was taking on my government as a victim of a nuclear accident at the power plant. Ōno was manager-housekeeper of the support group for those accident victims. But our sexual relationship lacked any psychologically sound basis. I wasn't really serious about political struggle. I more or less fell in love with Ōno, and that was why I continued attending political struggle sessions later on. At the time I rationalized to myself that I was in love with a woman who was definitely not run-of-the-mill, and that I admired her distinctive personality.

——She sure has character.

——You might say that. I also told myself that since I was in love with her character, I should actualize my feelings by making love to her. What we in fact did was clutch at each other's loose flaccid parts. That was how it went at our initial sexual encounter; and for the first time I experienced the horror of impotency.

Our children were playing completely harmoniously, each oblivious of the other's existence yet both perfectly synchronized with each other's unwitting movements, drawing clusters of tiny dots on torn pieces of paper. Neither Mori-father nor I had reason to feel uneasy about discussing sexual matters in front of *our children.*

Mori-father had become truly alarmed about how rip-roaring drunk Ōno got at the second party. For some reason, at midnight, none of her ever-present Ōno groupies was with her. Probably she herself had sent them to see the Spanish poet to his hotel. Just finished with an extensive lecture tour, unloading responsibility and getting loaded herself, she had let a novelist wash her feet in a toilet—this bit of news had been immediately broadcast, fortifying Mori-father's resolve to assume protective care of her. As day and the party both broke, Mori-father hailed a cab to take her home. But as soon as the cab moved, she got sick, so there was no choice but to check into a motel. Mori-father had often met with her since the onset of the political struggle, but they had never stayed at a motel together. When he saw that the scriptwriter-to-be was back in shape after getting a handle on the situation in the bathroom, he felt there was no alternative left but to make love. At any rate this was how he simplified the matter at hand and what he *insisted* happened. The first five minutes went smoothly. But those glorious five minutes passed and the lovemaking turned into Mori-father's one-man show, instantly degenerating. He whipped off the courtesy condom provided with the room but as soon as he felt potency returning, he slipped a new one on; again, his penis went miserably limp, retracting from the shriveling condom.

Why didn't he stop there? He pathetically feared that if he aborted things now the scriptwriter-to-be would remember nothing but their moments of sexual fiasco, making it difficult for him ever to get a crack at a sexual relationship with her.

——I've had enough, let's call it quits! Ōno said, but Mori-father kept at it persistently. She displayed a boundless loving tenderness that verged on self-punishment, magnanimously forgiving him who wouldn't give up mounting her.

Still dysfunctional, Mori-father began to fondle her butt—she had finally fallen asleep face down, cheeks up—while with the other hand he stroked his feckless penis. In short order the scriptwriter-to-be, as though instinctively sensing that she had to rescue her heart from under her enormous weight, bolted upright with a start.

——Who are you? Why are you pulling at your penis all day? she said and flopped right back to sleep.

Humiliated, Mori-father grew obnoxiously aggressive: he tried with his fingers to pry open her roseate *burn*like sphincter to ram his penis in. Once he realized that was impossible, Mori-father stuck in his fingers instead, engrossing himself in his revolting preoccupation. . . .

In the evening, when she awoke, Ōno again displayed that outlandishly loving tenderness, her self-punishment and essentially total humiliation for Mori-father.

——My butt's sore! I must have toyed with it but good in my sleep, she said. . . .

From experience I knew that my power to elicit from Mori-father this loquacious confession was an occupational hazard. When you lead the life of a novelist, you often get visitors who shoot off their mouths nonstop: what they've gone through, what they've daydreamed about, what they've aspired to, and so on. Just because I am a writer they expect me, the listener, to fill in the blanks and grasp the full meaning of their prattle—even though it escapes them.

The way Mori-father spoke definitely fell into this category. A science graduate and my contemporary, he had the conventional techie's tendency to look down on those in the humanities (we spent our boyhood in the era of the sanctification of scientific technology that started with the defeat after the atomic bombings, followed by Dr. Yukawa's[*] receiving the Nobel Prize). At the same time Mori-father credulously exaggerated the power of the written word, and especially the sway of fiction. Two sides of a coin. He seemed to appeal to me wordlessly as follows:

——I'm trying to project the full integrity of who I am through the prism of my entire subconscious, using you as the projection screen. I want to see in sharp focus a montage of all the snippets of my premonitions and dreams. The skillful use of the catalytic devices of language and imagination. Isn't that the skill a novelist has to learn?

In the meantime we noticed *our children* fidgeting as they raised their chins in silence with an urgent look on their faces, the look of being suspended in midair. When we took them to the bathroom, they stood at either side of the commode trying to urinate, but since they had held their piddle too long, their penises were now as erect as a cobra's head; the urine sprayed everywhere, wetting their thighs and our pants.

——It's my job to change his diapers and help him urinate at midnight. I'm always shocked by my son's atrociously erect penis.

---

[*]Hideki Yukawa (1907–1981), Japanese physicist awarded the Nobel Prize in 1949 in quantum theory and nuclear physics for predicting the existence of the *meson*—a subatomic particle heavier than the electron.

——Same here. When I think about it later, I find there are two reasons for it. One of them is this: my son was born with a hole in his skull because the Persuader of the Cosmos has a plan for us, for humankind; at midnight when we're eyeball to eyeball with the thought of death, my son's erect penis is an antenna receiving a message from the Persuader. That's what I think. The cryptic message is stored like genetic coding in my son's cells. And one day, with all the codes deciphered, some vital information will come to light. Under cover of the midnight darkness enveloping Tokyo, the Persuader's telescope beams down a tiny pinprick of light that cruelly oscillates one antenna—my son's erect penis. In insect communities, the lower strata often get deliberately destroyed to protect the higher echelons, right? By analogy, isn't that why we change wet *diapers,* to seal and conceal the phallus in a plastic wrap? Ha, ha!

——What's the other reason?

——The other one? . . . As you know, there's an inkling of it in my lovemaking with Ōno: while I'm becoming increasingly impotent my son's erection gets more and more futilely vigorous. . . . That's how I feel.

This whole day, the other visitor, Mori, had been silent; at the end of the visit, however, he suddenly cried out. I had been telling Mori-father, who was worried about the bathroom splattered with urine, that it was no problem when, bare buttocks breaking out in goose pimples, and with mechanical precision, Mori uttered this cry of criticism:

——**THIS WON'T DO, PISSING ALL OVER THE PLACE, IT WON'T DO!**

6

Mori-father was terribly rude to my wife when he visited, and Mori-mother, on the days she brought the child to school, persisted in complaining to me how her husband and Ōno were carrying on their sordid relationship, leaving absolutely no grounds for my wife to feel friendly toward him. This didn't mean, however, that the rest of the mothers, including my wife, felt any sympathy for Mori-mother. When one of them, with whom Mori-mother herself had engaged in an intense discussion, tried in turn to express an opinion, Mori-mother cut her short, furiously launching into yet another tirade about how her husband and Ōno were fomenting a vile conspiracy. When the long-suffering listener tried a second time to open her mouth in response, Mori-mother just turned a deaf ear, quivering with downcast eyes.

——With her teased hair, and the make-up crusted around her lips, she looks like a tiny cross-eyed bird glaring straight down the tip of her beak-nose! This, according to my wife, was what a widowed mother, a cabaret hostess by night, said about Mori-mother. The dark-complexioned Mori-mother sputtered saliva that instantly turned to powdery white slag when she spoke, and coagulated as ashen scum in the bristly hair around her lips. For the mothers of *our children* dying to talk about the full particulars of their plight, Mori-mother's handiwork in conversation was a terribly unfair violation of the rules. One can't really blame the widow-mother for maliciously criticizing Mori-mother.

One day my wife, who had participated with our son in a "shopping" workshop, came home an hour later than usual and told me excitedly how greatly she respected Mori-father. Even my son, his feverish cheeks dancing with joy, repeated over and over—as usual, parroting my wife.

——**A GREAT MAN! A SCIENTIST! AN ENGINEER! A GREAT MAN! A SCIENTIST! AN ENGINEER!**

Led by two teachers, one male, one female, *our children* had set out to participate in the "shopping" workshop while their parents trailed five or six meters behind. The day's "shopping" was a trip to a local supermarket, an activity in the curriculum designed to let the more able ones buy and pay for something on their own, and the less able at least manage to enter a store by themselves, by going through the automated door. And behold, one of the boys got his arm caught in that very door. The child screamed at the top of his lungs not so much from the pain as from the terror of constraint. Neither the female teacher, who under normal circumstances was full of vim and vigor, nor even the male teacher, a man of absolutely calm disposition, could figure out anything effective to help the boy. Likewise the supermarket clerks. However, Mori-father, who had been standing at a distance from the band of mothers, and following the procession half-heartedly without paying much attention to what was going on, suddenly swung into action and successfully disengaged the boy from the automatic door.

——When the hullabaloo was over, the area around the door was strewn with a plastic bag of toys, lumber for do-it-yourself projects, blankets, and other things Mori-father had bagged at the store. It looked as if they came pouring out of his pockets, one after the other, while his relief effort had been under way. The door, unhinged from the wall, was dangling from disconnected electric wires; Mori-father's clothing was spattered with blood. You see, my wife continued, while Mori-father was working on the door, the child's arm started getting badly pinned, so Mori-father safeguarded against that with his own arm. That was how he got injured.

The following day, a meeting was convened to express gratitude for what Mori-father had done and to offer some explanation of the accident to those parents who had not been present. Although my wife strongly urged me to go, I didn't. Why? Because it was a foregone conclusion that Mori-father would somehow stir up trouble, especially at a meeting that the principal and the headmaster would attend. Just as I thought, at midday my wife called from the school—Mori-father's begun to wage war, arguing with both the administration and the parents; they're having a hard time bringing this thing to a close. Our boy's hungry and stressed; he must be feeling insecure about the situation here. I'll stick it out until everybody's had their say, but would you please come and pick him up. The tone of my wife's voice was simultaneously agitated and yet strangely unfeeling.

When I arrived, a small number of parents were clustered in the back of the room like a band of refugees, each guarding his own child. Never mind *our children,* the parents all looked stunned and overcome by hunger and the utter asininity of the arguments. Mori-father was standing alone in front of the blackboard, yakking away at the group of administrators, the principal, and the rest of the audience, all perched uncomfortably on child-sized wooden chairs. As I entered the classroom, the principal shot me a glance that read: You! Parent! Friend or foe? We've got a war going here, and the outcome's still up for grabs. Unlike everyone else's pallid look, the principal's beefy face was flushed deep red, with steam about to shoot out his ears. No doubt he was the one to bear the brunt of Mori-father's attack. The female teacher, who typically exuded confidence no matter what, was glaring at Mori-father with a poisonous look, cheeks aflame; for his part the male teacher crunched himself deep down in his undersized wooden chair, folding his upper body over in half, looking for all the world like a supplicant throwing himself down at Mori-father's knees.

—— . . . Our children should be the center of this school! I think the principal deliberately misinterpreted me a while ago, I don't for one minute mean we should place them above *those who are not our children.* Simply put *our children* at the center of attention! If the administration doesn't want to do that, why does it set up a special class and agree to take care of *our children*? Again, although the principal went out of his way to distort my words, I'm not saying that *our children*'s attendance at this school is totally disregarded. But for God's sake, what's the advantage of *our children* coming to school to learn about the dangers of a supermarket door if none of the teachers in charge, let alone the store clerks, are any help when arms get caught in the door? What's the use of such a workshop? An hour after the accident the only thing *our children* will retain will be incoherent, terrifying forebodings and images of horror! Will *our children* ever learn anything useful in this classroom before they have to go out into the world? The only real help any teacher can give them is to tell them what the world is really like out there, what they should keep an eye out for! That's what you should be telling them. Are any of you teachers doing this for *our children*? *Our children* are not even being taught how to keep their arms and legs out of harm's way so that they can at least live an independent future, as imbeciles stuck away in some corner of society. Who knows, this system might accommodate itself to the future. With the education they're getting here, *our children* might end up learning how to dispose not only of their arms and legs but their whole body, in other words, ha, ha, how to commit suicide. If we really care about the future of *our children* we must teach them now about how to take up arms and defend themselves, to drive back the tyrannical force that would weed them out of the future society! As long as this planet continues to be radioactively contaminated, there's nothing we can do about the skyrocketing number of those like *our children* in the population. *Our children* reproduce and become an eyesore to everyone, everywhere. And one day officially fomented mass hate will be directed violently at them. *Our children* will be the fall guys for the pent-up horrors and fears in the rest of the dispossessed, discriminated-against populace. They'll be the despised, easily identified symbol of the nightmares awaiting everyone else. Of course, that's not to say that none of *our children* will learn to rebel; but, is this school with its special program teaching *our children* how to defend themselves?

——The dictates of all educational theory and practice will not allow us to do anything like what you're proposing, and you know it! You say these special students must eventually create an autonomous zone, even possess an atomic bomb?! You're talking absolute rubbish. What you're proposing is totally contrary to the principles of primary education. My long career as a teacher of physical education, and as a principal, has brought me to the belief that **EDUCATION IS THE RECONCILIATION OF NATURE WITH SOCIETY, THE UNITY OF MIND AND BODY.**

——Well, if that's the case, I won't demand that you teach *our children* self-defense, to work against the forces in society that would weed them out. What it all boils down to is that each of us parents must train *our children* on our own, on the sly, in our backyards. This training can't go on at school, after all—suppose someone squeals and a riot squad storms into a classroom in the middle of a lesson on proper use of a machine gun; after *our children* put up a little resistance, they'll get hauled away, ditto the teachers; well, well, we don't want that to happen, do we? Besides, all those regular *children who are not our children* are

nice little geniuses, and potential informers, I might add, ha, ha! Therefore, along the lines of what the principal just said, to bring about
reconciliation in this school, I repeat the proposal I made earlier: *our
children* must be the center of attention of this school!

———Specifically, how are we going to carry this out? My wife raised
the question as if she took the goings-on very seriously.

Mori-father had a split-second lapse and fell silent. But, perhaps this
was merely a diplomatic brush-off preceding the sidelong look he gave
her, rolling his pink tongue around his lips as if to lick off a fleck of salt.
His sensitive mannerisms reminded me so much of Mori-mother, it was
almost as if they were twins. Parents of our children often closely resem-
ble one another. In my own lovemaking, I sometimes feel my wife and I
are committing incest.

———Music! We can do it through music! You know *our children* have a
good ear for music. We'll train them to become proficient musicians.
The entire school will be alive with music composed by *our children*! I
have with me a memoir written by an Indian musician; when you've
read it, it'll become obvious what role *our children* can play at this
school. Plus, as a natural consequence of the learning experience, think
what sort of social graces they'll pick up! (Then, proving that this was
not an idea that came to him on the spur of the moment but was part of
a plan, Mori-father whipped out the insert of a record jacket and almost
shouting—he must have really been excited—read aloud the first few
lines of English, and then switched to a translation.) *I am always afraid
when I play; I pray I can do justice to my guru, to my music. . . .* "I sense the
bountifulness of all India in our music. A raga illuminates the many
spiritual hopes of the masses, the endless struggle for our survival. It
captures the melody of our many prayers recited at the temples, and of
all the lives at the bank of the Ganges that runs through the holy city of
Benares. I hear the resonances everywhere. When I was a child, my soul
was sated at this place with all kinds of trembling sounds. Our music
spells out to me the entire process of life, from infancy to death. . . ."

———**WHAT THE HELL IS A GURU!?** What the hell do you mean
by India? Raga? You talk these kids blind with bullshit; they're sitting
here perfectly still, not understanding a word, exhausted and hungry.
**WHAT THE HELL DO YOU THINK YOU'RE DOING, WHAT,
WHAT!? YOU. . . .**

A mother who until now had been cringing in fright, sort of fat but
not yet flabby, a miniature dark-skinned tank, began to shout, churning
the air with both arms. Her lipstickless lips were a ferric oxide color, but
the inside of her mouth (which until now had been tightly shut) was so
scarlet it looked like a fire raging in the darkness: she was a widow

called Saachan-mother. She may have been a miniature tank, but I once saw her aboard a train on the way to work, nicely made up, with a wig that made her head look two-and-a-half times its normal size, her eyes as dark as a molten moonless night, the pupils barely detectable.

—— . . . When we held a whole series of meetings to get rid of the prejudicial setup that shunts *our children* off into special classes, you only showed up once; we thought we could count on you, but you never showed again! **WHAT THE HELL ARE YOU TALKING ABOUT!** You say we can make *our children* music specialists? How about a kid like Saachan who's hard of hearing? Are you saying we're going to discriminate against her even in a special class? No more discrimination! Pray to your guru that you don't make a mistake! Why don't you just feel up your TV personality's ass! You sexual pervert!

The principal, a gymnast by training, had already slipped out of the classroom. He was agile as a monkey. The meeting was fizzling out while the parents busied themselves taking their children out to the restroom, or cleaning up the mess caused by the ones who couldn't wait.

——Your language is inappropriate in this classroom! Saachan-mother, you've got to be a little more considerate! The female home-room teacher meant now to rein in both the widow and Mori-father, who had gone totally over the teacher's head moments earlier. She made it very clear to them: I want you, Saachan-mother, to keep your trap shut, and in no way do I want a repeat performance of your eloquence, Mori-father.

While waiting for my son and wife to come back from the bathroom, I hung back in a corner of the classroom, doing my best not to attract Mori-father's notice. After a string of curses, Saachan-mother changed tactics and began instead to monopolize the female teacher, probably pressing to her to do something about changing the class format on behalf of Saachan, who was hard of hearing. That was her immutable topic of discussion. Still seemingly prostrate, the male teacher cast an eye at the dispirited Mori-father, who was gently rubbing his bandaged left wrist, injured the day before. The male teacher suddenly stood up and thrust himself forward to speak to Mori-father; something deep down in his sunken eyes shimmered; some decision had finally been reached. But as if wishing to ward him off, Mori-father called out to me, whom he had chosen to ignore up until that point.

——Mori and I won't be coming to this school anymore. I considered reforming not only the special class but the entire school system; but the way things're going now it doesn't look like there's any chance of that, so Mori and I won't come here anymore. What can I say, when not a single soul considers *our children* as being chosen for a special mission? . . .

Mori-father strode toward his son, passing by the male homeroom teacher whose head now drooped like a beaten dog's; Mori sat quietly alone, wetting himself. I left Mori-father behind with his son and escaped from the classroom, taking my wife and child.

——After that noisy manifesto, Mori-father won't be able to come back to this school, will he? I wonder what he's going to do next.

——He'll probably go in search of a guru, to train Mori to become a musician.

——You think he was joking, don't you. I think he meant everything he said, he was in earnest.

——**HE MEANT IT! HE MEANT IT!** my son repeated.

* * *

Nine months later, on a wintry night, two letters arrived in the final special delivery dispatch. One of them was from the "dead monkey," in a handmade envelope, a piece of torn paper patched together with scotch tape. Enclosed were three failure notifications for employment exams given him by the Asakusa Trust Bank, the *Reader's Digest,* and some company which apparently hires part-time workers to grade college entrance exams. The other letter was from Mori-father, who had dropped out of sight since our last meeting. It was written on the letterhead of a nuclear power plant in California. I read it searching to somehow purify my emotions, feeling defiled by what the "dead monkey" had sent me. It was as though Mori-father's absence were already summoning up a strong surge of nostalgia.

* * *

I'll tell you why I'm going to be writing a number of letters to you, and why they'll be no ordinary correspondence; and why I'll be sending you research notes (plus, at times, even my own creative writing, ha, ha!), and why I'll be calling you time and again, talking endlessly to you about myself. I got the idea from the "dead monkey" you told me about. Let some other "dead monkey" bite into the scruff of your fat neck. You might refuse, but you already know how tough it is to pry off a "dead monkey," ha, ha.

But my becoming your "dead monkey" also means you become my "dead monkey." Of all the "dead monkey" candidates around, as the person providing the resources, I must be the one closest to you, even though I'm into the sciences and you the humanities. From now on I want a constant data feed into you, to influence every bit of output that comes from you. You'll finally get sick of me, I'm bound to affect your consciousness and body. I don't mean to offend you, but my information will do more than just harass you. Who knows, it might, in the end, enthrall you. Once I integrate with you like this, it'll be like being my own ghostwriter, won't it?

Why do I need you as my ghostwriter? Because I need someone to creatively elaborate my actions and thoughts, to record them beforehand in a "memorandum." I'm about to embark on a new adventure with Mori; without a chronicler, I feel that the adventure-to-come (and therefore Mori's and my life) will be nothing but a maddening illusion. I've got a premonition that our adventure will be a phantasmagoric event, and you know if my "memorandum" ever ends up in the hands of the police, it would be considered drivel.

A fear mounts in me as I approach the onset of that adventure, filled with hopeful anticipation. That's the truth. I'm not asking you to rescue me; I simply want you as chronicler to enlarge upon what I'll keep reporting, everything that my consciousness and body will experience. At least that's what I want to believe you'll do. After all, if this adventure of Mori's and mine invites death, don't you think more than ever I'll need a ghostwriter to speak on our behalf?

Speaking of death, for some reason these days before he falls asleep, Mori gets into a bad mood. I don't think it's because he hasn't been to school. I suspect it's the same with your son because both Mori and your son are *our children.* Mori, who's never crabby except when he's sick, gets in a bad mood when I tease him just before he falls asleep. It reminds me of the time my dying grandfather got angry at me as I clowned around trying to get his attention. An old man about to face death, *our children* about to fall asleep . . . how can the promise of regeneration and awakening possibly be an encouragement to them? It may well be that they can feel themselves dying and wish to sleep forever, you know. So, when old people and children face eternity, they devoutly long for its quiescence.

What sort of adventure awaits Mori and me? I'm hoping it'll involve the total renewal of consciousness and body because that's probably the only adventure Mori and I would ever seek!

What's man's most fundamental wish? Isn't it to have his own consciousness and body continuously revitalized? I want you to imagine for a minute the everlasting immutability of consciousness and body in the world after death. It's a dead-end. I imagine we can only, at best, make a cul-de-sac of it by facing our despairing hopelessness head on; that way we might gain some access to the true meaning of nothingness. Standing rooted to the bedside of the humorless Mori, frozen in the act of clowning, I'm completely at wit's end because, you see, I've no idea how to acquaint Mori with that *nothingness* which we should be receiving with open arms. Don't you flounder around like this time after time? As a father of *our children,* you too have to grope in the dark! **DON'T YOU? (YOU MUST!)**

2

The Installation of a Ghostwriter

1

Sometimes I've said to myself and others something like this, paraphrasing Lady Macbeth.

> These deeds must be thought
> After these ways; so, it will make us mad.*

This is the way we must think, for **IF WE DO SO**, we'll go mad.

As a ghostwriter, I know that Mori-father's quote from *Macbeth* omitted the word "not," that it should have read "must not be." Suppose I put the "not" back in; let's say I revised his Japanese translation to: We must not think that way, for **IF WE DO** we will go mad, what good will it do? But, all of what I'm going to set down in writing comes from Mori-father's dreams and experiences. Misquotes like this idiosyncratic translation might be motivated by Mori-father's desire to have some fun, to take me in. Although the ghostwriter's job begins with the words of the other, the sticking point of it all is that he must record them, yet filter them through his own consciousness and his own flesh. Through this process I'm to steal into Mori-father's secret world, learn about it in

---

*Shakespeare, *Macbeth*, Act II, Scene I.

34

minute detail, and, however fleetingly, grasp the essence of his existence. But not the other way around! I couldn't stand Mori-father occupying my world!

When do I act and speak in the manner of Lady Macbeth? When I read a news item in a foreign newspaper. Take, for example, when a newspaper printed a photograph of a contraption that looked like a round, oversized plastic toy, in the center of which sat an old friend of mine, Malcolm Maurier. He used to be really skinny; the only thing about him that this picture reminded me of was his narrow forehead. I bet the thick black frame of his shades and his mustache were to camouflage the melancholy brought about by his outlandish corpulence. The article said something like: At the controls is the thirty-eight-year-old *former* University of California professor of aeronautical engineering who designed and manufactured his own flying saucer. That's it, that's it! I said. No doubt about it, he's a *former* professor. Two and seven-tenths meters in diameter, equipped with eight twenty-four-horsepower engines, the two-seater flying saucer can fly at speeds of 270 kilometers per hour. It should pass the FAA test by next summer, the article continued, and he will start marketing them at $10,000 apiece.

Someone at a news agency, or a copy-editor at a newspaper—it's obvious it's a newsperson of some sort—is poking fun at Malcolm's prospects; I don't think his business venture'll pan out smoothly, either. Malcolm Maurier's intention—which I know quite well—has nothing to do with the manufacturing and marketing of a flying saucer. Two hundred and seventy kilometers an hour, what a joke! At that snail's pace, imagine it pioneering the way for the exploration of the Andromeda Galaxy? So, what was this alleged flying saucer all about? He meant to create a symbol in the guise of a *fake* flying saucer. That's all.

At the University of California's nuclear power research center, Malcolm and I, on the lookout for empty chairs and carrying loaded aluminum food trays, almost bumped into each other, but instead came upon two adjoining vacant places at a table. Malcolm grabbed my upper arm. Stay put right here, he said and disappeared in the crowd. He returned with two large glasses of milk and began a bubbly sort of chatter, the tone of his speech as frothy as the milk.

—— Just eat and listen! I hear the highland aborigines of your country have dragged a gigantic wooden airplane up to some denuded mountaintop. Their attitude toward appropriating a symbolic flying machine only highlights the alienation of civilized people, denied true flight because of PAN AM or AIR FRANCE. In their collective, tribal imagination the reality of flight is the soaring aloft taught by the gods. Right?

I was really thrown for a loop, but I couldn't help but say, I've heard something along those lines, but isn't it a tribe on a plateau in New Guinea? I had to correct him.

—— Well, my uncle was a pilot during the Pacific War and told me about it. Every time the Japanese lost a fighter plane, they'd line up a wooden mock-up on the airfield. Don't those wooden planes and the highland aborigines' originate from the same power of imagination?

—— I've heard the story about the Japanese dummy planes. I know for sure it's a true story. It's different, though, from that of the New Guinean tribe. Those fake kamikaze planes were more than just wood and canvas, something to fool the enemy; they were also a symbol—especially since the manipulation of that particular symbol, the "Divine Wind," was the basis of our militarists' suicidal and murderous ideology.

—— Then you can understand why I want to set up planes on an airfield in California so I can attempt to communicate with the "gods" soaring in the Cosmos, can't you? At critical junctures, humankind produces a universally understood symbol—and this is my route to ultimately understanding the totality of the me who lives and dies in the Cosmos.

True to his word, Malcolm showed me many blueprints of his flying saucer, and also told me about Jung. "We always think of a flying saucer as our own projection. However, we have now become its projection. The magic lantern projects me as a C. G. Jung. But the question is, who is operating the machine?" For Malcolm, Jung's question was transparently easy: the "gods" who've come to inspect an earth on the brink of annihilation are operating the magic lantern, ha, ha. I rooted around in my files and fished out an old Christmas card—a print of a flying machine M. M. himself had engraved on a copper plate—and sent a telegram to the address I found on the card, with some words of encouragement.

> These deeds must be thought
> After these ways; so, it will make us mad.

Malcolm Maurier was a leading light in aeronautical engineering, but he chucked his professorship at the University of California to pursue his dream. He took the plunge, and began producing and marketing an airplane with eight twenty-four-horsepower rotary engines, a hopelessly primitive machine by today's standards. When I think it over, I can't help feeling it's no good to set all your hopes on one singular adventure, a real adventure, staking everything on one precarious pre-monition. Yet, I also feel the might of my premonition waxing ever more powerful with time.

It appeared first as a dream. In the dream-adventure, Mori and I had aided and abetted an old man—whom I'd dubbed the "Patron"—in gaining absolute political power in Japan. Mori and I were in charge of a massive victory pageant celebrating the old man's conquest, and modeled on the German stormtroopers' torchlight march of January 30, 1933, in which the Nazis celebrated Adolf Hitler's successful confronta-tion with President von Hindenburg, ha, ha. The Patron stood smiling by the window of a VIP lounge on the twentieth floor of the Keio Plaza Hotel, gazed down at the sea of torchlights below him, did a little hop, skip, and dance as he listened to the reverberations of thousands of booted feet; his smile went wet with tears of joy, and then became a roar of hysterical laughter.

Of course his behavior was influenced by the historical model for our pageant: utter madness. In the dream, Mori and I had shown no inclina-tion either to control the Patron or to pay obeisance to him in his role of political fixer in Japan; symbolically he stood not so much for the citi-zens of Japan as for most of the human race. I understand the Koran contains this passage: "And we cried out to him. 'Abraham! You be-lieved in your own dream! That's where the indisputable evidence lies!' " In the dream, the Patron summoned the whole human race, "My fellow human beings! Believe in your dreams! That's where the indisputable evidence lies! In your dreams you see me suspended in space, like a figure in one of William Blake's* engravings, as though I would envelop every inch of the earth!" Mori and I were planning to transform the Patron into a symbol of humanity's understanding of itself and of the world. What a magnificent dream, ha, ha.

On the day I had this dream, I took a lot of time explaining the grandeur of the dream to Mori. It's my daily habit to talk to Mori—I'm sure you'd do the same if you were a parent of *our children*—about things he can understand and things he never will. Isn't it possible that the fine dust particles of my words—which Mori can't grasp now—like the dust accumulated over the centuries in a sealed cellar, might spon-taneously burst into flame one day? Mori never, ever, rejects what I say to him. After passing through the fantastic convolutions of the inner ear, might not my words, like grains of sand in an hourglass, eventually ac-cumulate inside the twilight cellar of his brain?

---

*William Blake, English poet and artist (1757–1827) who created fantastical engrav-ings, drawings, and paintings illustrating his mystic-poetic visions.

While we're on the subject of biological organisms, in prehistoric times a Cosmic Voice beamed a transmission to Earth, a place then devoid of anything which could have received a message from the Cosmic Dust. And my words fall on the bedrock of Mori's ear, fine dust accumulating, still uncomprehending of its own meaning, but with the potential to ignite spontaneously, becoming a life force—much the way the simplest organisms, amoebae, our remote ancestors, came into being. And to top the analogy off, the Cosmic Will might have composed out of Cosmic Dust a complex message that bore within itself the seed of every possible civilization, the stuff that would determine our DNA molecules and eventually lead to today's nuclear age, ha, ha.

Wait a minute. Hold on. Now I may be out of bounds here, but as your ghostwriter, I want to add a sort of footnote at this point, in the form of two questions. If today's nuclear civilization is the preordained course planet Earth and *Homo sapiens* were given to take, as willed in advance by the Cosmic Voice issuing out of the distant Cosmic Dust, if there was no way for us to take any other track, then wouldn't that mean Mori-father has shirked his responsibility not only as an ex-nuclear physicist but also as an individual? Isn't this the fundamental failure that's driving him and Mori to take refuge in dreams?

Don't be so hard on me, ha, ha. I can tell from your speedy rebuttal that I'm taking quite a risk just by talking about my dreams. Dreaming is a dangerous business in itself, let alone talking about it, right? Joseph's half-brothers said, We threw that master-dreamer into a pit in the wilderness, and a wild beast devoured him. Aren't there a lot of people out who'd do the same? When I talk to Mori about my dream, I fine-tune my description of the pageant he and I had staged in the dream. With Mori sitting quietly next to me, listening comfortably, giving ear to the whole sequence of sounds—not that he's trying to extract any meaning from my words—with Mori repeating a word here and there from time to time, I keep up the chatter and gradually succeed in spelling out the substance of my dream. You see, as I try to penetrate my own dream, I'm swayed by its twists and turns. In trying to figure out its meaning, I need a companion who'll keep me on the straight and narrow; and I've got Mori.

In my carefree dream world, I celebrated the political conquest of the Patron with a parade that I deliberately modeled on the Nazis' torchlight march of January 30, 1933, the day Hitler came to power. Why?

—— You see, Mori, in the dream, you and I tried to make the Patron a somebody, a man who's successfully seized immense power, who's superimposed the image of Hitler on himself. You know how uninhibited dream logic is. I'm sure if the Patron ever gets wind of this, he'll have a good laugh. I've never felt any ill will toward him, but on the other hand I can't help harboring hatred toward Hitler.

But a dream's a dream, its logic its own. Within the flow of my dream, how did I slip past the contradictions? Whatta ya say, Mori? You were with me in the dream, you know, ha, ha. Why don't you tell me? Once, when I had woken from the dream and was grappling with the Hitler issue, I tried to think of him as a buffoon who, in the final stage of playing Antichrist, bombed. In the beginning of *War and Peace*, Anna Pavlovna Scherer, speaking of Napoleon, says he's the true Antichrist; that's what I mean. An Antichrist appears right before the coming of the genuine article and goes around spreading false words: *The day of the Lord is coming. On the penultimate day there shall be apostasy. A man of iniquity, the child of destruction, must come before us*, remember that? *For there shall rise false Christs and false prophets who shall show great signs and wonders insomuch that, if it be possible, they shall deceive the very elect.* That's how he's described. But Napoleon the Antichrist? Everyone knows he sank into oblivion in the end, utterly routed. But Christ, the genuine article, never rose to destroy Napoleon and his troops; no nation of God was built. That particular Advent of Christ was canceled.

And wasn't Hitler also a failure, another one of those who bungled their attempt to be the Antichrist? He of course did succeed in sowing and bringing forth the seeds of mind-numbing horrors all around the globe. But again, it wasn't Christ who came back to destroy him; man did that. That in itself should be sufficient proof that Hitler was not the Antichrist, ha, ha. The fact that man snuffed out Hitler—caught with his pants down—means once again that the Second Coming of Christ was postponed. In light of that much-postponed Coming of Christ, it seems that the human virtue of taking up arms to beat the hell out of likely candidates for the role of Antichrist is relatively important, wouldn't you say? Christ is quite probably on tenterhooks about missing his comeback altogether. I would say, in short, that the battle to defeat each Antichrist is an existential necessity, a battle, furthermore, that is aided by God. And we must carry it out, Mori!

Now, back to the dream flow. I'm not sure yet how this battle fits in with objective, logical reality, but let's start, at any rate, by recognizing that the Patron is on a par with the almost-Antichrist Hitler. You see, while he was listening to the orderly reverberations of thousands of boots in the river of light, and while he gloried in all the echoes that bounced off the three colossal skyscrapers facing each other, the Patron stood by the window on the twentieth floor of the Keio Plaza Hotel, hopping, dancing, smiling, weeping for joy, and roaring with maniacal laughter. Wait! I've just remembered something else in this sequence of events, Mori, something which up till now escaped my mind! It's as if I'm slowly zooming in on the scene: the one hopping, dancing, smiling, weeping, and roaring with laughter isn't the "Patron." It's the two of us. Apparently we, the pair who until then had helped the Patron to take power and who staged the victory pageant, mutinied at the last moment. What's more, in the zoom shot, Mori and I, both of us almost the same height, look like two comrades-in-arms. So, putting the "Patron-as-Antichrist" theory aside, do you think this dream is totally meaningless, Mori?

Now as for dreams, this ghostwriter—while transcribing the original account—is of the opinion that it makes no difference whether it's a fabricated story or an actual dream, since fiction and dreams are fundamentally alike. Therefore, raising no questions, I transcribe as a dream this tale which Mori-father calls a dream; I ask nothing, even when the narrator furnishes me with no background information about the Patron who, for all I know, may be a real person. What I suspect, however, is that many tales to come, whether they're taken from real-life incidents or the reading of dreams, are already poised on the threshold of Mori-father's consciousness.

For a ghostwriter, what in the world is the function of words anyway? Whether they're the dreams Mori-father actually saw, or dreams he says he saw, in which case there's no way to substantiate his claim, or those sly verbal maneuvers in which he toys around with creating a subplot, those words—which I continue to write down—stab through my consciousness and body, yet remain unaffected. If words that touch on truth and fabrication are to remain meaningful, what sort of structure would make it possible? I wonder how that structure fits in with my consciousness and flesh?

2

To live on and on knowing my life is a fiction, rationalizing that as long as I'm aware of it there's no danger of the real me ever being deceived, I'm bound to end up suspended in midair, dangling in the wind. I'm saying this from experience. Not that this is anything to be proud of, though.

I've really got nothing to brag about despite the way I put on airs—speaking to a novelist makes me very self-conscious, ha, ha, because after all I'm about to divulge to you my relationship with my wife, with my co-workers at the nuclear power plant. Ethically, when hanging in the breeze, a person can't tell up from down. Is there any substantial difference between being hung from a crossbeam in one's backyard or in outer space? Now, when I say "backyard," I mean the one that belongs to the nuclear plant where I used to work; rumor has it that the storage tanks buried behind that plant began to leak plutonium and strontium 90, with cesium seeping into the local aquifer, but let's assume that's irrelevant here. I've been receiving a paycheck while on an unofficial extended leave of absence for the past ten years. I even signed an oath of secrecy; I start talking about this stuff, and I get lockjaw.

What shall I say, is this story bizarre or ordinary? Ten years ago when I had an accident at the nuclear plant, all I could think about was myself. I also expected my wife to think only of me, but just to make sure of that, I consciously put her out of my mind. I pitied, pitied, fervently pitied myself. Besides, because the radiation burns healed rapidly, I didn't think the nuclear exposure would kill me right away—although the specter of death constantly hovered over me. I didn't know anything about radiation medically; but nuclear physics being my specialty, I'm not totally ignorant of the dangers of radiation. Still, since radiation poisoning doesn't hit you like an iron pipe or a knife, I simply didn't think of it as a death blow.

With regard to my death, I dreamed, vaguely but persistently, about being saved by some magical force, just the way most children do the minute they're cognizant of their own mortality. In any case, I'm still doing it as a grown-up. From the moment I realized I'd die someday, I have stubbornly and irrationally believed that no simple accident could finish me off; only some devious and confounding karma-like force could manage to snatch my life away.

What was another ominous thing mixed up with the radiation exposure I suffered? I actually was quite aware of it from the start: the worst cancer will manifest itself anywhere from several years to a decade later. Plutonium is the most virulent known carcinogenic, far beyond any other yet known on earth. There may be a more virulent one in space, but we have to wait until one of those kangaroo-hopping astronauts picks it up off the moon's surface, ha, ha. At any rate, I felt consciously the magical power of that particular strain of lethal cancer, and as I thought about it, I was terrorized by the feel of its icy talons plucking out my soul, and there was nothing I could do but break out in a cold sweat. My wife brought an old sea sponge to the hospital room—come to think of it, she might have superstitiously relied on the intrinsic supernatural power of that weird object, ha, ha—in any case, she used it to poke at my forehead and nose. I wanted to tell her to lay off, but I couldn't muster an ounce of strength to say it, my terror and my stupor were so deep. If a radiation victim had said that he'd castrate himself to forestall further genetic contamination of humankind, I think I'd have willingly followed suit. Unable to allay my terror or bring me out of my stupor, my wife bore an embittered look in her eyes; as for me, I couldn't even begin to communicate what I felt. While I racked my brains out, obsessing over the plutonium-induced cancer to come, I trampled all over her feelings.

Two years later when Mori was born, I in turn ended up watching my wife completely absorbed in her own depression—nothing else caught her attention. Whether her eyes were harsh, bloodshot, glazed over, or steely, . . . it all depended on how she read the expression in my eyes; at any rate I kept vigil over her. In the meantime I felt I had to do something, so, I finally intervened, trying to open the heart closed off to me. Strange though it may be, the key I used was my nuclear accident of two years earlier. With infant Mori in the intensive care ward, my wife had no way of letting her maternal instinct blossom. There was no other way for me to draw her out of her shell but to go back to the time when I had retreated into my own; this is how I felt.

Rereading what I've just transcribed, I find as a ghostwriter that the previous passage is not quite convincing. Probably that's because Mori-father chooses not to mention the specifics of Mori's birth defects. Whenever Mori-father leaves something out—in his correspondence if he omits a return address, or on the phone where he yammers away nonstop—as long as he maintains silence on a subject, the ghostwriter is left totally helpless. I wonder why he doesn't talk about it? Is it because my son was born with the same defects as Mori and he considers it unnecessary to go over the details with me?

I personally can't say with any certainty whether I suspected how utterly off balance my wife's psyche was thrown when my son was born abnormal. Flat on her back, forcibly prevented from peering down between her thighs, she heard the nurse gasp, Yiii! the moment her child came into the world.

It wasn't until five years later that I started picking up the feeble pulse of electricity within the closed circuit of her psychic world. I happened to be right next to her when, at the time of the normal birth of our second child, she told a nurse: It took me a lot of courage to go through another pregnancy after *that*, to hang on for nine months and face labor again. While I had ejaculated without giving a thought to the possible repetition of abnormalities in her second delivery, my wife, who seemed at the time also to be reaching orgasm, let out a single groan from deep within her pent-up circuit of enmity and terror.

What stratagem did I use to break into her closed world? I kept telling her a lie that was an outrage not only against *former* colleagues of mine at the nuclear plant but also against the victims of Hiroshima-Nagasaki: I told her Mori's skull abnormality was caused by my exposure to radiation; because of *that,* all this *happened.* I almost went so far as to say that my plutonium-induced cancer cells were transferred to Mori's head where they proliferated. And my wife believed me. What was the short-circuited result of this? Her decision never to have a baby again. This meant that she threw away the opportunity to exorcise her womb by having a healthy delivery.

I of course knew it was a lie the moment I uttered it. That's why, even though all the buds of a plutonium-induced cancer were rooted out as far as I know from all the cells in my body, and never transformed themselves into a cyst in Mori's head, I've been hounded, hounded ever since by the dread of a recurrence of a stigmatic cancer. Besides, in my life with my wife I renew this lie daily, so the only thing I can do is twist in the wind.

My wife has a very logical mind. She is imbued with a sense of mission, driven to carry out matters to their logical—and consequently attainable—conclusions, however awkward those conclusions may be. To wit: if I impregnate other women, out come more babies with abnormal skulls; in her estimation, you see, this would harm the well-being of all humankind; in a word, taking up the cross of global justice, she began to stymie my love affairs, ha, ha.

It may well have been my own lie and my wife's confidence in its validity that reduced me to impotence with Sakurao Ōno. If you live knowing a lie is a lie, you end up twisting in the wind: an axiom. My wife's righteousness was based not upon mere jealously, but on the higher obligation to eliminate inferior genes from future human stock, a mission to safeguard my affairs, ha, ha.

As a ghostwriter, I reflected on the behavior of Mori-mother, viewing it in a different light as she waited in the corner of the playground for *our children.* She criticized Sakurao Ōno with great solemnity as though talking about an impending world food shortage, never stooping to the ugliness of jealousy. She seemed to harbor a powerful albeit unhealthy passion in the guise of someone driven by a grand obsession. Mori-father certainly observed that himself. Whatever their current relationship may be, I feel the evidence is clear that they've at least rooted around in the very bowels of conjugal understanding, a situation the birth of *our children* drives all of us parents into whether we like it or not.

Now I want you to know specifically what my daily life twisting in the wind was like. As a result of joint efforts by the labor union at the nuclear plant and the Ōno contingent, I am now an *ex*-employee who's still on the payroll but doesn't have to go to work. An investigative report on radiation victims in the fledgling nuclear power industry is worth every penny it costs, which is why the labor union was very enthusiastic about such a report and management took the initiative in offering me an excellent deal, I'm sure. But to cut the deal I had to sign an oath of secrecy, so when I tell you about my accident—later on—I can't go into great detail, you see. Anyway, paid but with no job, I have no reason in the world to go to bed at any particular time, but since I've held a part-time job for quite a while now, I'm up at least till midnight. When I start drinking boilermakers at one in the morning, just before drowsiness takes hold, the alcohol reenergizes me. Relying on this brief surge of energy, I go over to Mori and call out.

—— Mori, Mori, get up, time to pee!

In the fleeting instance before and after I wake him up, depending on Mori's physical condition and the kind of food he ate at supper, I sometimes find him wetting his *diaper*. I must take him still half-asleep to the bathroom, change the *diaper* before he's through urinating, and wipe dry the plastic lining for the *diaper* cover: don't you do the same? At Mori's or your son's age, to cover his buttocks requires an enormous *diaper*, and when it's wet, mopping the cover off with a *diaper* that still has some dry spots becomes quite a chore, I must say. With the kind of stamina I have, I definitely need a boilermaker's help.

The ghostwriter can't help thinking at this time of the plastic sheeting problem. Whenever the supply of plastic runs out temporarily, the first item to disappear from the store shelves is the large vinyl sheets that can cover the buttocks of a fat eight-year-old. After asking around, I ultimately chase some down somewhere, and anticipating an uncertain future, I try to purchase the vinyl in large quantities. A veritable army of accusatory eyes turns on me: a man who on the spur of the moment, with some nefarious scheme up his sleeve, is buying up all the extra large-size vinyl sheets. Mori-father must have experienced those same hostile stares, the eyes of strangers condemning something highly irregular. Wave after wave of insult and humiliation lie in ambush for fathers of *our children.*

But what tests my stamina the worst is when Mori hasn't yet wetted himself, holding his urine to the very limit of endurance. His penis, like the head of a snapping turtle, is poised to take a bite out of me. I don't mean that it takes stamina just to hold down this turtle head, ha, ha. But to brace for the assault of his young body with that distressingly hard, hard penis of which I catch a glimpse as it slams into my stomach with a bang, that's why I need the stamina.

Am I referring to a semi-impotent man, to the seat of desire, my solar plexus? No, that's not even remotely the case, but I don't have to tell you that, do I? When I was seventeen, eighteen years old, I had to poke a hole in my pants pocket so I could keep the penis that would stay rock-hard all day down with my hand, ha, ha. Even after Mori's through urinating, when his erection hasn't quite gone down yet, I've got to hold it while putting him into the *diaper.* Its dazzling bounce shakes me up. Of course, Mori is innocence itself. Lately he's the "time demon," trying to assign a time for every step of daily life; wrapped up in a blanket, he peers at the clock.

—— **ONE TWELVE!** The minute he says this, he's out like a light.

What kind of signals was my wife receiving from Mori's engorged penis? At this moment I go back to the kitchen, tend to the spot Mori has messed up, and to gird myself for sleep, I keep knocking back the boilermakers; but cooling my guts like this only smooths the way for chronic diarrhea.

Just the other day, I woke up to find my bed shrouded in morning mist—I can tell you for sure, I wasn't camping out in the highlands, ha, ha. I usually sleep with the partition door between Mori's bed and mine open; my wife, who's always careful not to disturb me when she gets up to dress Mori, was obviously doing something with the window next to Mori's bed wide open.

Mori's penis, stiff with the itch to urinate, was slapping against his thighs while he lay on the unbuttoned *diaper* cringing with his eyes shut tight, dead-still, just as a small, cunning animal plays dead to escape.

At the foot of the bed, level with Mori's abdomen, crouched my wife. Hiked up around her skinny thighs was an old-fashioned slip I'd never seen before—the only thing she had on. Her genitals, exposed in bold relief, hung cold in the morning mist. She peered down at them intently, immobilized. I then noticed beside the *diaper* cover her left hand clutching a razor—she's a lefty—a memento of her father's, a curved Solingen he had brought back from Germany, where he studied.

3

I wonder if you've heard the rumors about the **YAMAME CORPS**. I happened to be right there, at the exact spot where history was made, exactly at the time of the Corps's birth. I feel a certain sense of pride in the fact that my path and that of the Yamame Corps have crossed at least once by my reckoning. When the Yamame Corps first armed itself and set off on a long march to a place where no police manhunt could ever find them, it just by chance originated at the Kuma River, a mountain stream in Azuma County in Gunma Prefecture, where I was trying to get as much *yamame* fishing done as I could, right up to the day before fishing season ended.

I've no doubt that the Yamame Corps is still out there somewhere, persevering in their collective lifestyle. Unless of course they've destroyed themselves in some factional bloodbath en route to some isolated mountain refuge. In the Corps, the legend of their radical first act that autumn must get recounted again and again as the touchstone of their history. It has always stirred my blood and continues to do so whenever I think back on those days. It's even possible that listening to that inspirational legend gives new recruits to the Corps their first lesson in guerrilla training. Although that formative mission was carried out under the collective command of an organization, the Yamame Corps, it was at the same time an expression of intense personal passions.

This episode appears in a letter, so far the most passionate and meticulous of the messages sent in by Mori-father. After making me transcribe those rather depressing domestic scenes, was he trying to cheer me up, fearing that I might get sick of ghostwriting? It's perfectly possible that the following, as relayed in one of Mori-father's letters—which I'm now going to rewrite—may be a total fabrication.

As I told you before, I fished for *yamame* from the summer through the autumn of that year at a mountain stream, the Kuma River—not that I was some kind of freshwater fishing maniac. Although it's true that going after the *yamame,* unlike other types of fishing, requires one to sacrifice whatever profession one might have as well as all other pleasures to single-mindedly concentrate on wading deep into a mountain stream, putting one's whole life on the line to catch that powerful, elusive fish. There's very little room in this sport for someone with my background: born into a poor country family, earning a physics degree—with a lot of difficulty—then landing a job at a nuclear power plant where I slaved my ass off over every assignment just to outshine my co-workers.

However, after that accident at the plant, the management and the union both begged me to take it easy, essentially to sit on my behind and do nothing from summer through autumn of my convalescent year. You see, I couldn't go back to a workplace that still posed a radiation hazard; I was deprived of an excuse to resume my work-and-slave routine. So I stayed that summer at the company dorm, living the life of the sinecurist, the keep-him-on-the-payroll convalescent.

An engineer had stayed there the previous summer—an elderly man, a consummate engineer, they said—and left behind an entire outfit for freshwater fishing. Like me, he'd never in his whole life had anything to do with such a demanding sport. I also found quite a few primers he had stashed away on the subject, which I pilfered without pangs of conscience; that the engineer would never again take up the sport was a pretty sure thing. He'd been spared exposure to radiation; what he had suffered was a nervous breakdown: he became a paranoid, obsessed with the fear that nuclear material would be stolen from a reactor by terrorists, and that an engineer would be kidnapped and forced to manufacture an atomic bomb. He spent one whole summer in the company dorm trying to recuperate, but his depression worsened and he hung himself right after finally persuading his family to emigrate with him to a country where there were no reactors, or so the story goes.

Toting the plastic rod left behind by this man who fretted himself to death about vulnerability in the nuclear age, I walked among the birch trees down to the Kuma River. Since I had no intention of moving along the river the way a pro at mountain-stream fishing would, I simply chose a convenient spot near the forest road. I scooped up some caddis-worms from the shockingly frigid water, letting my line out into the *depths* where the broad shallows change into eddies. Before I knew it, I had snagged a powerful, writhing *yamame*! Though the water was clear, it conducted dark milky shadows—sand, no doubt, kicked up by whirlpooling eddies. The *yamame's* skin displayed the same dark milki-ness of the water, striped in vermilion, with flecks of black. There's no freshwater trout in the region where I was brought up, you know; I was dazzled by this trout's coloration, and the savage line of its jaw. That fifteen-centimeter *yamame* packed such a wallop it was a while be-fore my ears again tuned into the sounds of the river.

From then on I hooked a fish a day, always at the very same spot where I had my first encounter with a *yamame*. On Saturdays and Sundays the real pros converged on the stream, continually moving upstream with the river's flow, quickly and effortlessly catching fish, while the local anglers scored just as easily with their flies. Only I stayed behind at my spot, where the pros would cast out a few times before moving on, and time and again I would plop the caddisworms out into the *deeps*, a really unlikely spot indeed to catch any fish with a fly. But you see, all I needed was one fish a day. And every descending dusk brought a shower. Those meteorological changes did something to the *yamame* swimming near the riverbed, probably made them eat the worms which always showed up in the same spot. I never failed to catch *yamame* there. After I had thoroughly immersed myself in the primers, I had the urge to go at the sport in earnest; I once went into the river in waders, waders left behind by the man who fretted about the future, and proceeded upstream past a salmon hatchery, but no bites. Unable to go on because of fog and the rapidly gathering dusk, I started to come out of the rapids, searching for signs of a trail to the forest road, when I ran into an angler in full array, casting his fly into the deep water. I couldn't get over his reaction when he finally did notice me. A strange reaction. Strange indeed.

—— Well, look at you! Say, you didn't catch anything, did you? It's dangerous, you know, where you've been, there's bear! said the man with a sneer.

BEAR, that's the key. A bear was what had given the Yamame Corps the impetus for the myth of their own early history!

You see, Azuma County is in the highlands, and autumn arrives very abruptly. First there are downpours for four or five days, and the river gets muddy and overflows its banks. Since I was really getting into *yamame* fishing, I had to go out to take a look at the river when the rain finally let up, but found the river in a phase totally unlike that of the summer. Uprooted trees hung over the water's edge, landslides from the forest road had altered the river's course, and the once dense bushes lining the riverbank were now on a sand bar. The sand is quite extensive, according to a farmer's wife who used to come to the dorm to sell vegetables.

And this same sand bar was eventually to gain a lot of attention in the news; at any rate, early the following morning in the dense slow-drifting fog—the rain had let up completely—two young men came down the forest road, running for dear life. They really had to scramble just to get away, they said, and had come in search of help at a nearby hotel which was just about to close now at the end of fishing season. The two young men were camping out with some friends, so the story goes, to catch small *yamame* at the end of the season, but the rains had come, stranding them on the sand bar created by the rising water which I mentioned earlier. But the rising waters had also marooned a large female bear and her cub: realizing their predicament the young people froze in terror. With some effort, the two-man suicide squad had finally crossed the river and contacted some people at the hotel. The remaining five campers, including a women, were still stranded with the bears. Now it so happened that thirty executive officers of the Shinshu Hunting Association were at the hotel having a get-together. When they heard the news, they marched downstream en masse, of course carrying with them their most prized possessions, hunting rifles, and plenty of ammo.

However, once the entire party had crossed over to the sand bar, their guides, the two young men, promptly turned right around and took the guns one by one from the startled executives. The rest of the seven campers emerged to help collect the guns and ammunition. Disarmed, the executives were then ordered to remove their waders, so we're told, and dump those into the river. The executives were at a distinct disadvantage, not prepared to shoot humans in the first place. And how could they put up a fight when those youths had seized their guns, two or three of them holding those very weapons ready at the hip? Now without waders there was also no way they could cross the rapids in the shockingly frigid water. The six boys and the girl loaded the thirty brand-new hunting rifles into a rubber boat and made their get-away, cutting across the current. The executives say the gang leader even made a fine farewell speech saying something like, On behalf of the Yamame Corps I want to thank you for donating your weapons. The thirty hunters then sat stranded on the sand bar, waiting for some passersby on the forest road—of course, after building a barricade of rocks and trees, just in case there really were bears, ha, ha.

This story really hooked me, and so I tried to follow up on any rumors I heard of the fledgling "Yamame Corps," and the new myth that had suddenly sprung up around the Kuma River. But although those seven youngsters had been responsible for the group's mythic beginnings, they seemed to have been very reticent activists, indeed leaving not a word behind that might give someone a lead as to where they'd come from and where they'd gone.

But why, you might ask, didn't the newspapers exploit this juicy bit of gossip by reporting the incident? It could only be because the legal authorities felt it their duty to put a gag order on the newspapers, fearing the news of thirty rifles in the hands of a group of young men might panic the public. But since I happened to be at the right place, at the right time, I was able to follow up on the myth and rumors.

Now I mentioned gag orders because nowadays I believe that authorities all over our country use them—it would be my guess that an alarming number of incidents never make the newspapers in our country. I know for a fact that something like this is going on in relation to the Nuclear Regulatory Commission. As I told you before, I myself am being paid compensation as an *ex*-researcher at a nuclear power plant, bound by an agreement *not* to leak the specifics of my radiation exposure to the mass media. I still need the money to survive, so I won't tell you now about the core of the incident, ha, ha.

I think there are more people out there who've been exposed to radiation the way I have. I can't possibly be the only one who's been persuaded by management and the union to keep the whole thing a secret, who's maintained silence on the subject. No wonder nuclear power costs so much, ha, ha. Whether you talk about the nuclear waste the plants produce, or the superheated waste water, the environmental destruction is obvious, but nuclear power is touted as *the* energy source, humankind's hope for the future. To say that I had a minor accident makes me feel somehow shabby, as though I'm continually finding fault with humankind's future. Silence has become my mainstay.

However, I can give you one actual example of a newspaper reporting such an incident. Remember awhile ago? An electrical engineer at a nuclear plant in the Tohoku region died of leukemia. He'd been hired by a subcontractor specializing in reactor safety control. For four years he inspected and repaired the reactors. Hospitalized last May, he was dead by the end of this year. For me the arcane details of the disease don't matter, but they reported it was a kind of leukemia that destroys individual cells that produce leukocytes. The company had already asked the mass media to keep a lid on the case, and the bereaved family also wanted it kept secret, or so they said. During his six-month stay in the hospital, even the engineer had kept the matter to himself, never speaking to any of his fellow patients about his condition. If he went public and his compensation were cut off, he'd lose all outside financial help, and in the midst of the nuclear-power-for-peace boom he'd surely be isolated and ignored, the only person to suggest putting the commercial use of nuclear power on the back burner. Now do you think a dying man could withstand such pressure? There are many such silent victims out there, *ex*-technicians, who are ill, secretly convalescing from their exposure to radiation.

Because of my binding contract which I already mentioned, a cartoonization of my predicament is the only way for me to talk about my accident; the actual incident I was involved in, however, occurred outside the plant. That was the first of many reasons why management and the union decided to keep things hush-hush.

It was like this. I was on a moving truck loaded with enough nuclear material to make twenty atomic bombs. There were only three of us, a driver, his assistant, and me, the supervisor from the plant, cruising down the highway, out in the open, without a single armed guard to escort us. What a daring feat, ha, ha!

According to preliminary research done by the ghostwriter in an attempt to understand the basis of Mori-father's "cartoonization," the technical particulars go something like this. At a nuclear plant, the vast heat created by a radioactive element undergoing fission is used to convert water into high-pressure steam that drives a massive turbine generator. Rods of "enriched" uranium—uranium in a more concentrated and volatile form—serve as the fissionable fuel. But the very process of fission itself transforms the uranium atom into an even more volatile and radioactive element: plutonium. Once a year the uranium rods, partially now plutonium, are taken out of the reactor and chemically treated to "wash away" the plutonium.

Ralph Lapp, who worked on the production of the Hiroshima-Nagasaki A-bombs, and after the war became a vociferous critic of the nuclear establishment—though not calling for a total ban on nuclear proliferation—wrote that the rods in the gigantic lead containers were extremely heavy and too "hot," radioactively, for any gangsters to steal. However, the green liquid chemically dissolved at the retreatment plant, the nitrous plutonic acid, has relatively weak radioactivity, and is often transported in containers by truck. Gangsters would have an eye out for those.

The ghostwriter, presuming that the nuclear material for twenty nuclear bombs is in that green liquid, feels confident of the plausibility of the above scenario, regardless of how jumbled together fact and imagination may be in the tale. But even if one succeeded in stealing the liquid, one must then refine it, requiring large facilities and expert engineers. Still, if one were to keep on insisting that, given all those complications, a nuclear thief would still go for the barrels, that would indeed be very plausible.

We were driving a large truck back to the nuclear plant from the treatment facility, where we had received a load of nuclear material. After finally fighting our way out of a traffic jam, we entered the private road that led to the power plant on the coast. Little did we know then that we were already captives. A small canopied truck—it must have been tailing us since we'd left the retreatment plant—passed us, honking, and then pulled us over; that was how everything started. Without an armed escort, there was no use resisting, was there? First of all, I had no idea what was going on; probably a speeding ticket, I thought. When I look back on things now, it was odd that police would be using a canopied truck. Our driver simply thought that the other truck was calling our attention to something that was wrong with the truck bed and wanted to let us know about it. The other driver made his appearance in front of our truck, wearing white gloves, and obviously confident of his actions as he signaled us to stop. The other truck's canopy flap flew open, and five, maybe six young men jumped out, vividly recalling the Tin Man in *The Wizard of Oz*, right down to the rattling and clanging. The sight of a group of men brought immediate outcries from the company driver and his assistant when our vehicle came to a halt. The two barked out their anger and embarrassment at the group.

—— **WHAT, WHAT, WHAT?** What the hell is that?

—— **WHAT, WHAT, WHAT?** What the hell is this?

You might say the Tin Men looked agile, yet clumsy; they certainly were energetically hopping helter-skelter around us, but their movements were also very awkward, as if they didn't quite know what they were after. Every one of them carried a two-pronged pitchfork, just about as long as they were tall.

—— **WHAT, WHAT, WHAT?** What the hell is that?

—— **WHAT, WHAT, WHAT?** What the hell is this?

The Tin Men held the door on the driver's side shut tight with their pitchforks, and the driver and the assistant uttered those cries, even more angered and embarrassed than before. At that moment for the first time I was seized by an intense fit of anxiety, an anxiety brought on by our assailants' strange outfits. Then I was overcome with a foreboding: Whatever these guys pull off, there'll be a terrible disaster. The Tin Men getups—definitely G.I. surplus arctic parkas attached to heavy-looking metallic sheets—may have been intended as radiation suits but they were more the product of vague, instinctual fear than scientific know-how. Still, those Tin Men messing around back there in the truck were our country's first nuclear hijackers. . . .

They began banging on the driver's door. The driver and his assistant once again took up their noisy chorus of anger and confusion.

—— **WHAT, WHAT, WHAT,** banging like that, what the hell are they doing?

—— **WHAT, WHAT, WHAT,** banging like this, what the hell are they doing?

There was nothing I could do but sort of editorialize on the point being made by our assailants.

—— They're telling us to open the door. Looks like they've masked themselves with towels underneath those hoods, their voices are muffled. But I don't think they mean us any harm. No need for that.

The pitchforks kept on banging; the driver had a distant, preoccupied look on his face as he pulled open the door. Heat rose off the pavement and wafted up with it the body odors of the Tin Men, assailing our nostrils. One particularly rank Tin Man reached out with his bulky metal-covered arm and jerked the key out of the ignition. A sweaty patch of salmon-pink skin between his army glove and the parka's sleeve was visible.

The Tin Man who'd grabbed the key slammed the door and ran back clink-clank to the driver's side of the canopied truck. Giving him time to hop on the running board, the hijackers backed around to the rear of our truck. Their driver, a pale-looking guy, was the only one not dressed as a Tin Man and instead wore a shirt unbuttoned at the top. Well, I only caught a glimpse of him because the Tin Man on the running board threatened me with his pitchfork to make me back away from the truck. This small truck is for transporting school lunches, I said to myself, and my mind began to take off on a tangent with a life all its own. The primary school markings triggered everything I did after that. Isn't it just a little bit funny? I didn't have a kid then, and had no interest in having one.

But when I saw the markings, I felt as if, deep inside my ear, I was hearing loud voices shouting, *GO, GO, GO.* In other words, I found myself in the very state of agitation that a pinch runner would be in, confronted with impending terror, while a pitiful ambition simultaneously tempted me.

Despite the fact that I was an engineer at the nuclear plant in charge of transporting radioactive material, I had already detached myself from the hijacking incident, and wasn't as indignant as the driver and his assistant. All I had was an uncomfortable premonition of danger, vast and vague in its contours and potentiality. However, the instant those echoes of *GO, GO, GO* flashed to mind, all the blood in my body rushed to my head.

These Tin Men are loading the primary school lunch truck with radioactive material; that means they're probably going to refine the stuff into plutonium at a school gym vacated for the summer recess. Chances are some punk science teacher who's just gotten a spot at the school will be supervising the process. But can this inexperienced gang possibly pull it off without botching it? Even if they make it, the gym will be contaminated: refined plutonium oxidizes spontaneously on contact with air, so the dust of plutonium oxide will be scattered all over the gym. Children will inhale the dust, and the school will be filled by children with lung cancer.

After I figured this scenario out, I said to myself out loud, **GO, GO, GO,** scrambled over my driver and his assistant, and jumped out of the truck through the unguarded door, shaking off their angry shouts.

—— **WHAT IS IT, WHAT IS IT?** Man, you're pale. Don't drag us into anything!

—— **WHAT IS IT, WHAT IS IT?** Man, you're pale. Don't get us into a fix!

By the time I'd made my move, the Tin Men had already loaded all the barrels they'd wanted. They stood around staring down at the green liquid dripping from the truck bed. At least one of the containers had broken.

Now that it was too late, these nuclear thieves foolishly began to brood over whether or not the leaking liquid would penetrate their Tin Man suits—they hadn't even brought a Geiger counter with them. One of the Tin Men guards noticed my escape and chased clink-clank after me; this alerted those who were looking at the green stain on the ground. I started screaming incoherently, trying to intimidate them. I was immediately cornered and forced to jump into the canopied truck.

—— **CONTAMINATION EVERYWHERE!** The truck, the pavement, everything's contaminated! All of you are contaminated! If you drive this truck around, all of Tokyo'll be contaminated! **STAY AWAY, STAY AWAY, STAY AWAY!**

Too scared to step up on the truck bed, or do anything else, all the Tin Men could do was stab at me with their pitchforks, provoking me to scream at the top of my lungs as I squatted behind one of the remaining barrels. But they kept stabbing: I was now beginning to feel the pain from the rain of blows, and the chemicals around me started to burn my skin; I wouldn't quit shouting. I would neither give in to the clink-clank of the Tin Men's armor, nor give up my shrieking.

—— **CONTAMINATION EVERYWHERE!** You've been exposed! I've been exposed! I'm one mass of burns! Are you going to drive this thing all over Tokyo? Give every kid lung cancer? You'll contaminate everything! **STAY AWAY, STAY AWAY, STAY AWAY!**

The canopied vehicle was not moving, and the pitchfork assault, more perfunctory, continued haphazardly. Suddenly I heard thunderous, frantic clink-clanking as the Tin Men began to run. The burns hurt so much I didn't even have strength left to come out from behind the barrel. I could no longer shout about the contamination. I shook violently, barely able to respond to the voices that continued to ring in my ear, **GO, GO, GO.** This was how I came to be exposed to radiation.

3

But They're Ancient History

1

But they're ancient history; I mean absolutely gone, dead and buried. Because they're what happened before the "switchover" of Mori and me. What is a switchover? I sometimes believe I keep on going, hanging in there, overcoming all kinds of post-switchover hardship just to talk about it, ha, ha. But to narrate this story in a convincing manner to you, or to the unseen masses through you, seems such a difficult thing to do! I can't just generalize about my experiences. That's why I've only talked tentatively about past history, about those things that are absolutely gone, dead and buried.

That's also why I need you, the ghostwriter. You see, the me who's spoken to you up till now is the already switched-over me. If I'd put down a pre-switchover history as a post-switchover man, there's no way an amateur like me could've made it realistic enough. You see, this chronicle of the distant past was a prerequisite for you to understand the switchover of Mori and me.

So far I've chosen not to talk about it. I did drop a hint now and then, though, about a weird premonition I had, describing the way this transformation happened to the pre-switchover me, the way it happened in my life as reality merged with dreams. After the "switchover," a ghostwriter was the only channel I could use to open up communication with the Other, the unseen masses. What's more, the ghostwriter's role will

become more and more crucial, because the post-switchover me—
even while he takes upon himself the task of talking to the whole
human race about the true meaning of the switchover, must act rather
than write, again for the sake of humanity! I'm damned busy, ha, ha.

Now that the ghostwriter's role has been clarified for the reader and
me, so has the nature of this transcribing task, with Mori-father as the
central figure. Therefore, commentaries—prompted once by the in-
compatibility of Mori-father the narrator and me the scribe—will hardly
be necessary. Besides, with my interest now keenly aroused, I'm drawn
to this idea of a switchover, or to Mori-father, who insists on it. Unless he
suddenly falls silent, I doubt if I'll ever relinquish the role of ghostwriter.

* * *

Well, back to the switchover of Mori and me: How did it begin?
First—I want this etched indelibly in your mind—it happened in the
early spring, on a day when the snowfall was so heavy that the seasons
seemed reversed: undoubtedly this was very significant. When I awoke
in the pitch-dark room I immediately sensed, by the nature of the noise
around me— different from what I heard on normal days—and by the
chill in the air, the presence of the snow blanketing the outer world. In
those days depression set in every time I woke up, and I usually felt as
though something inside of me was crumbling; but on that morning—
or rather, a little before noon—I got up in high spirits, bursting with
vim and vigor.

Mori was also ebullient over the snow, apparently up since dawn
watching it lightly touch down. It appeared as though his consciousness,
fettered in semidarkness, had expanded in its exhilaration, and, however limited, his movements had become more lively, his daring heightened. I think that was the direct cause of what happened on that snowy
afternoon, the last big event before the switchover. No matter how
erratic Mori's behavior might have seemed, once it had gone through
its own processes, you could clearly trace its own causal chain. There's
no capriciousness, no trial and error for Mori, which is of course *the*
main problem with *our children*, ha, ha.

My dear wife, however, was in particularly bad shape that day. At
dawn, Mori had come to wake her up so she would change his wet
diaper. To make matters worse, someone from Ōno's civil rights group
happened to call me up. Looking like a grumpy bird, she crawled into
her mental shell and didn't even bother to look out at the snow that
had piled up on the ground. With nowhere to go and the outside

unnaturally bright, all the shadows congregated in one spot; I had the illusion that they'd taken my wife's form, ha, ha. In matching heavy overcoats with identical long wool scarves, and with Mao caps covering our heads, Mori and I stepped outside in our knee-high boots. Strangers—their long-dormant imaginations stimulated by the snow—gaped at us in astonishment as they passed us on the narrow, shoveled road. When they got back home in a festive mood, owing partly to the snow, it's possible, you know, that they said something like,

——I ran into a weird pair today, a little guy and a big guy, dressed alike from the tops of their caps to the tips of their boots. When we got a closer look, even their faces, one regular, the other a scaled-down version of the other, were alike as two peas in a pod. They flipped out their penises, one tiny, the other huge, one partially erect, the other limp, and both urinated energetically! They weren't parent and child, but more like grown-up brothers, one normal, the other a dwarf. Ha, ha. Mori and I would never urinate in the snow. I just now made that bit up; it's something which a man inside me—who's my obsession—said off the top of his head.

That day, Mori and I went out to pick up the leader of the antinuke movement in southern Shikoku, who was to meet us after taking a ferry boat to Honshu and transferring to a Bullet Train. It was all because of my ten-year off-and-on association with the Ōno group, you see. The members often use a phrase, "ten years since the radiation exposure"; activists at informal gatherings put questions to me like, What sort of physical and psychological pains do you have now? Of course, it's impossible to tell them what I really think and feel when I'm depressed, so I make small talk instead. Local activists are particularly diligent and frantic about their note-taking, probably because they've got to send reports to their fundraisers back home. As an engineer with experience at a nuclear power plant, I can't help correcting them when incorrect information is bandied about. After all, my existence can't be totally useless to them.

Of course Ōno was the real reason I went to those antinuke meetings. My wife would've done everything possible to prevent me from going, but, how could she, a sensate hominid in the Nuclear Age, possibly oppose a fight against the nuclear industry, which, as she understood it, helped bring about her own husband's radiation exposure, disrupted his chromosomes, caused her to give birth to one of *our children*, and to top it off, precluded her from having a normal childbirth? She takes pride in the fact that she once was a medical student; deep down, being a woman of principle, she can't turn her back on a civil rights group which is at the forefront of protest against the nuclear industry just because its leader happens to be Ōno.

And what's so grotesque, even absurd and sad about it all is that my wife sometimes suspects that her own womb was somehow the cause of the accident, not the plutonium irradiation. That's why she feels duty-bound to renew and reconfirm her own rancor.

——We're going to the Bullet Train platform. The Bullet Train we rode when we went to Grandma's house, Mori.

——**BULLET TRAIN!**

This was how our dialogue proceeded as we were jostled by the crowd at the ticket counter; then I let go of his hand which I had been clasping all along. I had to purchase tickets to get onto the platform. I tried going straight up to the ticket window, but it suddenly dawned on me that four or five people were already in line; I almost stumbled as I did an about-face, and joined the end of the line. . . . The temperature inside the station was broiling; I felt woozy as I waited my turn, dressed suited for the snow, and besides, crowds tend to make me react like an epileptic. With two tickets in hand I turned around to give one to Mori: **HE'D VANISHED INTO THIN AIR!**

The crowd's momentum was propelling people to the right, away from the ticket counter, toward the main exit of the station. I yelled for him at the top of my lungs but my voice was drowned in the throng.

——**MORI, MORI!** I cried out in vain.

While shouting I almost lost my balance, and as the crowd surged on, it carried my body with it. I managed to halt in front of the main exit, but remembered Mori had no ticket, you see. I squirmed and peered through the gateway; soon another wave of people scooped me up and hurried me onto the passageway that led to the gates for the Keihin, Yamanote, and Chūo Lines. I ended up making a circuit of the whole station, and here I was back at the Bullet Train gate, but there was still no sign of Mori. It was way past the arrival time of the Hikari, the Bullet Train I had come to meet. Totally flustered, and feeling utterly incompetent, I went through the gate, running bowlegged upstairs to the Hikari platform, and saw two young men waiting, displaying the Ōno organization flag.

——Thanks for coming! I understand his train'll be delayed an hour because of the snow. They reported their data, looking typically collected and composed.

——I've just lost my son somewhere over there.

——Lost Mori? I bet it's an AEC conspiracy! You know, the U.S. Atomic Energy Commission?

——Are you nuts?! I'd finally lost it.

——Why not! Why does it seem impossible!

But they set aside their global persecution complex for the moment, and employing the same practicality as they would, let's say, in preparing for demonstrations, immediately stopped a security guard on patrol. He'll surely take down the name of the missing child, his age, sex, address, even the parent's profession, they said. Mori's eight years old, all right, but he won't tell you his name if you ask him. Besides, he won't show any of the anxiety that might tip someone off that he's a missing child.

——He's eight, all right . . . , with a cranial birth defect . . . and he may be aware he's lost, but he won't cry or yell. . . .

——You mean the abnormality's that obvious?

——The lump's already been removed if that's what you mean! Had to be!

The guard wanted me to come to the railroad security office, but how could I sit around at a time like this? One of the activists, full of practical suggestions, volunteered to go on my behalf. I started combing the platform again, beginning with the area around the ticket window, and eventually scoured the whole station. The structure of the building itself is rather simple, but Tokyo Station has a tremendous depth to it, a perfect labyrinth for children like *our children*; besides, you know that down there tracks shoot off to every part of Japan.

An hour after the hunt began, the young Ōno men came down the stairs flanking a small middle-aged man, the leader of the Shikoku antinuke movement. Already briefed by the young men about how my son's abnormality had been radiation-induced—a deception originally meant for my wife—the small man was determined to aid in the search, and kept pestering me about Mori's physical features.

——You'll know right away he's an idiot, two-thirds my size! A sad look in his eyes was his only response to my crude retorts.

While we poked into every nook and cranny for two hours, something came to me, with no logic or coherence of its own, something that took on a new meaning that flashed in my mind time and again during the switchover that was to occur shortly. I couldn't shake an obsessive image of Mori dumped at Tokyo Station like an abandoned orphan in a coin-op locker. I was also bedeviled by the possibility that Mori had chosen a train at random, taken off to a faraway place, and would be brought up by a stranger. Even if lost for only a few weeks, he'd lose *ties* of friendship with his own father and be completely transformed; by the time I found him, he might have turned into one of those children with the vacant stare of a stray dog, with a strange scar on the lower part of his abdomen. . . .

When I thought about the possibility of him falling from the platform, of being run over by a train, I felt my entire inner self gutted. The child, abandoned, missing, not quite understanding what had happened to him, lingering alone in a strange place, that missing child was none other than me—when I realized this, I knew there'd been a reversal, I was switch*ed*-over. Shaken to the core by this thought, I roamed round and round in the station until I saw the Shikoku antinuke leader approaching me, eyes full of pity, yet without reproach, and calling out, Mori! Mori! as he would do to any child standing alone. Every time I met his gaze, I felt more abandoned than ever in the midst of the throngs of people: I mumbled a line of Blake's "The Little Boy Lost"— I'd seen the quote in one of your stories—Father, where've you gone, abandoning me. Once those words escaped me, I felt like a heathen seeking salvation in some mysterious Other (ha, ha, maybe the father?), and burst out with an impromptu, stopgap prayer:

> Father, father, Where are you going?
> O do not walk so fast.
> Speak, father, speak to your little boy.
> Or else I shall be lost.

Out of breath, as if trying to catch up with someone who'd leave me behind, I went hurriedly round and round inside the station, almost at a run, ha, ha, in search of a father on the run?

Now as for the all-important Mori, it was those same two practical and capable young men who finally found him. Mori, who'd gone up onto the Kodama platform, stood squeezed in a space just large enough for him next to a kiosk, leaning his bone-tired body against the stand— a nuisance to no one—looking very calm, they said. For the last three hours, he'd taken refuge in that tiny corner after being shoved around by the hordes on the platform. Come to think of it, we did take the Kodama when the family made that trip to visit his grandmother. He must have slipped past the ticket-checker as unobtrusively as air. When the young men went to the security office to report their discovery, a minor official mentioned offhandedly to one of his colleagues over his teacup:

——I too thought it might be the boy, you know. The platform for the Kodama, right? I saw him, for sure.

The young activists who, out of habit, never failed to raise a ruckus at the slightest opportunity, especially when it came to government authority or abuse of it, vociferously challenged the official, If you saw him, why didn't you follow up on your hunch and report it? At that, the official got up, looking as if he were going to arrest them, so they ran away, ha, ha.

2

Although I'd more or less forced the antinuke leader—the man I'd gone to pick up, after all—to stay put inside the station for those hours while I hunted for Mori, and even though I'd accepted his offer to assist in that search, I decided not to attend the informal evening get-to-gether in his honor and went home instead. I made that decision after asking, in rather bad taste, whether or not Ōno would be there.

——Old man, what're you really in the movement for? The minute you find Ōno's not around, you take off. You old farts have no shame! Well, naturally I sensed their unvoiced reproach.

Anyway, I was dead tired; on the way home I savagely lashed out at the equally exhausted Mori as he slipped and fell countless times in the slush, getting more and more begrimed and besmirched. I hovered close by while my wife, still out of sorts, changed his clothes; then I herded Mori to the unlit study and began to beat him. Cringing in fright, Mori squinted his eyes and ducked his head, elbows up to protect his face. Where in the world did he pick that up, how to ward off punches? In our collective memory—somewhere in the human genetic code—is there a string that refers to the defense of the helpless against beatings? Although I was despondent, the way Mori tried to protect himself struck me; but still I kept hitting his face. I even resorted to some really low blows: in an attempt to weaken his defense, I either grabbed his arms to wrench them free from his face, or punched him in the chest.

As a father of one of *our children,* you might get offended and ask, What did you do that for? Mark this down as the hysterical cry of a lunatic, ha, ha: it was for his **EDUCATION!** Five hours had already gone by since the incident. How could Mori possibly understand that those hours he spent as a missing child were wickedness, and for that reason he must be punished? Still, I wouldn't stop beating him. Nothing to apologize for, ha, ha, just educating the kid! I was teaching him it was bad to abandon me, it was bad to get away from me, to walk so fast that my legs couldn't keep up, it was bad to take off to a faraway place I didn't know about! Ha, ha, a miserable education indeed, with questionable results!

When I whacked him the first time, Mori's face flushed beet red, bright as a light bulb on a Christmas tree; a few teardrops ran down his cheeks, which he slapped hard as if to confirm the absurdity of the beating. He uttered not a sound. And all because with my first blow I'd threatened and yelled, No crying! O my God, what had I done? How cunning! I'd savagely beaten a submissive creature who clumsily shielded himself as he shivered in the chill air that had moved in with the melting snow . . . savagely beat him as he clenched his chattering teeth so tightly that his jaw seemed to go numb. . . .

All the while I felt it was me being beaten by an invisible violent hand; no matter how I defended myself, a huge unseen fist kept coming back with more, and to understand the meaning of these blows, I was slapping my own cheeks (that is to say, Mori's cheeks!)—it all stood my hair on end.

——**WHAT THE HELL ARE YOU DOING IN THE DARK?** A hair-raising blast came from behind me. I whipped around to see the pitch-black gape of my wife's mouth. Three glistening lights shaped like willow leaves gleamed in the shadowy space concealing her body: a pair of eyes and a razor in her left hand.

——Why did you hit him when it was your fault Mori got lost? You told him about Grandma, that's why he went right to the Kodama platform. Mori waited there for three long hours, waiting stock-still until you figured things out! Why are you abusing him? What the hell are you doing in this frightening, dark room? Her voice had become a screech; she was as terrified out of her wits as Mori and me, in this unlit, frightful retreat.

——What do you intend to do with that razor in your hand? Secretly shaving your beard or something?

——You went to Tokyo Station to dump Mori, didn't you? The anti-nuke leader would be your witness, a perfect alibi. You went to dump Mori!

——That's not true!

——When you called the first time and said Mori'd disappeared, you were excited and happy because your scheme had worked! The second time around when you'd discovered Mori, you sounded disappointed! Are you still lying to me?

——The search went on for three hours, I was dead tired.

——I bet you were, because that evil wench didn't show up! She wouldn't come to see you! She had a live broadcast to do on TV. Why did you have to beat the child when he'd even returned after you dumped him? Just because you couldn't get to see her? Pervert!

When my wife was changing Mori's clothes, she kept her eyes averted from me while I described that afternoon's happenings; I'd figured she was still in a bad mood and didn't think anything of it. Apparently, though, between the two calls I'd made, between Mori's disappearance and discovery—in other words, for 180 minutes—she was steadily downing shots of whiskey. She was stinking drunk. As soon as I'd put things together, angry that she'd caught me by surprise, I blew up. For a whole year guilt had kept me on pins and needles. That's why I'd ordered Mori not to cry—for fear she might hear us.

——I can see why you hate me so much that you've got to flash a razor. But you can't fool me, I know what you tried to do the other morning. What's worse, hitting Mori or castrating him?

My words had hardly left my mouth when those eyes, those twin willow leaves blazed in the shadows. And she began forcefully swathing a wide arc with the other willow leaf, the Solingen blade!

——You lost your nerve when you tried to castrate Mori, you got yourself off with the Solingen handle instead. Don't deny what happened!

Although she was crocked, and lost in the darkness, I could tell her dumbfounded expression. The windmill motion of the blade stopped for a second. I of course knew she hadn't done anything with herself. But I was still simmering, and all I really wanted at that moment was to cruelly mock my wife's pathetic situation that morning; maybe that would defuse the problem at hand. Of course I loved my wife, in fits and starts, my wife who always fought like hell with me over everything. Well, that statement is rather convoluted—and convulsed too, I guess, ha, ha.

——I'LL KILL YOU! You started it, you insisted on making love to me after you got irradiated! I'LL KILL YOU!

By now the slashing motion of the blade was in earnest, and she leapt at me. I pushed Mori down, my head just barely dodging the razor's descent. On the rebound, she sprang and vaulted about the room, crashing herself against one of my bookshelves.

——*Oooo ouch!* she screamed pitifully.

A maniac on the offensive, she rebounded from that collision, spun around, and made another lunge at me.

I meant to dodge her assault again at the last second, but just as I was about to do so, Mori groaned at my feet. He's slashed, I thought; the moment I froze, her razor-gripping hand dealt its blow, landing just below my right ear. Out of sheer fright more than pain I knocked my wife down. The fact that the razor had actually cut something shocked her; a no *ooo ouch!* escaped her as my punch sent her crashing against the glass patio door. Then she let out a *psssshuuu, pssshuuu,* probably trying to breathe through a bloodied nose. On the floor was Mori, moaning *mmmooooo,* suffering painfully in the clash between my wife and me.

I stood groaning in the dark. I thought the impact I'd felt below my right ear, across my mouth was simply a glancing blow, but blood oozed out and a fresh, sharp pain shot through me as though my nerves were being stretched taut on a rack. At that critical instant of my life, I must have been groaning in imitation of Mori, for my own sake, for my salvation. My wife's moans might have had the same motivation behind them. Our groans were in perfect harmony with Mori's.

Blood began to spurt out of my cut jaw, and like a leaky faucet dripped down my chest, belly, and feet. I opened my mouth to lick the wound, and blood streamed over my rigid tongue into the back of my throat. In a paroxysm of coughing I spit up a blood clot. The razor must have sliced a muscle in my cheek; anxious to see if my false teeth were exposed, I moved to turn on a light, dripping blood all over the floor, and thinking: I've got to show this gash to that murderous Solingen female! But it turned out to be not a matter of showing, but of being shown up. Still on her feet in front of the glass door, her face crimson, nose bloodied, head drooping, my wife was poised to slash her right wrist with the Solingen! Right next to the light switch was a mousetrap, which I grabbed and threw to knock the razor out of her hands. It missed the razor, but snapped down on the fingers of her right hand. My wife, no mouse, screeched as she tried to unspring the trap, ha, ha. Mice used to chew the coolant pipes for the nuclear reactor at my old job, you see, so I'd designed a specially constructed mousetrap. Over time I'd stolen quite a few odd items from the plant, but nothing proved as useful as that designer mousetrap.

With four fingers in her mouth, all of which she'd finally managed to yank free from the trap, my wife staggered out of the room. When I sat down on my bed I felt the skin all over my body turning unnaturally cold. I once read in a book that analyzed the effects of stress on employees in the nuclear industry, that at a certain level of stress, the subcutaneous blood vessels dilate to allow the maximum amount of blood into the muscles and brain, readying them for action. I was terribly moved by my physiological response. What heroic vessels! In my case, though, the blood wasn't being pumped into the muscles and brain, but out the gash.

Still feeling stone-cold, I looked down at Mori lying on the floor, moaning, both of his arms pressed to his head as if holding down the plastic portion of his skull. Could Mori and I revive our former relationship? What was that relationship about? Remembering how Mori slapped his own cheeks as if to confirm the beating, I also slapped mine to keep active the memory of what I'd done. However, my fingertips went right through the gash and smacked something really hard—my own jaw; I let out a yelp of pain and astonishment. At this my wife snapped to, and grabbed the first-aid kit. I wanted to let out another yelp, to seek compassion from Mori whose rotund body was completely still, except for the moans. . . .

In sumo wrestling, a draw is called when one of the contestants is injured; for the time being my wife shelved our dispute, and applied first aid to my gashed cheek. By marrying me while still a resident at the Medical School Hospital, she sacrificed her chance to become a doctor; but the fact of the matter was—as I see it—she already felt too inadequate to go on anyway, although I never said a word about it.

I was afraid that while she gave the first aid she'd recover some of her fighting spirit and start jabbing the gash with a pair of tweezers. She announced after she spent a long time disinfecting the wound,

——I'll put on some gauze and dress it with a bandage. That should stop the bleeding. I think it's stopped, she said in a muffled voice. Even though the caustic taste of fresh blood was still in my mouth, I was no longer angry at being slashed. I almost felt liberated, the same feeling one would get, I suppose, after a bloodletting. When that was standard practice in the Middle Ages, according to an article in a popular magazine, female patients would squeeze the hand of the doctor cutting into them, to ease the pain.

——I need to have it stitched, you know. I'll go to a doctor, I said, believing everything had blown over.

——**YOU CAN'T GO TO A HOSPITAL!** my wife shrieked. She happened to be bandaging my face at that moment. She straightened up from stooping over me and kept on shouting, her hot breath reeking of whiskey.

——Even if the authorities get me, **I'LL ADMIT NOTHING!** Lack of B-vitamins had slowed my brain functions, and the pain of the wound was awful, but my wife's combative style knocked me for a loop, ha, ha.

——All right, I won't go tonight. I can't leave Mori with you in the shape you're in, anyway.

Her head dropped, she looked lost in an alcoholic stupor, but then she began vigorously bobbing her head.

——Give me back the Solingen! You got your mousetrap back! she kept at me with increasing vehemence.

——I won't, I'll get you a Gillette safety razor instead. I don't mind if the other cheek gets slashed, but I can't let you go after Mori's penis. No sooner had I said that then I had to leapfrog away from a fast kick aimed at my crotch.

——You're the one who hurts Mori. Mori and I'll never let you off so easy!

Did she intend to give me another kick, or was she merely reeling from the alcohol? The way she was tottering I wasn't sure, so I two-stepped sideways to get away from her and that alcoholic haze.

——I'll go back to my parents with Mori! Go to Nichidai University

Hospital in Itabashi and get back the lump they cut out of Mori's head! That's yours! I won't let you take back anything else from Mori! **MORI AND I'LL FIGHT YOU!**

——Don't talk nonsense! Why, even the civil rights activists are toning down their rhetoric nowadays, you know.

My wife immediately read too much into what I'd said, her body still draped like a canopy over the cringing Mori but her glinting willow eyes turned on me; I know she thought I was referring to Ōno. Was it possible that my wife's sudden diatribe was psychologically driven, a challenge to Ōno?

3

Since my wife had quit halfway through bandaging over the gauze, I tried to do the rest myself but botched it. Couldn't quite figure out how and what to bandage. I went to get a black wool ski mask. I loved the feel of it when I put it on: the bandage secure in place, and hardly any pressure on the wound. I called out, Mori, Mori, the pain throbbing in my cheeks, and all I heard was

——*Yoee, Yoee.*

When I got back to the study, my wife was whispering something into Mori's ear, and seeing me come in, she suddenly raised her voice and began what became a kind of litany:

——Mori, with Mama, you're going to get out of here. Just Mori and me. Leave the loony who beats Mori all alone. Mori and Mama're clearing out!

Mori had stopped covering his head and was no longer cringing; he was even standing on his own. With her back straight, knees tucked demurely under her, my wife was hugging him tight in her arms. A head taller than her in that position, Mori, who cast his swollen squinting eyes up at me when I reappeared before him, didn't struggle to free himself from the hug.

——Mori, you're going to get out of this place with Mama. Mori and Mama, just the two of us, we'll go off somewhere! We'll leave the loony who ditches and then beats a kid like Mori; we'll clear out!

All I could do was sit motionless on the bed, shivering with cold—whether meteorological or physiological I couldn't quite tell—and waiting for my turn to speak, fearful that there might be no second chance for Mori and me.

When my wife, with Mori still cradled in her arms, lifted herself up to leave, it was quite clear he was resisting. With all her might, she tried forcing him to move with her, as if to take him captive. But like a stake wedged in place, he wouldn't budge, causing her to stagger.

——What're you doing, Mori? Come on, we're going!

——Mori, Mori, my feeble voice quickly broke in, echoing only *Yoee, Yoee.* Mori, Mori, stay with me! Mori, Mori, stay with me!

My wife was trying to *uproot* Mori: he planted his feet firmly on the floor like a nonviolent resister. Nevertheless, she kept on tugging, but as she did she teetered precariously, her stamina leeched by alcohol. All that time Mori looked straight at me who called out, *Yoee, Yoee, Yoeeyore!* Even though I felt embarrassed by the red-trimmed black wool mask I was wearing, Mori's gaze encouraged me, so I kept calling back, *Yoee, Yoee, Yoeeyore!*

——**WHAT THE HELL'RE YOU SAYING?** My wife turned to me with a crazed look and, unlike Mori, rather shocked at my appearance; my mask was getting to her, ha, ha.

——*Yoee, Yoee, Yoeeyore!* I cried out, and spit out a glob of bloody saliva on the pillow; it was the color of pyorrhea.

——**MORI, MORI, PAPA'S NO GOOD!**

——**PAPA NO GOOD, THAT'S WRONG!**

——**MORI, LET'S GET OUT WITH MAMA!**

——**YOEE, YOEE, YOEEYORE!**

——**WRONG, WRONG MORI'S GOING TO LEAVE WITH MAMA!**

Abruptly my wife unlocked the arms that held Mori, straightened her back, and moved a few steps toward me. As she halted, she slowly, stiffly raised her arms, like wings in an Ainu crane dance, not dancing, but threatening.

——Both of you are plutonium-soaked loonies! she yelled, and ran down the stairs bawling.

I took down some salami from a shelf strewn with research notes and reached for a bottle of brandy from the same hiding place, brandy kept for sleepless nights, and for those days when I'd be too lazy to go downstairs to get beer. On second thought I put back the brandy, remembering the wound, and cut the salami with a pocket knife, a tool treasured by anyone who loves to fool with gadgets.

——*Yoee, Yoee, Yoeeyore.*

Mori came straight to me, and began to gobble down the sausage slices which I placed on a stack of keypunch cards; he peeled off the casing with a fingernail, removed all the black peppercorns, grabbing each thin disk horizontally, and completely shutting off the outer world. His eyes seemed to darken to the color of deep water. Mori is the only one I know who can eat so naturally, treating food as a serious matter and showing the respect he has for it as a vital material substance, no matter what the food. Since I considered the momentary respite simply a hiatus in an ongoing battle, the joy I felt watching Mori scarf up the salami amounted to no more than a gulp of water I'd managed to swig from a canteen in the trenches. The lone female rebel downstairs was busy making a racket—packing, it seemed. Also, she made quite a few phone calls. We have two telephones; if you dial out on one, the other jingles a bit. I could've easily found out who my wife was calling by carefully picking up the receiver, but I didn't. Now with Mori on my side, I could almost feel victory at hand: no need for impatience. Besides, no matter how gently I might pick up the receiver, my wife'd catch on for sure and would blurt out, **YOU'RE LISTENING IN, YOU PLUTONIUM–SOAKED LOONY!** Ha, ha.

When Mori was through eating, I peeled his security blanket off the bed; it was an old favorite that had gone with him to the hospital during the second cranial operation. Too tired to put a *diaper* on him, I instead took him to the bathroom to pee. Mori and I—still dressed—then lay down together on my bed. The gash in my cheek began to throb with pain, toggling me to the "present," and with it, the sensation of periodic motion. The periodic motion of the always "present": it makes me think of the eternal recurrence, the eternal recurrence of pain! As a child, whenever I closed my eyes to sleep, all kinds of objects would go around and around behind my eyelids, separating and coalescing, always in a clearly looping cycle: a mandala. I remember how my entire life seemed to me to be foretellable, if only I could somehow decipher that cycle. When did I stop experiencing that? I really wanted to communicate this recapturing of something I'd forgotten for so long, to Mori, whose head next to mine was facing forward, his body burning with the heat of his own inner fires. But I thought better of it; I didn't want to disturb Mori; he'd gone through too many things in one day, and I decided instead to get that brandy after all. However, before I was even out of the bed, the sleeping Mori grabbed for my wrist: Was he saying, Never let me become a lost child, and I'll never let you become a lost child?

4

I was asleep. I was having a grotesque dream, pregnant with unhappy feelings, in which I was again dead tired—a rather complicated kind of fatigue, something more than just being *tired*. Ever since the Tin Men incident, my life had been like one long summer vacation, you see. In my waking hours I didn't do much physical work; could this type of dream-labor be compensation for that? I often woke up without remembering the content of my dreams, yet feeling utterly exhausted; I sometimes wondered whether the cumulative fatigue that pressed down on me equaled the weight of the vision I am slated to see on my deathbed, that flash encompassing one's entire life. But all this was only until the switchover. I get too carried away as I speak to you now, which is the reason I need a ghostwriter. Besides, the switchover was near at hand, so I've got to ask you to indulge me for now.

The dream went something like this: I'd just gotten back home after being mugged by some thug. It seemed as though that had been the only reason I'd gone out. I felt something disjointed in my mouth. The gash in my cheek and my pair of false teeth must correspond with this feeling. I couldn't pay my dentist after he inserted the temporary false teeth, so he hadn't yet replaced them with the real, permanent ones. Meanwhile the gums had grown stiff and retracted; saliva bubbled up through the crack between the false teeth and the gums. I found myself continually biting down on the teeth. At any rate when I got home, the minute I poked my fingers into my mouth, two upper premolars, already loose from the strain of the metal bridges which held the false teeth together, came out. When I tried to push them out with my tongue, all the rest of the teeth fell out, like dominoes. You know, it was rather weird walking around with those fallen-out teeth still in my mouth. . . .

The sound of my wife running up the stairs woke me up. She and I have this habit: inside a room, we both creep along as slow as molasses, but in moving between rooms, we tend to hurry, as though afraid Mori's lump or something waited in ambush. She flipped on the light and spoke fast and furious,

——**I'M GOING TO ABANDON YOU AND MORI!** Up till now I was afraid you and Mori might commit double suicide; I felt sorry for you, thought it too cruel to abandon you two. **NEVER AGAIN, EVER. I'M ABANDONING YOU AND MORI!** I'm going back to school, start all over again, start what I've sacrificed for you and a kid like that! Then I'll have a real marriage, and a real kid! If I marry some other guy, the baby's bound to be normal. **HYPOTHESIS 1!** If Mori was the result of plutonium contamination, since my next husband-to-be won't be contaminated, my future baby'll be normal! **HYPOTHESIS 2!** If Mori was merely accidental, it's already happened once, so odds are my next child'll be normal! **GOT THAT? I'M ABANDONING YOU AND MORI, I'M SPLITTING!**

——But you can't do anything about it tonight. Why not wait till tomorrow morning?

That was what I'd meant to say, but the only sound that came out of my mouth was, *Yoee, Yoee, Yoeee.* My wife—who's carried out 2,500 copulations with me, by conservative estimate—immediately retorted.

——**WHAT THE HELL'RE YOU SAYING?** The director's already here with his car; the tires are chained in case there's ice on the road. He's waiting outside because you might bring breaking and entering charges against him, and prevent me from leaving. Now get your ass out of bed and carry my suitcase! **I'M ABANDONING YOU AND MORI, I'M SPLITTING!**

Her use of the generic term *director* without any explanation snatched away my will to stop her. The front door was ajar and beyond it I heard the sound of a trumpet playing in the crisp midnight air, a golden oldie from the forties. I had read in a gossip column in some theater magazine that the New Theater director had installed a musical horn in his souped-up sports car. After putting on one hit play after another, his troupe was hailed as the harbinger of a renaissance in the theater; my wife, years ago, had dated the troupe's up-and-coming director.

——There's the suitcase! Quit your dawdling! **I'M ABANDONING YOU AND MORI, I'M SPLITTING!**

The living room was a mess. Piled up around a suitcase I'd used once for a business trip abroad were belongings that she, though unwilling to part with, was unable to cram in: one was a skillet, a wedding gift from her med school classmates; we never had a chance to eat a steak thick enough to cook in it, though, ha, ha. Pretending to check whether the suitcase would close, I tried to shove the skillet in; my wife, who stood arms akimbo, roughly snatched it away from me and flung it aside. I really wasn't sure why she suddenly hated the skillet.

In a way I was glad she hadn't put it in. The pain in my cheek and the aches in my joints from sleeping on a too-narrow bed with Mori made the weight of the luggage unbearable.

——**WHAT'RE YOU WAITING FOR?** Already taking a breather? **IMPOTENT!**

With or without pain, I hustled like hell to get the suitcase outside. What a thing to say within earshot of my suitor-rival; it had been ten years ago, hadn't it? Impotent, mind you, ha, ha.

The director, a small, melancholy looking man, stood next to an old Citroen parked under a streetlight, sporting slick clothes which matched the style and color of the car, and a pair of shades despite the dark.

I put the suitcase down right in front of the gate, took a step backward, and waited. I hadn't been ordered to carry it to the Citroen, had I? I had followed her instructions to the letter.

——Quick, get the luggage! He might not want to part with it, and haul it right back into the house!

Still in the doldrums, the director walked slowly toward me, hurrying as he closed in on the suitcase. Out of the blue he made a move to punch me. Didn't they—he and my wife—know any tactic other than ambush? But there was no need to dodge him: before I knew it he'd slipped on the ice and was sprawled all over the pavement. Too bad he didn't put chains on his slick shoes as well, ha, ha. I must say, though, it was admirable the way he got back up, seemingly unruffled, and carried the suitcase to the car.

——You don't have to beat him up, I'm the one who's abandoning him! **I'M ABANDONING YOU AND MORI, I'M SPLITTING!**

After the engine started up, the Citroen pulled up to me; the director gave me a parting shot,

——You loony!

I went back inside my wasteland of a house. I was further depressed by the fact that the director, who had opened his minuscule mouth to abuse me verbally, looked much older than I imagined he'd be. He definitely did; I too must look much older than I really am. Look how the aches and pains in my joints linger on although I was long done lugging the suitcase. This sensation of irreversibility, as if every part of your body is being worn out, was unthinkable when I was young; that's the nature of the pain I was feeling at that moment, don't you think? If I hadn't pictured Mori sleeping in my bed, I'd have broken down in tears right there, ha, ha.

I returned to bed, and was about to lie down when I realized Mori had wet it through. As I woke him and began to clean up the mess, I stole a glance at his penis, still steaming from the hot urine, gaining in strength and size. Too bad that shrimpy director, no longer young, couldn't have seen this. I'm sure he'd have felt threatened, body and soul! I pushed out my pitiful pinch-runner penis, ridiculed as impotent, next to Mori's. Ha, ha. I took him back to bed, and put the blanket over him, almost folding his erection in half at the base. His battered face was swollen. It reminded me of the time when, because of the lump, and with his head further disfigured after passing through the birth canal, his bruised face looked like that of an old man.

——Sleep tight, Mori, I wanted to say, but instead I said, *Yoeee, Yoeee.*

——**MORI SLEEPS!**

I almost wailed a lamentation, Mama's gone, abandoning you and me; I loved her more than anybody else, more than Ōno, we were comrades in this painful struggle together! but swallowed the words on the tip of my tongue. What was I to do with the wet mattress? My wife gone, faced with the day's problems already at hand, I gave up trying to figure things out, covered myself with the only dry blanket around, and

lay down on the floor. After all this, my sleep was a terrifying experience. I don't mean I had a horrible dream. I was immersed in a pitch
blackness that allowed no dreams. A brutal act, like being turned inside
out, was taking place in my body, which wouldn't rebel against a consciousness held in terror. The terror. As though my own body had
begun to give birth to a clone. Its progress almost impossible to impede.

The next morning I woke up and found not only the gash in my
cheek but also the burn scars of the Tin Men battle healed and gone.
The false teeth were gone too, replaced by my good old teeth. No need
to look in the mirror: a cocksure sense of identity told me that I was
twenty years younger, that I had the body of an eighteen-year-old. Now
twenty-eight, and twenty years older, Mori came over to see how I was
doing, his favorite tattered blanket tied around his head.

Simple mathematical equations represent the switchover: 38 minus
20 equals 18; 8 plus 20 equals 28.

4

We've Immediately Taken Up the Struggle

1

The most symbolic meaning of the switchover has to be the disappearance of all radiation scars from my body, don't you agree? Plutonium, a substance that never existed before, is being produced day in and day out by nuclear reactors; its half-life is 24,000 years, you know. There's no chance plutonium will disappear before humans do. Symbolically, I'm foisting the body of an eighteen-year-old in its preradiated state—a young, healthy body, free from man-made contaminants—onto a world that man can never, ever purge. Anyone who considers the way I think and feel to be crazy will probably dismiss the switchover as madness, but I have no intention of speaking to those who regard me as mad. Is what I say crazy? I don't for one moment think so. I can't spare the time now to inspect and report on the state of Mori's body and mine. Isn't it enough that the switchover is infusing my words with a natural radiance? As long as I keep on talking about the task which the switched-over pair, Mori and me, are about to take on, my words are bound to express the essence of our switchover. In any event that's what the Other's supposed to perceive through your account. The only thing Mori and I should be doing is maintaining our autonomy during the switchover. Think about it: what kind of experience is it for an older person to possess the physique of an eighteen-year-old all over again? Ha, ha. Extremely pleasant. Wouldn't most people in that situation just let out a gasp, finding it hard to believe that they ever had an eighteen-year-old body? Although I was once thirty-eight, I'm now gasping deliriously in my eighteen-year-old body, ha, ha. Of course, I'm not without anxieties. At eighteen, the first time I was in love I tasted the agonies of a passion that almost boiled my insides. I want to die in peace without ever having to go through that again. I wonder if the switchover will be so intense that I'll have to relive the same agonies. Well, that probably sounds like so much hot air, ha, ha. Of course, the present me is not worry-free, but you don't feel it yet, do you? That's because my words are beamed to you by an eighteen-year-old.

By the way, which direction will my flesh take from now on I wonder. Seventeen, sixteen, fifteen . . . zero? In the end will I just pop out of existence floating in the amniotic fluid of an artificial womb? Or, if my body-clock has been set back to eighteen and stopped there, does it mean I'll become an immortal in an eternal future? I'd still have the option of committing suicide when I wanted in the future, and escaping the hell of immortality. Once my switchover becomes public through your writing, won't I become the most sought-after personality on earth? The Pope will have to grant me an audience to settle the matter of my existence one way or another, ha, ha. Thousands of others may have experienced this same event, you know; it's just that no one's reported it—and the fact still remains that Mori and I've been switched over. If it is a global phenomenon, doesn't that signify an impending crisis for humankind? The creator of the polio vaccine at the Salk Institute in California once reminded us that in Chinese the word *crisis* means danger plus chance. Is there a mass switchover in the wings for the unseen masses—including the already-switched-over pair, Mori and me? Surely a switchover of that magnitude suggests a being (or a phenomenon) that symbolizes the crisis of humankind. And if that's the case, the embryonic movement of the Antichrist may have already begun. To overthrow the Antichrist, to abort his coming, how and where are we to fight him? Or let me pose another question: Who's going to fight him? Leave it to us, the switched-over pair; that's my reply.

. . . I was preoccupied with such thoughts, but I couldn't just let them slow me down. I'm at that age where you feel your body fluids running riot at full boil, and you're compulsively hotheaded!

From the moment I became aware of the switchover, I was also seized by an *idée fixe*. It went like this. Some cosmic being aboard a UFO sets up a projector aimed at a certain spot on the earth. The projector beams light onto a three-dimensional screen that reflects two images. With this setup, wouldn't it be very easy to switch over from image A to B, with a twenty-year time gap between them?

If our switchover came about like that, then clearly the cosmic being's got some design on us, and as Mori and I see it, it would mean we've been given a mission. The switchover took possession of us with irresistible, overwhelming force detonating a time bomb within our flesh. Assuming, of course, our switchover is for real, isn't zero hour steadily approaching, hastening the realization of our mission? The switched-over pair—me in the eighteen-year-old body, Mori in the twenty-eight-year-old—stands ready for that coming mission. Seeing things thus, with my newfound optimism, and at the ready to right whatever complications might arise, I could feel how my spirit, not just my flesh, had been rejuvenated. At least that's how it seems. Should I be complaining about that? Ha, ha.

2

What's become of the switched-over Mori? Like me, he retains his pre-switchover spirit; no conflict there. Looks as if there's rapid progress on the physical front, fitting his age with his body.

He's quit parroting things, and is more reticent than ever. We share my wardrobe now because it fits his twenty-eight-year-old body. His natural reticence is actually very becoming, and he's already got a distinctive style, you know: expressive reticence. Before I make a move to do anything, I tell him what I'm thinking of doing next, what I'm going to do. When I experience something new—as an eighteen-year-old would—I tell him what it was like, ha, ha. He comprehends my remarks. Without saying a single word, he encourages me and reconfirms the totality of what he's taken in, all in one shot!

I'll be more specific as the situation unfolds. Switchover or no switchover, the earth continues to rotate and revolve around the sun, tides ebb and flow, and this whole cosmic cycle impels us toward action. Face to face with the switched-over Mori, I keep feeling intense nostalgia. I've never seen him like this before: this Mori is the real Mori, the ultimate Mori, the seminal Mori; as long as this Mori is a reality, I'll be able to live the switched-over life with him and carry out the mission ordained by the Cosmic Will. I am utterly tranquil.

Moreover, I also knew that Mori was fully aware of his own spirit slowly undergoing transformation to fit his new body. So, you see, there was nothing for Mori and me to discuss on the topic of the switchover. Suppose it were otherwise: let's say one of *the children* like *our children* had been switched over, but showed no comprehension of what had transpired; what a sticky situation that would be, wouldn't you say? Or what if Mori, catching sight of me the eighteen-year-old, thought what a weird father, or became enraged, and in a panic attacked me, armed with the solid musculature of a strapping young man? Remember, I'm just a squishy teenager, ha, ha.

With our relationship based on an unquestioned mutual acceptance of the switchover, I told Mori this story.

——You know the pinch runner I've often talked to you about? I remember something else. It happened on a blisteringly hot day right after a heavy rain—we started the ballgame the minute the sun began to dry up the puddles. In the clear bright light that succeeded the downpour, the rain-swollen muddy river was visible—red ocher snaking between the houses. The players could think of nothing but the game; I was seated on a bench waiting to be picked as a pinch runner. I remember the terror and ambition that came with being picked as a pinch runner, but for some strange reason I've avoided recalling how badly I wanted to be chosen. Now I remember that I wanted it to the exclusion of all else in the world. So I paid no mind to those kids not permitted to sit on the bench, who were yelling and shouting that dead soldiers from our village whose remains were never returned from abroad would come back floating on the swollen river. . . . At any rate, take your pick, get whatever fits you out of the dresser. It's cold today. Let's fix a bite to eat!

Mori retreated to the corner by his bed, where he seemed to be rummaging through the dresser. Remember how one objective of the special education class had been to train *our children* how to put on their own clothes? It's a bit comical to speak of it now, after the switchover, but Mori had somehow attained a modicum of success in that short-term training.

I hopped out of bed, and my fresh and strong eighteen-year-old penis rapped against my pelvis, ha, ha. Not just my penis was firm and supple, but my waist and buttocks too, so much so that my pants were baggy. Frankly speaking, this did make me feel insecure, as though someone had pulled the carpet right from under me. Don't you think accumulated fat is a form of psychological compensation, like an infant's blanket? You should know—an overweight middle-aged man, ha, ha. I wasn't thinking only about myself, though. I'd already begun to worry about Mori: I needed to hide the switched-over Mori from outsiders. Thank God there's no military draft in this country, but isn't there an article in the Constitution which says that it's a misdemeanor for an adult male, even one who suddenly jumps in age from eight to twenty-eight, to fail to register? But how to keep Mori a secret? Worst would be to stay shut up in the house; wouldn't it be better to get out into the town? To the masses! Into the deep and wide sea of the masses, where even the oddest of guerrillas get on swimmingly!

The phone rings. As I reach for the receiver, I suddenly flinch in fear. Now that I've been switched over, how should I answer the phone? The *present* me is the only me that physically exists. But temporally, is this *now* a continuation of the pre-switchover? I try to cheer myself up; the here and now is everyone else's problem.

——Asleep? How long do you need to sleep? **I'VE ABANDONED YOU AND MORI! I'VE SPLIT!**

Then the line went dead. The hangover didn't hamper her one damn bit; or perhaps it was the hair of the dog that bit her; anyway, the call was one of my wife's crazed blasts to let off steam.

——Good! The outside world's still in the same old disorder. Mori and I seem to be the only ones switched over!

Just as I said these things to myself, the phone rang again. This time I picked up the receiver ready to bawl out my wife—no, my *ex*-wife, ha, ha—but instead, a voice I'd never heard before launched into a monologue.

——Do you know today's meeting is secretly sponsored by a violent counterrevolutionary group? I suggest you stay away.

I got no opportunity to respond. An antinuke meeting was in fact scheduled for that evening, with the Shikoku antinuke activist—who arrived the day before—on hand as a consultant. Naturally the Ōno group jointly sponsored the event. I had consciously avoided conversations about who and what was involved in organizing this meeting, but it wouldn't be totally off the wall for the Revolutionary Party's leadership to split and for one faction then to realign themselves with the Ōno group. Except for that party, I'd never heard of any other group directly interfering with the Ōno organization's activities. *Good,* I decided on the spot, *I've no idea what political party's involved, but if there's anyone out there who might cramp Mori's and my freedom, we'll go to the meeting and find out.* I clearly had acquired the decisiveness of an eighteen-year-old, ha. ha. No matter how reckless the direction might be, I felt sure I could engineer the course of events to my advantage. I was a devil of an optimist. Besides, we two switched-overs would be venturing onto turf where forces were predisposed to block any move we might make. Wouldn't that ensure our smoking them out?

As I went down the stairs, I peeped into Mori's room. There, as if in a fairy tale, teeny-looking clothes, shoes, whatnots, were all over the room. You see, I was already accustomed to the post-switchover Mori.

——He hasn't left on his own, has he? A twenty-eight-year-old man with the experience of a retarded eight-year-old . . . ?

I'm in the habit of talking to myself, and I could hear how my voice took on the timbre of a frantic, hurt kid. The eighteen-year-old me trembled in fear at the thought of Mori abandoning me. But then my teenage body raced lickety-split down the stairs. No need to panic: there was Mori!

Until then I had always done the cooking, while the child Mori looked on holding a bag of noodles in his hands; but now he was cooking on his own. In high spirits Mori, bent over a gas burner, was carefully checking the water boiling in a large pot; he'd already minced garlic, and set aside a chunk of butter. His body in my pants, sweat shirt, and windbreaker, the nape of his neck and the bulging shoulders made for a familiar sight—exactly what my body was like in my youth. Reassured, I went to the bathroom. Seen for the first time since the switchover, my own face was nothing like what it had been when I was eighteen. Rather it was the very face I wanted at that time, a real face, smiling back from the mirror. The two eyes that looked embarrassed at their inability to project confidence, and at their childish curiosity, were the only details that spoiled the harmony of the face. But when you step away from a mirror, you can't see your eyes any more, ha, ha.

3

Although it was brief—by the time we'd finished our meal it was past noon, by four we'd left home for the meeting—Mori and I spent a leisurely and peaceful afternoon together, synchronizing the organisms that were our young, vibrant bodies with the motion of the Cosmos, much the way one might try to get over jet lag after a long flight.

Mori and I were like brothers who, after a long absence, drank and caroused all night, and the next day tended to say very little to each other. Of course, I was cast in the role of the enervated, embarrassed kid brother who went too far and drank too much, while Mori played the generous, even-tempered older brother. I put away pots and pans which my wife/ex-wife had left behind; Mori was listening to a record in a corner of the living room. I felt I was tidying up the mess to atone for my disorderly drunkenness.

Mori often sat quietly with a smile on his face when he listened to music. That was his habit even before the switchover. The fact that he'd carried this habit over after the switchover was reassuring to me. It meant that I had a clue as to Mori's switched-over future. Whenever he listened to music, he seemed to defy the very definition of amusement.

Once the music is on, his serene smile comes and goes—but that's not to say it's frivolous or flighty. So, let's say he was listening to Mozart's "Turkish March" performed by Glenn Gould, or by Horowitz, or by Gieseking. Mori smiles for each performer at different phrases of the same music. The three performers effectively enhance the repertoire of Mori's smiles.

That afternoon, as if recognizing the need to retune his switch*ed*-over self to the music, Mori planted his bulky body in front of the speakers and listened to the K.331*, Mozart's Piano Sonata in C Major, played by Horowitz. All that slapdash turmoil the night before must have affected the turntable; after two or three bars Mori adjusted the speed slightly. You see, he's got perfect pitch and remembered Horowitz's tonal quality at the precisely correct speed. Boy, it made me very happy to know the switched-over Mori still retained his gift. When children like our children grow up, they lose the marvelous gifts they exhibited from infancy. The phone rang again. I was through tidying things up by then and cautiously picked up the receiver. The instant I heard Ōno's voice—by instinct—I told her I had to go to the other phone: up the stairs I bounded. I thought it was possible she couldn't identify my switched-over voice, and if that was the case I decided I'd play a prank on her. But I didn't want Mori to listen in.

——Isn't Mori-father home? Who is this? Is there any way to get in touch with him?

He isn't here. He's left on a long trip with Mori, and Mori-mother's gone too, back to her parents. They had quite a row yesterday because Mori was missing for a while. After he was found, Mori-father came home and had a fight with Mori-mother. I guess they had to split temporarily so they could start all over. I'm just house-sitting. No, not alone, with my older brother. He's listening to music in the living room. We'll be house-sitting here for a while. We expect to hear from Mori-father, but we can't contact him. Mori-mother will also get in touch with us when she feels like it. When she feels like it is quite different from when Mori-father feels like it, ha, ha.

(Silence)

Who are you? I've heard about the mix-up with Mori. So glad he's been found. I wonder what Mori-father means by leaving on a trip with Mori. Who are you?

Me? Mori-father's sole disciple. The guy listening to music has been a

---

*Mozart's compositions are often identified by using the letter "K" followed by a number. The "K" stands for Kochel; in 1862 Ludwig von Kochel assembled a comprehensive catalogue of all of Mozart's works, numbering them in the order in which Mozart had written them.

friend of his for many, many years. I've been working and fooling around with Mori-father for a while; I'm his junior. To put it in classy terms, I'm his disciple of eighteen, ha, ha. Since this morning we've been asked to house-sit, to take care of the mail and phone calls. That's what I'm here for, ha, ha.

(Silence)

Really? So you've been answering the phone since this morning, right? Didn't you get a funny call about the meeting Mori-father was supposed to attend? Blackmail, or pushy advice, something of that nature.

I did, I did. I wondered who it was. The message was not to come to the meeting. No explanation. Clearly it came from some opposition party, or a splinter group from one of the sponsoring parties of today's meeting.

The meeting was called so citizens can discuss industrial nuclear pollution. There are a few young party members on the organizing committee, but there's no way it's going to be a political gathering. The opposition faction in the party apparently has begun to interfere even with a meeting of this kind. (Silence) Do you think Mori-father's been blackmailed and pressured to take off on a trip with Mori? It's possible, isn't it, that yesterday's incident was no accident, but the opposition faction's attempt to hide Mori, to effectively intimidate Mori-father. One could very well hear from a newspaper about the Shikoku antinuke leader's arrival at Tokyo Station. Well, in a Shikoku newspaper, of course. If you want to know the exact arrival time, all you have to do is call their Tokyo bureau office. I wonder if, without knowing it, Mori-father's somewhere kidnapped, and his wife and Mori have temporarily gone underground. Are you sure you don't know anything about the whole thing? Are you just playing dumb because Mori-father told you to? How about the older guy who's housesitting with you? Does he know anything? I'm Sakurao Ōno.

I knew from the start you're that famous Ōno, ha, ha. I know all about the affair between you two. Mori-father confided in me every time you two did it. Probably he felt insecure—about becoming impotent—and wanted to hash things over with me. I hear that the night he was with you, even after you went to sleep, he played with his penis the rest of the night, and it refused to get hard. He began to push the limp thing up your ass—you happened to be sleeping on your chest then— right? In the end he had to masturbate with his finger poked up your ass. Do it with me, Ōno, I'm only eighteen, and I don't know what to do with this raging hard-on I've got all the time, please, do it with me. Your erogenous zone's the tits, right?

(Silence)

You're Mori-father, aren't you? Why put on the squeaky routine, and babble on about such sick things?

. . . She abruptly slammed her receiver down and I was left laughing my head off like a monkey, with the dead receiver still in hand. And with a vibrant penis in my pants, ha, ha! I was on top of the world: to think I could trick an older woman with those lewd stories. After all, I was an eighteen-year-old brat, ha, ha. Not a shred of shame or embarrassment. And I'd never felt so free in all my life. I wouldn't have even dreamed of this kind of freedom when I was eighteen the first time around, let alone later when I'd grown older. To quote Goethe, and display some teenage pedantry, ha, ha!

"So that the whole world will be there to please me,

I will please myself."

That was the mood I was in; I took in the whole room, to bid farewell to my past, to the wider world, to my life, to all of me that I found displeasing: clippings from the "Nuclear Industry," National Regulatory Commission reports, papers on "Examples of and Policy for Stress Corrosion-Cracking in the Nuclear Industry." Even though my official career as a research engineer was over because of the radiation exposure in the Tin Men incident, I had continued to edit research reports of this sort as a freelancer. If they'd found out, the plant management and the union would not have been happy. To be sure, the quality of the research done by my contemporaries and their younger cohorts is leagues beyond anything the ex-engineer could do. Despite this, or rather because of it, whenever I heard of a nuclear accident—let's say the one at the Commonwealth Edison plant in Illinois—I immediately contacted my old workplace and requested data from the publicity department, harping on their slogan, "Always uphold the three principles of the peaceful use of the atom: Involve yourself; involve citizens; communicate with the public." This was the clincher in my strategy, ha, ha.

Perhaps in my compulsion to leave no stone unturned, I wanted to unearth another radiation casualty from the battle of the Tin Men. But now I was liberated from all data, from all the notes I'd gathered. I went through my clothes, picked the most suitable wardrobe for Mori and me, and went downstairs. In hopes of getting together with Ōno after the meeting, I transferred condoms out of a box of knickknacks and stuck them into my pocket, four of them, to test my rejuvenated sexual prowess! Ha, ha. Just the same, if I'd remembered the rest of the line by Goethe, it'd have dampened my excellent spirits. "I wasn't put in this high place just to have fun in the world."

4

That afternoon an earthquake hit the city while we were playing the boardgame "Bridging." On the board grid, you place T-shaped plastic pieces in holes arranged in fours in even-numbered rows, and in fives in odd-numbered rows. The opposing sides are colored red and white, and you can only span a bridge with a white-to-white or red-to-red combination. When bridge construction is blocked by an opponent's piece, the only alternative is to change direction. Or, you're forced to skip one hole. I took great pains to teach the pre-switched-over Mori how to play this game. It was also for his education! But what sort of education? To learn that he's got to fight obstacles to achieve things; that the Other is out to block his way. To learn what he should do to keep going forward, and how to get out of traps. To learn there will be times when he'll have to block the Other's move, times when he'll have to beat the Other. Isn't this a textbook game for life?

First of all, it was fiendishly difficult to teach Mori the rather abstract concept of a continuous bridge, a bridge you can span with five T's by going straight forward or one you can just barely make with twenty-five T's and only after many blocked moves. To comprehend the fact that both structures are still a bridge takes quite a bit of intelligence, you know. Then, on top of that, instructing Mori on how to place his own T's to block his opponent's construction was a hell of a job. Mori constructs a plan based not on the logic of the game but on his impulse to build something. Anyway, in the end he learned the basic moves, and if we started the game with three T's on his turf—a very simple format—sometimes Mori would win. Whenever I got stuck, unable to find an effective move, I would become mesmerized by the fact that I had to thwart Mori. Wasn't the whole game a rehearsal for the switchover to come? Now that it was really here, I wanted to plumb the depths of this idea.

As was our habit, we began the game with three T's in Mori's territory. I was immediately cornered. His offense is invariably the most plausible, leaving no room for a counteroffense. So I lost. In the next game I let him start with only two T's. I proceeded with caution, trying simultaneously to isolate them and to make sure he couldn't connect them with a third T. But that strategy could backfire and make my position vulnerable: the moves it would take me to encircle Mori completely might cost me the moves I needed to block his construction. My parched throat began to burn. I let him put down another T. But, to confuse his placement, I cheated. I'd lost all sense of decency—remember, I was eighteen, ha, ha. However, I was the one to be tripped up by the dirty trick—the fickleness of trickery, you know. I blew my stack and, sweating like a pig, smelled Mori's body odor at the same instant; the smell of a grown man, not my odor, not the odor of a young man. Mori also tensed up. Should we play fair, or what?

. . . Then, an earthquake hit us. It had a strange equilibrium to its up-and-down motion, as though we were aboard a large lurching platform effortlessly falling, platform and all. I began to yak away at Mori as I am wont to do, this time about earthquakes.

——This is an earthquake. The earth's crust is moving. How does such a thing happen? Generally speaking. . . .

Mori's face, vibrant and radiant, even with a three-day beard, was full of curiosity, his eyes so serene! All of a sudden I felt diffident. Mori, with his interest aroused, listening quietly to what I feel obligated to say, was like Socrates, a teacher who elevated his students' level of knowledge by letting them face their own ignorance. Fortunately, the phone rang and I was able to get out of this jam. As with the earlier threatening call, a young stranger's voice was on the line, but this one was extremely courteous; you know the young union activist-type, all revved up, who goes around disguising the pitch of his voice to make it lower, deeper, more mature.

——If this quake were eight on the Richter scale, Tokyo'd be leveled, and naturally, the Self-Defense Corps would get called in. Given such an opportunity I'm sure they'd stage a coup. Do we have the power to stymie such an event in this country? No, we don't. First an earthquake, then a coup—that'd be enough to crush the revolutionary forces in Japan. Only the Self-Defense Corps is in a position to take advantage of a situation in flux like the one created by an earthquake: no way the Revolutionary Party can take advantage of it, based on our current assessment of conditions. What would have to happen for us to take the next step? We'd have to have in the ready an enormously destructive force equivalent to an earthquake. We'd have to make clear our absolute willingness to use that destructive force whenever we considered it necessary. There's no other way. Humans cannot create the amount of energy generated by all the earthquakes happening within the earth itself. But if we limit our target to Tokyo alone, a whole slew of possibilities will open up for us. Under the leadership of the Revolutionary Party, the masses will have a nuclear bomb. At a critical juncture in a situation that we precipitated and that was in great flux, we would have at our disposal a bomb equivalent to the power of an earthquake that could level Tokyo: that'll be our trump card. The Counterrevolutionary Party is putting out the word that they too are formulating a similar plan. However, we, the Revolutionary Party, have been consistently agitating to implement this strategy for the past ten years. I tell you, the Counterrevolutionary Party's line is phony. Ours is the only revolutionary party, our program the only correct one, theoretically and tactically. We do hope you'll come to the meeting; don't be dissuaded by the scare tactics of those Counterrevolutionary thugs. We value the voluntary participation of specialists.

———Specialists? What kind? I'm just an inexperienced, unimaginative eighteen-year-old brat! I responded in a voice natural to my switched-over body. I'd been creamed in "Bridging" and really was beginning to feel like an eighteen-year-old in mind as well as body.

———**WHAT?** He dropped his disguise; his real voice, fraught with anxiety, sounded callow, coarse, and juvenile. **AN EIGHTEEN-YEAR-OLD BRAT?!** You playing dumb? You're an *ex*–power plant engineer, damn it!

———All right then, ask me something about my field. I wanted to find out if I still remembered any of the knowledge I'd accumulated over the last thirty-eight years. And whether anything of substance was retained in my adolescent head . . . .

———Hunh?! **BLITHERING IDIOT!** At first I thought I heard him speaking dialect, but he'd just blurted some old-fashioned cuss word and hung up, ha, ha. But all I'd done was speak the plain truth. Well, I imagine the Revolutionary Party will now put me on their enemies list: a cop-out nuclear specialist. Of course! Wasn't I already in the clutches of their archenemy, the Counterrevolutionary Party? Well, one or the other was bound to hate me. But in the end, hated by both?! The one they really hate is a thirty-eight-year-old who no longer exists: things are totally safe for the switched-over me, aren't they?

When we arrived at the meeting hall, a strange man was giving a speech next to a mound of thawed and refrozen snow in front of the building. I took him to be around thirty. Every time he paused in his speech, the meeting's young security team, who wore "Opposition Police" armbands, kicked him viciously, and he sailed headlong into the pile of dirty snow. Pale, somber, he looked smaller than he really was, like someone who wants to keep everything to himself. Yet he flaunted a flamboyant mustache. That was what forced me to do a double take: I zeroed in on the large pointed nose right below his handsome forehead. The content of his speech straddled the duality of simplicity and pomposity.

———For a revolutionary party to work to defeat its opposition is the most natural thing in the world—otherwise, you couldn't be called a political party, at least not a Leninist one. But why is it necessary to crush a man's head with an iron pipe, smash his bones, and ultimately kill him? Just sneak up behind him, grab him, take down his pants, and spank him. Then let him go. They're all intellectual geniuses; they'll eventually get sick of being spanked, and more than likely even decide to join your party. Those with bashed-in heads or smashed vertebrae will be totally useless to you. The dead even more so. All of you intellectual geniuses get the picture, don't you? (Thereupon, a few of the banded Opposition Police proceeded to kick the mustachioed man, *We don't crush no heads, we don't crack no bones, man, never kill nobody! What the hell you mean, opposition party? Spank a guy?* And as though he'd been waiting for his cue, the man dove headfirst into the snow mound, then got up, and shook off the slush and snow like a dog. He resumed his speech, this time a little out of range of the Opposition Police, but he soon found himself gravitating in their direction.) I've devised a plan, a mediation plan, and a well-organized one I might add. Party A and Party B should each exchange five members. With both sides having hostages, each side will have to think about their hostage-members' fate. Therefore, you all want to be as hospitable as possible. If you welcome the hostages with the intention of helping them change hats, that's what I call a real clever party. Mao Zedong always welcomed guests from abroad. If you think violence is the only way to eliminate the opposition, you're not very clever. That's anti-Maoist, isn't it? Let's say that each party's hostages realize that their enemy's theory and practice isn't so different from their own, or at least that the difference isn't worth a spanking. They become the driving force that'll push for the merger of the two parties. Isn't that so? If that's not the case, then what? (The Opposition Police leapt to the attack, falling right into his syllogism. *You've got no clue about true programmatic analysis of the world situation. You think there's only Revs and those Counterrev thugs!* And then they really went after him, kicking hard and mercilessly.)

The man with the mustache got up with difficulty and, shaking off the snow, walked toward us: we were the only spectators around. Like someone extremely nearsighted who takes off his specs for some unknown reason (in his case, to thrust his head into a snow pile, ha, ha), he looked at us through squinting, half-open eyes, and said:

——When the Revs target the general public for their campaign, they try to hold on to the intellectuals or specialists who've come from outside, don't they? Shouldn't it be the other way around? Unless you tear the stockade down, get over the barricades, and reach out, the party will never grow, will it? Just shackling a handful of intellectuals inside your own cordoned-off compound would be totally useless. Wouldn't you rather free them of their chains instead, and let them roam around as a sort of catalyst at large for campaigns targeted for the general public?

I first thought the mustachioed orator was speaking to me. But all of a sudden I noticed he was really speaking to Mori, one of those intellectuals the Revs wanted to keep fettered inside their compound! The twenty-eight-year-old Mori gave an ear to the orator and smiled a relaxed, approving smile, as though he agreed in silence, full of encouragement. It prompted a special smile from the mustachioed speaker, like that of a child caught in a prank, his nostrils clogged with dried blood. At that point the Opposition Police came over and made two entirely different announcements, one meant for us, the other for the speaker, both issued in exactly the same tone of voice, with exactly the same facial expression. I want you to see the difference between the two in written form.

———Would participants please step inside! *Hey you. Do you want to make trouble blocking these people's way?*

Just as the Opposition Police made a move to shove the orator aside, he thrust his hand to Mori, who confidently extended his own and shook it. This overwhelmed me, and I got a lump in my throat, as befits an eighteen-year-old.

5

At the entrance, two long tables with very little space between them faced each other; we squeezed through them as the people at the tables plied us with several leaflets—in exchange, of course, for monetary contributions. Boy, they get better and better each year at positioning their tables. As stingy as I am, it sure sets me on edge. When I put two one-hundred-yen coins in a collection box, one for myself and one for Mori, he pulled a five-thousand-yen bill out of his pants pocket—my pants till yesterday—and put it in the box. I almost choked, ha, ha.

On a banner hung from the stage ceiling was a slogan written for the meeting. It had to be the work of Ōno, her best shot at special effects I'd say—what workmanship. **"NUCLEAR POWER TO THE POWERLESS!"** Full of implications, wouldn't you say? It's one issue no government, East or West, has ever cared to address. Now that I think about it, those Tin Men were trying to make a go of it with their useless protective suits and god-awful clanking noise. And to think that I stopped them. Shouldn't I have just put on one of their Tin Man suits and helped them haul away the nuclear material? I suddenly felt sure that the Tin Men had infiltrated this meeting, which was organized by students and even had housewives participating. I must say, though, it would be impossible for the Tin Men to identify the switched-over me with the me they knew.

The minute Mori and I took our seats, the skin on my chest began to itch. It was a good thing my seat was right next to the aisle. I began to wiggle in my chair, enough I thought to cause a chain reaction of wiggling among those around me. I finally stuck my hand in my shirt and, feeling the tiny bumps of a rash, let out a breath, *Wooohhh,* the pain! Even taking into account that I was reverting back to the life of an immature eighteen-year-old, my memory of pre-switchover was still pretty good, and I don't think we had had an abnormal outbreak of woolly bears on the day after the heavy snow. The shirt was the problem. I'd wanted to look super cool, be the best-looking teenager in the joint, so I put on the most colorful shirt I could find. A wine-colored jersey shirt which I bought at the Research Institute Co-op in California at a time when I was in seventh heaven at the supposed takeoff of my career.

When I found the shirt in the dresser, it somehow made me uneasy, but with the rashness of a switched-over eighteen-year-old, I put it on my bare skin without bothering to identify the source of my uneasiness. Now that the terrible itchiness had begun, I finally backtracked to the source of the mystery. The last time I wore this shirt was when, just back from the States, I went to help the chief manager of the power plant move into his new house. Me, the gung-ho, scatter-brained clown, was hauling pieces of furniture when fine woolly-bear hair began to drop from every single camellia in bloom in the over-luxuriant garden. There were incredible numbers of them. By the time the itching got unbearable, my colleagues' resentment at and contempt for my show of excess zeal were so obvious that I couldn't very well ask them to scratch my back. Despite the merits of my research in the States, I was passed over for promotion at the power plant and was instead made the nuclear materials transport supervisor—a position at which I was exposed to radiation. All this began on the day I overplayed my hand. And to this day, the woolly-bear hair has persistently clung to that shirt. Unlucky days really exist, don't they?

By gingerly pressing my fingertips to the buds of the rash, I did my best to keep distracted from my itchy chest and underarms. As I did this, my presence with Mori at the meeting began to fade from my consciousness as though I was being sucked into some feverish world of illusions.

In the meantime, something uncanny about the atmosphere at the meeting was pulling me back to reality. Now, I don't mean to suggest that the party's enemies had somehow infiltrated the meeting. But there was clearly something unusual about the crowd: a granny with wire-rimmed glasses and frizzy hair, her face impossibly big and fat . . . a young boy in a European-style artisan's smock . . . a fortyish baseball-capped man with a goatee, mixed in with what appeared to be the usual assortment of activist-students and their sort. Everyone just knew that something fantastic was going to happen any moment and was waiting in anticipation of that moment. I stole a glance at the girl student sitting next to Mori; sure enough, she'd also tensed up. She had her hair pulled back tightly into a bun, her round face looking as if its pointed nose and mouth would pop off, and there were dark shadows around her eyes: she was also stealing glances at none other than Mori.

If you think I handled this bizarre situation effectively, you're wrong, because as soon as the key figures of the meeting came on stage, I lost all self-control and pined in my seat for Ōno, ha, ha. The first to appear under the banner, **"NUCLEAR POWER TO THE POWERLESS!"** was the Shikoku antinuke leader. His big eyes and nose jutted out from the tiny, tense lines of his face. Those eyes, wider than wide, scanned the audience. Next came four or five young activists whom I knew well, and then Ōno made her appearance. From behind large and sinister-looking frames her popeyed gaze—it could be from hyperthyroidism—swept over us. Both of them, the Shikoku antinuke leader (well, at that time I really didn't give a damn about him, ha, ha) and Sakurao Ōno, were searching for one particular person. Who? **ME!** Me the ever-absent power plant *ex*-employee, the pre-switchover me! She was so engrossed in the search that the hem of her skirt got caught in the wooden chair and she teetered a bit on the stage. The vestal virgin was immediately offered a steadying hand by a nearby activist. However, with a simple thank you, or something to that effect, she gently drew back. This set the switched-over teenager in the audience on fire: Cheers! Applause! I let out howls only a dog could detect: *Hey babe, neat, real neat,* **YIPPIE, YIPPIE!** Boy, too bad there was no dog around to answer me, ha, ha. The music went up. Beethoven! Before he switched to Mozart's piano sonatas, Mori used to listen to this string quartet all year round until it almost poured out of my ears: the F Minor *Serioso.* The cluster of sounds of the first bar shook the entire audience: how effective! A delicate chord then introduced the theme; what a touch, something Ōno would do. A blizzard of confetti floated down on us from above the ceiling. As I looked up through the swirl of confetti, I saw some figures switching the banners. **"NUCLEAR POWER TO THE POWERLESS, BUT NOT IN THE HANDS OF COUNTERREVOLUTIONARY THUGS!"** Then, following the soothing strings was a loud, intimidating blast that jolted those on the stage into a fright. Ōno cast aside her usual proud bearing, and began to yell in a panic:

——Opposition Police! Opposition Police! As I watched her lips move, I felt my heart choke with desire and pity.

But the Opposition Police didn't respond to her call, and the young intruders held the stage. Only the antinuke leader, as though faced with something morally unforgivable, took command of the situation and began to scold everyone in sight. When Mori stood up with me, I noticed he'd put his arm around the girl. She had completely entrusted herself to him!

The lights went out as if there were a short somewhere. Then a blinding strobe flashed in the direction of the opposition-intruders, and continued to go on and off in one-second bursts. At each sweep, the powerful strobe floodlit the hall like a bolt of lightning. In the dark between the strobe flashes, I saw the crowd begin to stir, its afterimage remaining in my eyes. But the image and the actual movement of the people a second before didn't jibe. It was like the jerky time-lapse shots of an old silent movie, and because the *Serioso* was playing so loudly, I couldn't make out what people were saying. And then within that silent movie, fist fights broke out in every corner of the meeting hall. Of course the brawlers were young activists from the two warring parties. Pushed out of the center of the brawl, the nonparticipants scurried to and fro. But in such a large-scale knock-down-drag-out melee, can "nonparticipant" status ensure any kind of safety, especially while bright light and pitch darkness shoot back and forth nonstop? Just as I expected, somebody finally socked me in the neck, and when I swung my arm around to retaliate, I hit a nose, God knows whose. I waited, scared, for a counterattack, but instead of someone standing there in front of me, all I saw in the flashing light was an empty space.

——Mori! I cried out in the dark, and turning back toward where he should have been, I yelled—God knows why—in rapid-fire punk jargon, Let's split, Mori, huh, before we get nailed!

But, the next flash showed no Mori! I was plunged into darkness and began to blink hard, so hard I could almost hear the click, click of my blinking, trying to focus on the afterimage of the crowd where I saw no Mori, the crowd disintegrated in a free-for-all. Then the next bolt of light illuminated Mori and the girl in complete composure, making their way down the aisle, eight to nine seats away from me. The two were not like any of the others—certainly not the victims, and even less like the victimizers, who were sliding around as if skating from fight to fight. The two slowly walked forward, arms outstretched, as though warding off a specter in a nightmare, and the throngs of people parted before them. Mori's arms seemed to possess supernatural power; they easily mowed down everyone in his path, and no one put up any resistance.

——Mori! I screamed out, trying to counteract Beethoven. Mori!

Mori! Where are you going all by yourself? The light flashed; totally indifferent to my signals, to my cries, Mori continued up the aisle escorting the girl in the denim shirtdress with a leather jacket slung over her arm. With the next flash, panic stricken, I again yelled out Mori's name as I tried to force my way past a row of seats—but I couldn't make it. Elbowed out of the way, writhing in pain, all I could do was thrust out my head like a snapping turtle and call out, **MORI! MORI!** When he finally turned toward me, there was absolute rejection in his glance— his profile with its three-day beard is all that remains in my memory— and then he disappeared into the crowd. Drenched in sweat, overcome by the painful itch of the rash, I stood riveted to the spot. I'll tell you why Mori's rejection stunned me so badly. I had refused to accept his past rejections as such, but this time I felt that the time had come, all accounts were past due. From childhood on, the pre-switchover Mori had continued to reject his father—me—with his own elusive will, and I had refused to accept that, always suppressed that. . . .

——The **"YAMAME CORPS"**! The chanting went up for the first time and drowned out the superloud string quartet. **YAMAME CORPS!!! YAMAME CORPS!!!**

My emotions received yet another stunning jolt. It was as though the words Yamame Corps had fallen into a hole—which the rejecting Mori had bored into my soul—but instead the words had formed a lid to seal it! In the next interval of light everyone's eyes turned to the stage.

And behold, a free-for-all had erupted on the stage! No, no, I don't mean those guys were having some kind of mass orgy in the debris up on stage, ha, ha. The stage was packed with people taking punches at each other, pushing and shoving. You couldn't tell who the Yamame Corps were. And lifted into the air above the bobbing heads in the fracas was the scriptwriter-to-be. A pair of large fat legs were kicking and struggling in the center of a billowing skirt suspended in midair, a cavern in the shape of a bell!

——**SHITHEADS! YOU UNGRATEFUL WRETCHES!** I yelled in a voice that reverberated through the sealed pit of my soul. And me, the eighteen-year-old, burning with a confused mixture of desire and indignation, charged at the bell-shaped cavern hanging in the air above the stage. A visual hallucination of fat thighs vividly shimmering in the dark! Fortified now by a set of young teeth, no longer temporary false teeth, I sprang forward.

6

I charged the stage, leapt into the rioting crowd, and was immediately shoved back. I gave it another try. This time I grabbed the edge of the stage, and the mob promptly stomped my hands; then I thrust my head and shoulders forward, and they kicked me. This happened over and over. I tried one more time cautiously placing my fists, not my hands, on the edge of the stage, dodging the rioters' battered old shoes which kicked the air in my direction, while I hopped to and fro trying to find a breach in their defenses, when a skinny man, forty-ish—probably a seasoned trooper in the Yamame Corps—came crashing down from the stage, his body hanging upside down right in front of me. His face, pale and doltish, his eyes the amber of a cat's eye, stared straight ahead. He must have been thrown by the sight of me. You see, from his position, my face was upside down before his head hit the floor.

——Oooo ouch! he cried out.

Another fallen victim on the floor was vainly fighting off a horde of stomping clodhoppers. As he hurriedly tried to get out of range after one assault, I realized, Good God, the Shikoku antinuke leader! His large mouth, set in a small head, was as puckered up as the wrinkles of an anus. He looked like an old man taking the beating for his son. That impression was restricted to the mouth, though: angry eyes on fire, nostrils flaring, he was white-hot, a veritable tornado of fighting spirit. As he fell down again and again, the antinuke leader swiped at the skin of a kicking leg with some sort of weapon in his right hand. When the weapon failed to lock onto a shin, it clattered like a pair of castanets. You guessed it! Somehow I just knew they could be used that way, so it was easy to put two and two together. That tiny man, harassed, beaten, stomped every time he tried to get to his feet, had spit out his own dentures, and was using them to bite the nearest shin. Boy, that spurred me on. Have you ever heard of a biting attack by remote control?

——**RIOT SQUAD! STAY COOL!** A concatenation of voices took up the cry coming from the back of the hall. Drowning out even the loud music, the outcries that reverberated through the hall had an immediate effect. In the blink of an eye the knock-down-drag-out ceased. The assault group's commanding officer must have ordered a pullout. The speakers also went dead.

With all the lights out, frustration and anger erupted—neither faction was trained to cope with a blackout. In the darkness I heard a bunch of rioters jump off the now quiet stage. The situation was very precarious for those offstage. I buried my head in my arms, and blindly tried to wedge myself into the space right below the stage, whereupon I heard a huge thud.

——**DAMN YOU FASCISTS!** I heard an indignant voice cursing, a voice that belonged to none other than a thoroughly mortified script-writer-to-be. **BLOCKHEADS! CREEPS!**

I scuttled on all fours in a charge toward the sound, through many pairs of shoes still tramping the floor. *Chommmp!* A sharp pain seared through my right buttock; the antinuke leader's denture had "bit" again, I bet. If I hadn't dashed forward wide-eyed in the dark at that moment, in one-tenth of a second my testes probably would have been bitten off, the juicy testes of an eighteen-year-old! Ha, ha. The antinuke leader was still fighting back. I charged, charged purposely bumping my head into the thighs and shins in front of me; careful not to get my fingers smashed, I crawled ahead on my fists. I then hit an overturned wooden chair squarely with my shoulder, and unwittingly knocked it away from me; somewhere ahead of me I heard a groan and a curse

——**DAMN YOU FASCISTS!** I didn't want to appear from the same direction as the flying chair, so I backtracked a bit, scuttling around like the clever brat I was, and then crawled over to the spot where I guessed she'd be, with my heart pounding. I swiftly put my arm around the stunned Ōno, who was barely sitting upright, almost falling to the stage floor.

——It's me! Let's get out of here! I said in a deep voice, hoping that it still had the deepness of the pre-switchover days. I helped her to her feet with my arm around her rather massive waist, and together we retreated backstage in the dark. Since the brawlers on stage had all jumped down into the aisles, there really was no one to stop us. As if she had been waiting for my appearance, the scriptwriter-to-be clung tight to me and trotted as fast as her high heels could take her: What a sweet, lovely sight! The surface of my chest itched painfully, whereas, deep inside me, my heart ached with a sweet tenderness, ha, ha.

In the meantime, we had stumbled into the drop curtains and were debating where to go next when a thunderous roar rolled through the meeting hall! The riot squad stormed in through every exit and entrance of the building.

The ancients regarded the breaking of thunder on the left as a good omen. Let's go right and create our own luck! I smashed into the handrail of a spiral stairway. Up above beamed a faint rectangular light. I looked at it more closely; sure enough, the words **DANGER, CONTROL ROOM**, were lit up in red. Ōno and I ran up the staircase rubbing against each other like two frightened sheep on the run. The red light was mounted on a control panel, and right across from it was a faintly illuminated doorknob. We let ourselves into a rather cramped space and locked the door from the inside. Below, countless boots thumped the floor, as though the first act of *Macbeth* had begun. I helped Ōno squat on the floor which was covered with a straw mat, and then helped her lie down; I said with a confident air—remember, I'm an irresponsible eighteen-year-old brat, ha, ha

——With their bulky metal shields and protective gear, the riot squad wouldn't dare come near this room!

So, what happened next? We made love, ha, ha. You see, the script-writer-to-be began to cough, so I kissed her mouth to muffle the sound so that the riot squad couldn't hear her. Although we loved to lick each other's asshole, we avoided kissing on the mouth even after we became more intimate—something unclean about it, we thought, ha, ha. Fearing an interruption, we immediately started a savage thrusting of our bodies at each other. The sound of Ōno's fat thighs banging against my butt drove me on, ha, ha. I came so fast that I didn't have time to get out the four condoms I'd brought with me! I pulled out my throbbing penis and shot what felt like an endless stream of semen onto Ōno's spacious belly. As I held my still-hard penis, the smell of the ejaculating semen overwhelmed me with the hallucination that I was a plant, oozing sap. For her part, her orgasm came with the help of my scrotum, which she vigorously rubbed against her vagina, while her other hand covered her mouth to suppress her moans. I had made a discovery: *Aahh, this is the way humans make love.* I truly get into Ōno's flesh in lovemaking, Oh, how I love the Cosmic life. My soul comprehends its meaning the way my body penetrates her flesh. And I reply to the Cosmic Will, *This is OK.* This was how I experienced the best orgasm of my life!

By the time we rearranged ourselves and sat down side by side, the darkness below had been completely conquered by the riot squad. We heard them climbing up and down the stairway by the switchboard. The engineer, after either being ordered to stay out or locked up by the assault group, was apparently back at work. The lights went on in the hall, the riot squad formed ranks and began to round up the participants who had missed the chance to escape. Rapid-fire commands were barked out, but compared with the earlier din, all was now quiet. In the meantime a light filtered in at floor level through a tiny frosted glass window to the spot where we were hiding. The police were taking down the double-crossing banners as evidence of the assault. In the filtered light the scriptwriter-to-be read all the tell-tale signs of the switchover on my body and understood. Suddenly she stretched out her long arm, caressed the back of my head, and said,

——Ah, poor thing! Why in the world did this happen to you? Ah, such a poor thing, why you?

She instantly accepted the fact that I was still me, and at the same time switched over, that I possessed the body (or, the spirit) of an eighteen-year-old.

I didn't have the ability to respond to her question; besides, there was no need for me to reply in the first place; I had my arms around her waist, now relaxed and soft, enjoying this sensation and that of her caressing the hair on the back of my head, the nape of my neck. Tears welled up in my eyes, as if describing for me the choking pain of the switchover. A teardrop, not from the eye touching Ōno's flushed cheek but from the other one, rolled down into the tiny dent at the end of my mouth. I licked it with my eighteen-year-old tongue. The sides of my nose began to itch at the spot where tears ran down, but now the pain across my chest was gone. Lovemaking had rid me of the woolly bears' poison.

5

How We Felt Left Out
of the Conspiracy

1

So the scriptwriter-to-be expressed in one gesture an innate tenderness toward my spirit and my flesh after the switchover, but that tenderness was given democratically, it wasn't meant only for me.

——Suppose those kids have been arrested; I've got to put together a rescue operation pronto! She even went so far as to chide herself.

It's me who needs the rescuing. I want only you to deliver me. No organization. Don't stop.

——The fact that the riot squad didn't find us hiding here meant they probably didn't take the brawl very seriously. Nothing really will happen to those who didn't escape. Besides, no one meant to pick a fight with the riot squad, did they? I'm sure they were just rounded up, taken outside, and then let go.

——Didn't you say before that the riot squad wouldn't dare come in here because of their metal shields?

——. . . If they really wanted to bust up this meeting and arrest the ringleaders of this free-for-all, they wouldn't have risked coming in here now, would they?

——Do you mean they would have had to take off their bulky pants and heavy boots to avoid electrocution, just to snoop around here? I think it was something else. I think they must have targeted the king-pins and arrested them right after they occupied the hall. And if that's the case, I've got to put together a rescue team right away and get down to brass tacks.

——But, who are the kingpins they targeted? Are those VIPs on the sponsor's side, your side, or the assailants'?

——Why would I start a rescue effort for Counterrevs who broke up the meeting? Even if their arrest were a frame-up, I wouldn't do that.

——. . . Then, exactly who among the sponsors are the VIP targets of the authorities? Of all people, you, the Ōno group leader, were able to hide safely.

——I'm not a key figure in the Party. No one, not Party members, or those CRP thugs, not even the Public Security Department considers me a bigwig.

——That's news to me. I even thought the Yamame Corps was under your command, not to mention the Ōno group.

——Why do you have to provoke me? How can you make such a statement when you know nothing about what's going on inside the movement?

——. . . You've got those "kids," the ones you say you've got to res-cue, in the palm of your hand. From what I've observed so far of the Ōno group's civil rights activities, I can't believe you've simply been a puppet. You see, in the midst of the brawl at the meeting, someone shouted Yamame Corps. Doesn't it mean the Corps is the Revs' military arm? I've heard about them for ten years now. . . .

——So what! Just because my group belongs to the "Yamame Corps," does that automatically make me their leader? I'll repeat myself again, Why do you insist on blabbing ignorant statements when I've got to start organizing a rescue operation for those kids? Are you waiting for your penis to get hard again so you can **FUCK** me? I've had enough.

Aaah, don't talk like that even if you decide not to rescue this miserable brat right under your nose; you saying FUCK destroys my memory of fantastic love-making, I wanted to say. My heart cried out in anguish. But instead, in a delayed response, I said the opposite. I wonder why I even had to say it! Could it just be typical teenage sentimentality?

——I don't want it, either. But you had your hand on my crotch, so I refrained from saying anything, ha, ha!

——Let's go then. I'm in no joking mood, that's for sure.

I wished the engineer had locked us in, but the door opened im-mediately. *Aaah, I wish I could stay in here alone with her until tomorrow!* a voice inside me—somewhere around the stomach, I should say—cried out, ha, ha!

——Isn't there an emergency flashlight near the control panel?

In preparing to become a scriptwriter, she must have been in a place like this before; she proved she was a professional and senior to me, because I immediately saw a flashlight as long as a billy club hanging at the side of the red warning light. As I attempted to light the way for Ōno, the beam fell on a skull and crossbones, **NO TRESPASSING, HIGH VOLTAGE!** on the door we had just exited! No wonder the engineer and the riot squad didn't dare go in. But we had gone in blindly, exposing our nakedness to tens of thousands of volts, to make love. Who knows, I may have felt I had the best orgasm ever because the organic stirrings inside my testes responded to the high-voltage currents stimulating them. Ha, ha!

When her glance caught the warning sign, the scriptwriter-to-be cried out feebly, *Aah!* and clung to me as if her body had turned to jelly. So I descended the spiral stairs, my arms protectively around my pitiful, lovable, sexual partner—the best I ever had—not some hateful, seasoned television debater who out-talked me every time. While she acted the unsteady dolt in shock, I was the stalwart, hand firmly clamped to the banister. Sensing that everybody would make a fuss over the valor of an eighteen-year-old, I walked on newly resolute, as if for the first time in my life.

Do you doubt the voice of experience? I'm an amateur when it comes to language, but if you do doubt me, I want you to put things down in such a way that the voice of your misgivings would reverberate over the voice of self-assertion that *insists* on being heard. Of course, I'm not saying that you, the ghostwriter, should supply a footnote stating "But, I don't believe you."

You silently record the words I *insist on*. But I want to convey to a third party—the unspecified number of readers—the dynamic relationship between the *stubbornly insistent* me and you who transcribes my accounts while doubting their veracity all along. As far as the third party is concerned, I exist only in a confrontational relationship between me (the *stubbornly insistent* man) and you (the man who quietly records my words in spite of his misgivings). If I were suddenly plucked out of this world, the only way I could be brought back to reality, to real time and my resurrected existence, would be through your words. I don't want the third party to read your words as just some gossip about a switchover. Our so-called switched-over fate, Mori's and mine, has to serve a higher purpose. Picture that purpose on a three-dimensional screen, projected as the fate of humankind, of the world, and of the Cosmos all at once. This is *the* fate, I *insist on* representing. This is what I want to bring to life in the creative *imagination* of the third party; this is what I want to actualize through him. You don't mind my using your favorite expression do you, ha, ha: only then will I be resurrected as a real ghost. And to make it all possible, the tension of the confrontation between my *insistent* words and your silent misgivings must sustain the narrative. So, if you keep on doubting as you do, the reader will ultimately rebel, damn it! And from that moment on he's bound to take my side just to compete with you. With your misgivings operating as a lever, a dynamic relationship will surely open up between the *stubbornly insistent* me and the reader.

This is simply a matter of applying the basic principles of mechanics, my specialty, ha, ha. You novelists do create verbal devices that activate something imaginative in a third party, don't you? The principle of mechanics is what's behind *devices,* anyway! For technicians, once the written word, with all its activating power, helps bring about a real, material result, what was written becomes a piece of scrap. Take, for example, the words I wrote down concerning the possibility of stress corrosion cracking in a nuclear reactor; once the technician in charge of the unit comes up with a solution that removes the danger, that's the end of it, and my words become totally useless.

But for you novelists, the words you write down are themselves the *device* that continues to activate something imaginative, right? And you don't have a technician on hand who'll scrap your words in the end, do you? To make the insistent words of a former engineer a prime mover for the imaginative process in a third party's mind—wouldn't you say that the *device* I propose is an effective one? Let me put it bluntly again: if you don't believe what I've got to say, for God's sake, don't pretend you do.

2

Negotiating our way over the dirty, packed-down snow, frozen into ridges and ruts resembling a dog's spine, we let ourselves out the service entrance and walked away from the hall, around the cul-de-sac of the surrounding buildings, and toward the front gate. I'd nothing to back up the hunch, but I was confident that Mori in his prime would be waiting for me in the dark on the pavement with or without his student friend. Probably not right in front of the building, since the riot squad had cleared the area—he'd choose a spot just as he did at the Kodama platform and wait for me, regretting he ever rejected me.

I really believed this, you see, and felt chivalrous enough at the time to listen to the mumblings of the scriptwriter-to-be, and even to attempt to comfort her after those warning signs gave her the shock of her life.

——. . . It's not that I feel left out by the citizen groups and the various factions of the Revs with whom we've been struggling together in the movement. The organizing and mobilizing efforts were quite successful, not counting the assault made by those damn fascist Counterrev thugs. With me at the center of things, my group took the initiative in laying the groundwork. Now that's a fact. But still, compared to the activists of five, six, or even seven years ago, today's young activists are really beyond me. They're marvelous when it comes to distributing flyers; and whenever I come down with a cold, they come and stay up with me all night; some of them even go to their part-time jobs without a wink of sleep. But despite all of this, it does cross my mind from time to time, that these same kids might be secretly making bombs somewhere. Who knows, they might be conspiring with kids from outside and making not just time bombs, but A-bombs as well. Digging a cellar somewhere. . . .

——You can't be serious! If they mean business, they'd need a cellar as big as an indoor tennis court. Besides, they wouldn't be able to do it without experts. Remember, you'd need a very high ceiling.

——All the same, those same quiet, sincere, terribly ordinary kids, if that's a virtue, who've been disciplined all their lives—including in the movement—might very well be secretly making A-bombs when they get together. It's those same kids who have *shouldered me out, who've left me in the dark;* that's how I see it right now. But that doesn't mean I can say to them, Are you making A-bombs on Sundays? Can I join in?

We were at the front entrance of the hall, but there was no sight of Mori! It was as if a cannonball had shot through the center of my body! You're thinking it's a repeat performance of what I went through the day before when I lost the pre-switchover Mori at Tokyo Station? No, nothing of the kind! Although I felt a big cavern opening up within me, it was quickly filling up with ghoulish green, scorching hot poison! I was jealous of the girl who'd taken Mori to a place I knew not where, of Mori who'd opened up a relationship with the Other, shouldering me aside!

——What's the matter? Is it the switchover? You don't look good.

Under the streetlight, she could clearly see the switched-over me, and realized how lost I was. And she said those kind words while she herself was still in shock.

——Mori's gone. I thought he'd wait for me here! Well, of course he's the twenty-eight-year-old Mori, not the missing child of yesterday. . . . When last I saw him in the hall, he was escorting a girl toward the exit. . . .

——I'm not sure what's going on, but . . . if what you say is true, wouldn't the riot squad have rounded them up? Come with me and let's start that rescue operation for the kids. Information on Mori's bound to leak out.

——No way, I'm not coming along! As far as you're concerned, Mori's just a number, one of many kids, but he's the only one I'm concerned about. I'll look for him myself!

——That's not true, every one of them is important, Ōno said sadly, but immediately reverted to the well-drilled expedient tone of an activist: Go ahead and take that cab. Make the rounds where Mori hangs out. If I hear anything, I'll give you a call no matter how late it is.

However, I found myself emotionally regressing even further, switched over almost to infancy. My knee-jerk rebellion in declaring that I'd go look for Mori alone totally collapsed when the rather un-friendly-looking taxi driver turned around as I got in. I just gave him my home address.

——Buddy, you don't have any gas on you, I hope?! Tear gas, that is. Those students somehow slipped by the riot squad, but do they ever stink of tear gas. My fares complain about it all the time.

I kept silent. No doubt about it, in terms of age, I was switched-over, a high school street-fighter. I did look awful after that brawl in the hall, but since I didn't have a crowbar on me to give the driver a good whack, I stayed low-key.

——You sick or something? The way you're huffing you'd think you owned the place. It's midnight, you know—man, you scare me! He continued to needle me; of course he might have meant it humorously.

But by that time, like Ōno, I was in no mood to laugh about any-thing. Worse yet, I began to pity myself. *I didn't ask for the switchover. Mori who's also been switched over has rejected me and run off with some girl. I want to go back to the good old pre-switchover days! I'll pretend it all never happened. That's it. Just a dream I want to wake up from to go back to the life of a middle-aged man with a kid, a man whose wife slashed him and then aban-doned him!*

. . . This was how my mind wandered until I got out of the cab in front of my house, and took my key out of my pocket. When I tried to insert the key into the lock below the doorknob, I found a gaping hole; my fist went through where the keyhole should have been!

——*Ooo ouch*, I mumbled something and immediately stepped back in fear.

A Rev hit squad wrecks the door to its rival party's hideout with a crowbar and metal cutter. You read about this type of violence in the newspapers all the time, don't you? And where can I go to escape impending danger in this fine metropolis at midnight? I doubt if I can weasel my way out of this. I even botched the search plan for Mori and ended up coming home. As I stood rooted to the spot on the brick walkway, the door was opened from the inside and a light shone through the hole in the vandalized door! This was too much for an eighteen-year-old. I froze in terror. With a three-day growth of beard covering his cheeks and chin, Mori stood at the doorway, as though letting in an exhausted tomcat in heat after a night of caterwauling and prowling! As surely as I was displaying my adolescent brashness, Mori now seemed to have settled into his switchover, matured in mind as well as body.

I went inside without greeting him, but was at a loss over how to lock the door I closed behind me. The lock and the plywood around it had been gouged out. From behind Mori, who was observing my predicament, came his girlfriend and she immediately began to work on the door. She squatted down on her haunches like a dog. She wound a piece of rope around the handle of a pick, passed the pick through the gaping hole, looped the rope end to the outside knob, wedged the pick handle in through the hole, and secured the other end of the rope to the inside doorknob. She gave a push, once, twice. The door was completely secure. I was overwhelmed—much the same as I was at eighteen by a girl, two, three years older who took no notice of boys her junior— by her dexterity, by the way the girl's hands fiddled with those tools. I didn't recall having any picks or ropes in the house. This quick, nimble-fingered girl must have brought them in. The situation was obvious even to the brain cells of an inane eighteen-year-old.

——It must have been a sight to see when she broke the lock with that pick, Mori. Are those her party's tactics: breaking and entering, pick and rope in hand, knocking down anyone who resists, and then tying them up? Are you telling me that our house is occupied by a hardcore activist who's been through commando training?

—— I couldn't help breaking the door! You took the key with you— it's right in your hand, the key we needed! Mori quietly sat back and watched, letting his mouthpiece handle the reply. He was in his prime. He'd lost all traces of the distorted appearance imposed on him before by the necessity of covering up the damage to his skull. Apparently his natural physical structure was developing now in keeping with the true generic plan encoded into his genes. My wife/*ex*-wife is small and morose compared to her brothers—giants in the Yamato tribe, with large bodies and faces exuding confidence—and their genes were transmitted to Mori, bypassing my wife/*ex*-wife. Their bloodline was clearly manifested in the switched-over Mori.

——This young woman won't raise a fuss if I come in, Mori, will she? Well, after all, this is my house. I tried to deliver those words in a self-assured voice, but it cracked with resentment against this man in his prime who showed neither joy nor shame at my homecoming.

Mori quietly smiled, eyes quizzical—reflection, maybe? Once more the girl's head popped out from behind Mori, glaring at me with a stare that could kill. She bared her large—really not that large—front teeth; with her response, we immediately became verbal opponents.

——Your house? Don't chew me out over petit-bourgeois ownership! Don't be hung up on that stuff. Why not come in and have a bite? By the way, I approve of an offspring's right to speak to his father as an equal!

What, what? I'm the father around here, Mori's the son! True, we've been switched over and our ages are jumbled. Does this apply as well to the parent-child relationship? And what about the genetic lineage we share and the idea of descent as a direction? Stop being absurd, ridiculous! I tried to scream back, but I didn't know how much she knew of the switchover. I couldn't afford a careless slip of the tongue. My joints were aching all over, and I sluggishly bent down, took off my shoes under the watchful gaze of Mori, and followed him into the living room. The young woman who'd attacked me seemed to be of the school that holds a tongue-lashing is always a winning strategy; but it apparently wasn't in her character to beat a dead horse. She was already in the kitchen working. She had placed herself under Mori's protection in the midst of the chaos at the rally. Now she was no longer in her denim shirtdress. She was wearing a sweater and a colorful skirt in a sort of Spanish pattern. I found that rather weird but when I looked a little closer at her back, my eyes almost popped out of my head. She was naked from the waist down and had just wrapped one of my bath towels around her like an apron. A quick movement as she bent over the sink to pick up some plates presented me an eye-level view—I was sitting on the floor—of the bony crack of her butt, and the black shadowy area beyond. Something entirely different from resentment set my head ablaze, and my heart pounding with excitement. I couldn't lift my gaze from the sight. I'm not sure whether Mori had also caught the dark sheen of the crack, but his large body sat crammed into the corner where as an infant he used to listen to music—acoustically, the best spot in the house—expressing in his face the total absence of repression in his soul. My eyes carried a message, intended to restore my parental authority. *Quit acting like you're on cloud nine.* But Mori was now his own man who could instantly vaporize my cold optic tidings. Before the switchover, he had been very sensitive to those nonverbal signals in my attitude and tone of voice.

——Too bad we couldn't marinate this overnight, the girl said apologetically as she brought out fried noodles topped with pieces of roast pork—apparently cooked in my oven—Mori said this was the best roast pork he'd ever had.

I wonder whether he meant better than all the pork he's ever had before the switchover. Every year around New Year's Day, I took Mori to Eisho's in Yokohama to buy bright red-dyed roast pork—he's saying hers is even better than that? I was tempted to make some snotty remark, but hunger in an eighteen-year-old body is a ravenous force. Dazzled by the fried noodles placed in front of me, my eyes caught the perfect symmetry of color in the roast pork, the onions, the bean sprouts, the oil, and the noodles.

——By the way, don't ever call me Miss. I detest male chauvinism. Call me Sayoko. The name my parents picked for me shows contempt for women. So I made up my own name. You know the characters for chemical reactions, *sayo?* My name is gender-neutral, you see? . . . Water or beer? Well, you own the beer in the fridge anyway, so there's no need for you to stand on ceremony.

——Please, may I have a beer, Sayoko. I placed my order, delighted that requesting service this way didn't seem to have any male chauvinism about it. And when I saw Sayoko, with an air of indifference, stand up to get my beer, reaching behind with her left hand to hold the ends of the towel in place, I got a bit flustered by the thought that she might have guessed I had peeked at the crack in her ass, ha, ha.

Oh, the meal? Boy, was it scrumptious. Wait, I'd better qualify that—it was good, by the standards of a teenager's taste buds. When I'd finished all the roast pork bits, the sensitive advocate of women's rights at the table displayed her practical sort of kindness. She brought out the whole roast on a cutting board, sliced off more pieces and put them on my plate. I'd made a new discovery. Until I was in my thirties, I had believed that the long reddish black roast was just a chunk of muscles, but now I knew it was shoulder blade roast cut into long strips like so many Yi Jing sticks. You never know when you'll learn something new, ha, ha. With just a twist of sarcasm typical of an eighteen-year-old—I was slightly tipsy after the beer—I complimented her cooking even though that was unnecessary.

——Say, Sayoko, have you been reading up on how to cook roast pork as you studied the Thought of Mao Zedong? Her eyes narrowed in an instant; a beam of light concentrated by her pupils darted out and pierced through me. She didn't open her mouth to speak until she'd found a way to channel the indignation within her. By sheer willpower she prevented the dry lips that encircled her shiny front teeth from loosing a torrent of anger at me. Why was she trying to overcome the anger inside her? Was it simply because she held the lamebrained clown in front of her in contempt?

——I have no intention of discrediting the workers who make a living roasting pork. But I can't accept putting the study of Mao Zedong's Thought and Chinese cooking in the same pot. When you say Mao's Thought, just what do you mean?

——Hmm, hmm. What I'm referring to is Mao's scientific thought. The Chinese have produced A-bombs based on that thought, right? I've analyzed in detail the actual footage of the Chinese nuclear tests. I don't think they were being careful enough when it comes to the danger of radiation exposure for the test observers.

——You're shifting the focus, aren't you? It's OK. Let's concentrate on the test footage. Did you also see the medical data with the film? You didn't just take a quick look at those film strips shown to foreign journalists and then compare the film clips for the tests held in Nevada, did you? The Chinese are self-reliant, beyond comparison. Are you saying you've seen or heard about cases of radiation poisoning in China?

——You see, Sayoko, reporting in China's severely censored.

——Nowadays, they've got no choice. They're preparing against counterrevolutions from both the South and the North. The matter of censorship and the question whether or not radiation victims exist are entirely different issues. You can say that censorship occurs but there wasn't exposure to radiation. One premise does not follow from the other.

——Hmm, hmm. Provided that your party—which seems to follow Mao's line on self-reliance—or the opposition party for that matter, did succeed in making an A-bomb on your own, in testing it, I certainly hope you won't harm your country by exposing it to radiation.

——Why do we have to test it? If a genuinely revolutionary party goes nuclear in Tokyo, if they go public with all the photos and scientific data, that'll be enough to mobilize people for revolutionary conditions. As long as control of nuclear power is the fundamental issue of the revolution, we can't let the Counterrev thugs succeed in making an A-bomb first. Along the same lines, don't you think a revolutionary party armed with the correct program should beat the authorities to the punch before they develop nuclear weapons?

——You take nuclear armaments so lightly; it's not impossible to make an A-bomb given a large enough group with access to engineers and researchers. But that's nothing more than laying the groundwork for establishing a nuclear nation. Just take the problem of transporting the bomb in question. How are you going to pull it off? With your Revs using their correct line?

——We don't have to transport it, do we? All we have to do is keep the bomb at some liberated area within metropolitan Tokyo.

——You mean you'd threaten to self-destruct, to blow it up? And that will mobilize the city and its suburbs? Once you've terrorized the masses into submission in Tokyo, you think that'll pave the way for the blood-less triumphant reign of the Revs? Not really much of a reign though, is it, if the liberation army has to sit tight, right next to the bomb. Hmm, hmm.

——You think that *hmm, hmm* just might add a little luster to your character, but you sound like some old fossil—well, it's unimportant.

——If it's not important, don't say it! No matter what the nuclear arms strategy is or what party's involved, I predict they'll come to a dead end. Long ago, Mrs. Roosevelt, in a speech broadcast on the BBC, said that the majority of American citizens would rather see the world de-stroyed than allow America to go communist, and of course her com-ment had severe repercussions. I'm sure an A-bomb would force people to mobilize even in Tokyo. But if the new "silent majority" of housewives insisted that they'd rather die in the atomic blast than face a revolution, then you'd lose, right? Even then, you couldn't set the bomb off, could you? A lesson: a nuclear war doesn't have the power to overcome a people's war!

——The multitudes of housewives? You're a male chauvinist pig through and through, aren't you? Jerk!

Objectively speaking, am I? Hadn't I finally put this female activist down, theoretically speaking? Counting the round I had with the script-writer-to-be, one win, one loss, don't you think today's debate with females is tied? But the third party, Mori, who sat observing the "young-sters" arguing, knit his brows and smiled, giving no sign as to who he considered the winner in the debate between Sayoko and me. I sud-denly decided to discharge at Mori the hostile feeling that was pent-up inside me.

——How're you feeling, Mori? Did everything go all right with Sayoko? You look so composed! You're treating me like a kid still wet behind the ears. In the days before the switchover when I couldn't throw my wife out, I tried to negotiate with her—for the day when you'd be sexually mature—to do it with you, Mori. You'd say, of course, that it's a crime; but the supreme supernatural being, the arbiter of all crimes, foreclosed the future on you; so wouldn't the crime be written off? As long as she practiced birth control, she wouldn't risk warping the future of humankind. It's a humane procedure, less violent than castration, or so I tried to persuade her. In return, I received her stare, a look that said I was a madman. Now that you're switched over, and all of a sudden confronted with the matter of sex, I'm so glad to know you've made it with Sayoko.

——Even a loony isn't that gross, you're such a sicko jerk, so disgusting I feel like throwing up, the girl said in a merciless tone that trampled my touchy eighteen-year-old sensibility. Tell this drunken jerk to go to bed, Mori. After all our waiting and worrying for him, thinking about how he'd come home hungry, he gets drunk and gives us grief!

I had not forgotten the rejecting gaze Mori gave me in the thick of the chaos at the meeting. Although I was now in a verbal wrangle with him, I didn't have the courage to look him straight in the eye. Instead, I stared down at my own slightly red hands. And on them, as though written in neon electric letters, I read a telepathic message from Mori: *Unless you stop drinking and go to bed right this moment, you'll ruin your health, and won't be able to carry out the mission of the switchover. Isn't that so?* Of course it was—it was like a slap on my forehead. I stood up quickly and tottered forward, banging my head against a wall. Neither Mori nor the girl laughed. And now, come to think of it, I remember that when I was eighteen, I had never drunk even a half a glass of beer. I found my way in the dark to the bed where I dropped. The sheet that touched my cheek was caked with the dry blood I'd lost before the switchover, and the dampness from Mori's urine began to penetrate my pants. I was already half asleep, though. While the outside world was perpetuating itself in every detail, only Mori and I, who'd both undergone the switchover in body and spirit, endured our utter displacement.

3

Well, although all along I've been adamantly pouring my heart and soul into recounting my story, now I'm stuck. . . . What I mean is, the words I use to describe Mori after the switchover sound too lackluster, too mundane. I'm adamantly relating what's going on, but I really feel so wretched that I want to cry. When I talked about the pre-switchover, I was never like this. It might have something to do with my upbringing, but I always believed that children like *our children,* by virtue of being retarded, would invite fundamental respect. When Mori was born, I told my grandmother about his abnormality and what we would have to expect in the future; her reply was full of encouragement: She told me that she'd enshrined Prince Sukunahiko* and lit a votive candle for Mori.

If my words merely portray Mori as just another young man in his prime, wouldn't a third party who'd been fascinated by the switchover instantly become disillusioned? Have I really grasped the essence of

*A god of medicine and wine in Japanese creation myths.

Mori after the switchover? Up until now I've talked rather idly about the post-switchover me. Maybe without my knowing it, I have become an inane jerk, incapable of understanding how captivated Mori's really become after the switchover. After all, it's a measure of ability, you know, one person's capacity to touch the soul of another.

At any rate, I'll continue to speak my mind as I have in the past. The subject himself is a living being full of energy, in the real world. On the morning of the second day after the switchover—the noon after, to be exact—I woke up on a sheet caked with my own blood and stinking of Mori's urine. In spite of the stage fight the day before, in which I was hit, kicked, and actually pushed off the stage, and the frenzied lovemaking—of course, in the missionary position—only certain muscles ached and, knowing that I'd quickly recover, I woke up full of energy: Why not let this young, vibrant body do its thing! Think about it. Of all the eighteen-year-olds in the world, I'm the youngest. (Compared to the ordinary eighteen-year-old, I was born twenty years earlier, you see. A teenager born of a human seed before it aged, ha, ha.)

The telltale tip-off of this newly energized organism just awakened, full of verve, was a morning erection. Since I don't want to keep this subject up—that would be sarcastic—I'll let it go, ha, ha. A full bladder is not something that can be ignored; it's physically related to the morning erection, thereby creating a new dilemma, a typically basic one for an eighteen-year-old. What should I do if I go downstairs to urinate and run into that girlie? Last night I got drunk and even made a snide remark about her making love with Mori. What should I do if she misinterprets my erection? She might blurt out something like, Are you the type of father who gets the hots for his own son's lover? Man, what a lousy punk! Or, would she say the opposite? Are you the type who gets the hots for your own father's lover? Either way, the outcome would be the same, I bet, and I'd still be a lousy punk! In the meantime, my bladder's at the bursting point. I couldn't afford to suffer indefinitely with this dilemma. I got out of the bed, hunching my back as I shuffled around the room collecting a fake Campbell soup can pencil holder, a baked-clay Mexican frog with its mouth open, several glasses of various sizes, an ink bottle three-fourths empty. I lined up the entire collection on the edge of my desk, and I began to urinate. First, the vases and glasses, then the fake tomato soup can. . . . By the time I started filling the Mexican frog, I was moaning in fear that it might overflow. But this frog could hold all I had and more! I wonder if it was an Inca urinal? Ha, ha. As I looked down at the frog's mouth through the vapors steaming from the hot urine, I felt like the legendary thief Jiraiya,* who had just made a narrow escape!

In the post-urination calm, I lost myself in a reverie about what I mentioned earlier—how to comprehend Mori's switchover, how to plumb the depths of my soul. Had I lost my ability to touch someone's soul, an ability I'd had until the switchover? As soon as I began to entertain this doubt, I plunked down on the bed and felt my whole self shrinking along with my withering penis. All I could do was mope about it all. If the outcome of the switchover meant the loss of my ability to touch Mori's soul, what significance does that hold for me? The event itself defies logic, and therefore, it should contain a clue that would push the human struggle forward, shouldn't it?

. . . While I was turning these things over in my mind, sitting alone, distressed, a revelation hit me: Although I may have become an obnoxious jerk, there can be no doubt that Mori's been actually switched over to maturity, that he's been switched over with a special mission! Didn't his telepathy confirm that to me last night? I've also been switched over, but I am to be the eyewitness at the scene where this mission is to be carried out. The body and spirit of all humankind may be nothing other than a shadow beamed by a projector aboard a UFO, but as long as Mori's shadow, among 3.5 billion shadows, was selected and entrusted with a mission, and is trying to fulfill that mission, I, who've been switched over to keep vigil, to give testimony on what comes to pass, can't just remain idle. . . . Tears began to well up in my eyes as I thought about these things; I opened my mouth wide, panting heavily, so that I wouldn't break down and cry. That's what it means; even a foolish teenager, for all his lack of experience in touching others' souls, can grasp something very fundamental through the medium of the bountiful tears streaming from his own young tear ducts. Letting my tears flow, I daydreamed that I'd go downstairs, and beg Mori for mercy. *Mori, Mori—addressing him as befits our upside-down relationship— Mori Papa! Don't hide anything from me, tell me your mission! Why have you been switched over? But if you can't reveal the secret of your real mission, that'd be all right, too; then don't reveal anything, just tell me what to do, to do this, or that! I'll prove myself to you, I'll work like a dog and obey all your commands! Mori, Mori, Mori Papa! Are you listening to me?*

---

*According to legend, Jiraiya became the chief of a band of robbers after fleeing his destroyed home (the castle of his father, who was murdered). He is also known as Ogata Shume, and for those legends that deal especially with his youth, goes by the nickname Young Thunder. In the various episodes of his legendary exploits, he is closely allied with the Toad Spirit, which sometimes appears as a female and sometimes as a male, and which bestowed on Jiraiya the power to control frogs plus taught him all kinds of toad magic.

Once this fanatic, sentimental convulsion had run its course, I could no longer sit still on the bed. A moving force—*une force qui va,* an expression I picked up in French class—had me tingling, was impelling me to take reckless action. Was I also this impatient my first time around, during my first adolescence? In this state how was I ever able to study for the college entrance exams? Wasn't I a better human being at eighteen, the first time? You can't rely on the quality of anything nowadays! Ha, ha.

As was my wont in pre-switchover days, I hurried down the stairs. In the living room Mori and the girl sat gloomily looking at newspapers spread before them on the floor.

I barged in on the pair, with an all-knowing air of confidence,

——Reading the morning editions? No way yesterday's incident would have made it into the papers.

——Evening editions! The girl replied tersely.

Mori was freshly shaved, and, in sharp contrast with my boyish middle-aged look in the pre-switchover days, his handsome face expressed an assurance born of maturity. Gone was yesterday's smile. With a deeply melancholic look he handed me a newspaper. He certainly had a sense of fairness about him, not at all like the girl. *Let me see one, let me see one.* I wanted to bound over to the Mori-Sayoko pair and snuggle up to them.

4

I looked over four different papers, one after the other. It was already afternoon, but not yet time for the home delivery of my evening paper. Mori and Sayoko had gone out to the local train station and bought them. I wondered if they let last night's incident go to their heads and overestimated its significance for the press, thinking that all the newspapers would be full of reports of the incident? Ha, ha. What a laugh! The newspapers aren't Rev newsletters, you know. I was pretty sure that the papers would devote only a small piece or two to the event. Of course I never let on how comical I thought Mori-Sayoko's elaborate intelligence gathering and analysis were. Three of the four papers before them had only the barest of headlines devoted to the incident, something like: **FACTIONAL VIOLENCE BREAKS OUT AT ANTINUKE MEETING. RIOT SQUAD CALLED IN.** But the fourth paper carried the report as a special feature. **FACTIONAL VIOLENCE: THIS TIME A LITTLE BIT DIFFERENT. BOTH PARTIES KEEP SILENT. HORDES OF CONTENDING SCHOLARS AS CHEERLEADERS.** In what way *a little bit different?* Although 300 participants were involved, unlike the recent factional violence, there were no deaths or serious injuries. Minor injuries occurred only when the riot squad attempted to quell the fighting. This point was emphasized in an interview with Sakurao Ōno—ridiculed as one of the contending, screaming cheerleaders. *You've launched that rescue mission. Have you had a chance to sleep?* I let these thoughts reverberate through my love-stricken eighteen-year-old heart.

Thirty-five brawlers were detained but all refused comment; none of these men and women are on the internal security list. In past instances of factional violence, both sides immediately claimed responsibility, but this time no word was issued by anyone. Was it really factional violence then between two opposing revolutionary parties? Why was it that neither party used their usual weapons, crowbars or iron pipes? Wasn't the violence paradoxically meant to explore the possibility of unity? . . . Not a word about the Yamame Corps in the article.

The cheerleaders, the contending scholars—and there were only two actually interviewed—were quoted in the article. The first statement by Ōno had logical consistency: she started with a criticism of the riot squad's handling of the situation—as I mentioned earlier—and went on to say that the meeting was a rally held by citizens calling for the reclamation of nuclear power from the authorities, and was not directly organized by the Revs. Those who came to disrupt the rally were not only fascists and thugs, but a bunch of mercenaries who supported nuclear power. As for the second cheerleader's statement, what first piqued my curiosity was the title he gave himself: the "Volunteer Mediator." Rather outlandish, wouldn't you think? To further impress the reader, the reporter documented the Mediator's conduct at the scene of the incident. Sensing that a brawl had broken out inside the building, the Mediator tried to crash the meeting but the security people kicked him out. No wonder the Opposition Police were of no use to Ōno; they were exhausted from their numerous encounters with him, ha, ha. So he waited outside and continued to protest, careful not to get arrested for interfering with the riot squad who brought out detainees, the article said. And after a large police van had hauled away the riot squad and those arrested, he made a statement which was appropriately entitled, *One Hundred Screaming Scholars Contend.* He said: In the meeting which just disintegrated, there are frail, defenseless youth among both the sponsors and the infiltrators. They are like modern-day Children's Crusaders* who are trying to resist the present worldwide

---

*The Children's Crusade (1212) was a tragic episode in medieval European history, much chronicled and replete with legend. Thousands of children went to their deaths

nuclear madness. What a cruel waste for them to try to destroy each other! I'm volunteering to mediate their disagreement.

——A Children's Crusade? Wasn't that a group whose annihilation was predetermined by history? I felt obliged to interpret this event for the Mori-Sayoko pair. Just another reflex action on my part to educate the pre-switchover Mori.

——You can't say the Children's Crusade was absolutely futile, the girl said. And remember this time around it's meant for both the present and the future. Of course I disapprove of anyone's putting Counter-rev thugs on the same level as the Revs. I'd rather hold off my criticism until I can make a fair assessment of the Revs.

——He's the one, isn't he, Mori, the man you shook hands with. That weirdo who wouldn't quit making speeches even after being beaten and kicked into a snow pile when we arrived at the meeting hall yesterday.

——That Mediator is no weirdo. I may disapprove of his conclusions but I give him credit for the logical process by which he reaches them. I've listened to his speech ten times. It's only been a little over a year since I really became active, and even when I was just a political observer at meetings, he was always there.

——Logically speaking, how can you oppose his conclusions, yet still give credit to his reasoning process? And isn't he of the opinion that we should heed and accept the goodwill of the Children's Crusaders in both parties, and in the end do away with factional violence? If you talk like that, you're liable to end up being just a number in the party.

——My party? You don't know anything about it. You heard the Mediator speak for a short while yesterday, and that was the first time for you, wasn't it? Although Mori did shake hands with him. What you should be reflecting on right now is the slogan "No investigation, no right to speak."

——Mao Zedong!

——Everybody knows that. Right, Mori? When I say I give credit to the Mediator's thinking process, I'm basing my assessment on my own experience. Even before I had a grasp of revolutionary theory, his way of thinking things through encouraged me to become a Rev activist.

---

following a young boy prophet who promised to lead them to Jerusalem across the Mediterranean Sea whose waters would be miraculously parted by God so they could cross. While none of the children—who may have numbered as many as 50,000—ever reached the Holy Land, and great numbers were captured and sold into slavery, their march, generally chronicled to have been up the Rhine, across the Alps and over to Italy, is popularly remembered as a great and fervent expression of the poor and dispossessed, allegedly evidence of the power of innocence and purity, historic record notwithstanding.

——The Children's Crusade—you're one of them!

——. . . Once one makes up one's own mind, no one can step in and change that basic decision, because the human mind is a closed system, he said.

——Formalism! No, pseudo-formalism!

——. . . According to him, one faction attacking another would be utterly pointless, but this is where he goes wrong. I do agree with him, though, when he says to those who struggle within the actual Revs to treasure their initial decision to join, which stemmed from their closed-system reasoning. Because when you first join, you're at loose ends— who knows what the latest line or analysis is on the current situation, or where to start? When the Mediator talks about factional violence—although his interpretation of the revolutionary struggle is wrong—he is saying, just take my word for it and try to overcome the confrontational struggle. He once quoted something from a Japanese classic along these lines: "Being persuaded by Hōnen. . . "*

——Shinran!†

——. . . Mori, why is this kid babbling to himself? The Mediator also said, "Even if you are a nonbeliever, if you go to mass and get blessed with holy water, you become stupid and start believing in those things." That does sound altogether reactionary, though.

——Pascal! *Abêtir, abêtira!‡*

——This kid babbles like a madman! What are you trying to say? You see, Mori, the Mediator uses the quotes to illustrate the positive meaning of his thinking process. He's saying that to arrive at the correct end result, it's all right to be carried along by the process. For instance, being *persuaded* by Lenin to join the revolution was the right choice, wasn't it? Or, if a Red Guard acted out of simple, blind faith, as long as he followed the correct line of Mao, it would be all right, wouldn't it? What it all means is that to make history, to influence the course of history, it is more opportune to believe—however blindly—in something and act upon that belief than to remain impotently apolitical, doesn't it?

——Materialist gambling à la Pascal!

——**NONSENSE!** the girl finally burst out. But she regained her feminine composure and continued. You see, Mori, I think you said those things about the switchover really believing them, and I believed you as well. Remember, when I first met you, you said, *If the Cosmic Will does not exist, why is it we've been switched over?*

---

*Hōnen (1133–1212), founder of Pure Land Sect of Buddhism.

†Shōnin Shinran (1173–1262), founder of True Sect of Pure Land Buddhism.

‡"Once a dolt, always a dolt." Blaise Pascal (1623–1662). French mathematician, scientist, and theologian/philosopher.

This hit me like a bolt out of the blue. In the girl's voice, Mori's words reverberated through my frustrated eighteen-year-old mind and body and resonated with those words of Ōno Sakarao: *Why in the world did this happen to you? Ah, such a poor thing, why you?* While I was upstairs brooding over the switchover, crying, imagining I was receiving a revelation, racked with uncertainty over what to do next, the switched-over Mori was not devoting all of his energy and body to lovemaking with the girl. He too had been meditative, in anguish, and uttered those words to the girl before they made love. After all, he had been abruptly jolted from his rather stable situation; his four-year-old brain, congenitally limited and languishing in the twilight of infancy, suddenly began to work. His sudden ability to think, to speak his mind, wasn't this tantamount to being thrown into a bottomless pit of agony and painful introspection?

All alone the switched-over Mori meditated in agony. But his words, coursing electrically through his activated twenty-eight-year-old brain cells, radiated out to harmonize with other, earlier words that had welled up out of Ōno's tenderness and sensitivity. A veritable duet began. As the one who will help out with the mission under the guidance of the switched-over Mori, why can't I *insist on* the fact that I've just received a signal from the Cosmic Will?

If the Cosmic Will does not exist, why have we been switched over? Why in the world did this happen to you? Ah, such a poor thing, why you?

——Well, enough of this useless debate; let's work on something practical! We've got to have a bite first. If being switched over means *we'll be a pinch runner for those who can't run, or who don't yet know that they've got to run, then we may have to start running very soon.* That's what you said, Mori. So let's get going. I want you to come along and join the rescue effort. We've got to make up for lost time!

Without the slightest hint of surprise, I became aware of the sure and steady din of the voices, *GO, GO, GO*—they had really arrived this time. The strident voices reverberated through me, body and soul, eating me alive with a desire to run while seizing me with a paralyzing terror; yet at the same time I was moved by another desire, to overcome that terror and run, probably triggered by the infusion of what had started in Mori's switched-over flesh and mind. How many times before the switchover I had retold my pinch runner experiences! They must have somehow worked that way into the core of his existence, into his subconscious, and were now activated in the post-switchover Mori!

The girl resolutely positioned herself inside the kitchen to start the preliminaries for the rescue operation; Mori and I for our part waited in silence for the meal, cheers and yelled threats ringing inside us: *GO, GO, GO, GO, GO, GO, GO, GO, GO, GO, GO, GO, GO*....

5

However, first there was a financial problem to attend to. We'd finally gotten our post-switchover lives in gear, but no matter how bizarre our lives were with all their ups and downs, we still had to worry about mundane matters. . . . I've probably just read your mind, and said what you wanted to say: the switchover? I accept that, even if it's an out-of-the-blue, crazy reverie. I'll transcribe your words at face value, since you *insist on* the fact that this is the reality you've actually experienced, you're still experiencing, you're going to continue to experience. But how about the financial side of all of this? You can't just subsist on air. Unless you tell me about your financial situation, I can't make my account come across as realistic, you'd say.

So, I'll proceed with my narration, this time concentrating on my financial situation. To tell you the truth, the event that triggered my having to confront this very problem—I didn't ask for it, you know—took the form of a giant in fake U.S. Army combat fatigues! Before the Mori-Sayoko pair left the house to join the rescue operation for the jailed Revs, I asked the girl, Was your party the assailant or the victim? And I was totally ignored. I wonder if she felt the question would trivialize her own party, make it just another political grouping. Me, the faint-hearted eighteen-year-old, unable to press her any further, stayed behind hoping to hear from the scriptwriter-to-be. Anyway, as long as they were going either to the Rev headquarters, or to some party hangout, the girl would never let me show her around.

Left behind, I pondered whether I could repair the hole in the door which the girl had ripped open with the pick. Once Mori and the girl had left, I began to worry in earnest about that unlockable door, especially about a "bombing by mistake" by the faction opposing Sayoko's Revs. At my old job at the power plant, my forte was the technical skill with which my fingers played the controls. I found an unused plywood bookshelf and carefully sawed off a portion. Right when I was attaching a padlock I'd found—God knows why I'd ever bought it—to the board, a man's voice hit me from behind.

——HEY!

Was I going to be "bombed by mistake"!? I cowered at the thought. With both knees on the board, my back to the street where the snow had long melted, could I defend myself? The man, noticing the drill, chisel, and other carpentry tools scattered around me, must have hesitated and decided to take the precaution of announcing his presence outside the gate. And to think that all he could say was, **HEY!** At any rate I egged myself on to stand up, picking up a chisel as I turned to face a giant in dark green camouflage fatigues. He had a crew cut and a look about him that said HEY! was the only possible way to express his melancholy. One of my wife/*ex*-wife's gargantuan younger brothers: although, except for his glaring, bloodshot eyes, he bore little resemblance to her. As soon as I recognized him, panic and confusion seized me and I felt my hair begin to stand on end. But his bloodshot eyes held the same panicked look, although slightly out of sync with mine.

——Who're you? Are you that . . . ?

That's it, I remembered I was switched over. Immediately, I was freed from my panic. I relaxed and responded to the **HEY!**

——Right! I'm a nephew of that plutonium-soaked loony.

——. . . *Hmmmm, yaaa,* is your uncle home?

——He's a real loony; after his wife slashed his cheek, he went into hiding. So I'm housesitting for him.

——**THAT'S BAD NEWS!** When did he say he'd be back? . . . Did he take his sick son with him?

——Well, to your first question, *I've no idea.* To the second, *Yes.*

——That's bad news, **BAD NEWS!**

The huge man in the combat fatigues hung his gloomy face even lower and seemed lost in thought. There was desperate savagery about him, just beneath the surface. You wouldn't want to run into a guy like him in combat.

His heavy breathing and flustered tone of voice were obviously mismatched with his deliberately courteous manner of speaking.

——I wonder if you know where your uncle keeps his seal? Your aunt told me to pick it up. I'm your aunt's real brother. If your uncle were here, he'd hand it over right away. She's got the savings book, but took the wrong seal. Do you mind looking around for it?

——Did you put on your combat fatigues just so you'd be able to wrench it out of that plutonium-soaked loony's hands if he were here?

——**WHAT!** My brother-in-law/*ex*-brother-in-law bristled. But despite his large frame and obvious impulsiveness, he was actually very much in control of himself. Dispatched by his adored sister, he was gung-ho to carry out his duty. He worked for an advertising agency where he produced commercials, and had contacts with the director of the New Theater. Probably sent here by agreement of a three-man ad hoc committee: my wife/*ex*-wife, her brother, and the New Theater director.

——I don't want to pick a fight with you. Well, since you've been asked to housesit, you must know something about your uncle and aunt being separated, don't you, son? Isn't it agreed that he'll support her?

——His cheek's been slashed by his wife, and he's got a sick son to bring up by himself; I wonder what the court would say about all that.

Besides, they say she skipped out with that trendy New Theater director with his pitch-black shades—you've heard the story, haven't you? The way I heard it my aunt slashed one of my uncle's cheeks, and the director tried to hit the other. Is this director some sort of militant Christian?

——**WHAT?** . . . My, you say interesting things, don't you. Well, so much for small talk. Go look for the seal, will you? Things have been settled between your uncle and aunt. Don't you think he'll feel more comfortable if you hand it over to me now, rather than to the aunt later.

——It's definitely better than being afraid that the other cheek might be slashed at any time!. . . . Once I hand over the passbook and the seal, how are my uncle and his sick son supposed to eat? All the paychecks from the power plant're directly deposited to his account.

——You do know a lot about the family, don't you? You must know where he puts his seal then, don't you. Go get it, won't you? If you do, I'll show you how your uncle can get by.

——Don't treat me like a little kid, I snickered at him.

——**I'M NO ERRAND BOY, EITHER!** . . . If I spill the beans to a newspaper about what he's really doing to his activist friends, he'd hand over the seal and everything without a hassle. Last night's factional violence has already been written up in the newspapers, you know. One television network even mentioned Big Shot A, in their commentary, got it?

——*Mmmmh!* I was in a bind. I retreated into the house, returning with the drill I'd been using still in my hand, and handed over the seal with my left hand. I told myself this precaution was essential because those under the influence of my wife/*ex*-wife seemed to have the habit of attacking on impulse.

——I'll tell my uncle you tore the seal out of my hands and took off.

——Say what you like. **HEY**, brat, quit poking fun at your elders, you've gone too far! **I'VE HAD ENOUGH!**

. . . Less than twenty minutes after the encounter, the phone rang and, without so much as a greeting, the voice of the scriptwriter-to-be assaulted my ear.

——We got an anonymous phone call at my rescue team headquarters claiming that you supplied nuclear-related info to Big Shot A. Also, some of my kids're saying that you were in disguise among the spectators at the meeting yesterday. This may mean trouble. Of course, we've heard such rumors for some time now, that the Counterrev thugs who attacked us were receiving money from Big Shot A. Do you have any idea why they're pointing the finger at you, saying you're an informant?

————My wife/*ex*-wife's younger brother came around to pick up my passbook and seal and insinuated much the same thing—I barely managed to deal with him. This could be his plot to slander me once he's secured the seal.

————Does it mean you have nothing to do with Big Shot A, or you do? . . . I'll be at the usual hotel three hours from now. Let's go over this problem together! You're no longer that safe sitting around the house doing nothing.

I immediately decided to follow her suggestion. Of course, what she meant by the "usual hotel" was where the script-writer-to-be and the pre-switchover me engaged in some fairly sleazy sexual intercourse. I resumed the repair job on the front door lock and my mind began to sort things out—the threats of my brother-in-law/*ex*-brother-in-law, Ōno's warning—and as a result the bolts I was trying to screw into the door kept sliding time and again through my sweaty fingers. As an eighteen-year-old, I'd already been exposed to an awful lot of danger and terror, and now I had no other choice but to leave the house, stumble about the town—and all without the help of a grown-up Mori! And now it was no longer simply a matter of being afraid of being bombed by mistake. I was specifically targeted for bombing!

6

This Is the Way I Encountered Big Shot A, That Is, the Patron

1

In spite of my fear of ambush by the Opposition Police or the Yamame Corps, in the turbid twilight shadows of rain drops and mist, I took the train and even began to suspect that the conductor might be a Rev. Instead of punching tickets, he might decide to punch my body full of holes! Remember, one of Ōno's activists had recognized me in disguise. Of course, it was a case of mistaken recognition. But after they'd beaten me up with crowbars and iron pipes, even if they'd discovered that I wasn't masquerading, but had really been rejuvenated, my eighteen-year-old skull would already have been smashed to a pulp—so what good would their delayed recognition do me? Even a rare switched-over hominid like me doesn't have a spare skull lying around. When I imagined the twilight brawl that might break out this fine spring eve, my fear heightened: I might well be disposed of in the fight without fulfilling the mission entrusted to me by the Cosmic Will, without ever really understanding what the mission is all about. If I'm wiped out like that, Mori's got to carry out the mission on his own, Mori who knows nothing about real life! But, hey, apropos of nothing, what signs of horniness did Ōno pick up—despite my troubled demeanor? No sooner had each of us walked from opposite sides of the hotel into the tall shrubbery out front than disgust flashed like a lightning bolt across her tired, gloomy face; there was clearly no chance of us going into the hotel; with her shoulder she prodded me into an about-face that put us back on the street. She muttered something through clenched lips that deeply wounded the soul of this eighteen-year-old!

——I've just had a hell of a time keeping those kids from holding an inquest right on the spot. How can you look at me like a dog in heat?

Both of us then tried to open our umbrellas—which we had just closed—but their spokes got entangled with each other. Frustrated, Ōno violently shook her umbrella and when I drew back, one of the spokes jabbed me in the crotch.

——*Oo ouch!* I groaned.

——Ouch? The angry woman, the skin over her cheekbones turning a ghastly chartreuse in the dark, stood towering over me as though my pain was just another insult! Let's not dawdle around, we should get going. I've got to hold my own preliminary hearing on your case.

——Where should we go?

——Where? Somewhere we can debate, naturally.

——That hotel back there would do just right!

——**I'VE FOUND ONE!** That one with the neon sign, *All* rooms equipped with saunas, that's it.

——**A SAUNA?** I started to object, but since getting a reasonable explanation from her was out of the question, I trotted along with the brazen scriptwriter-to-be. Once inside the love hotel she was ready to take off all her clothes in front of the employee who brought in tea, and by the time my pants were off, she had wound a bath towel around herself and gotten into what looked like an upright coffin made out of unfinished wood. I squeezed in after her, already ensconced on a bench, her head almost touching the ceiling, her bulbous body, fat without being flabby, settling on the benchseat, her eyes glaring at me, ha, ha. Since she came into this hotel to question me, the sauna was merely incidental, right? However, she couldn't keep herself from putting it to good use, demonstrating her practicality. Bruises, as colorful as any tattoo, stood out among the red-white blotches that were breaking out on her skin; technicolor vestiges of the previous night's riot. My knees were powerful enough to recover from any contusion, so I drew them together forming an "L" with my body and sat right next to Ōno; but my penis, overpowered by the older woman's businesslike determination, remained very quiet.

Immediately a cross-examination—rather than a debate—began in the sauna. Every time we opened our mouths, the quinine-laden air, heated to eighty degrees centigrade, seared our throats and lungs; Ōno and I, in a fit of coughing, expelled gasps as hot as fire. In air as hot as eighty degrees centigrade, words really don't come that easily, so I'll give a summary of how the scorching inquiry proceeded. As you'll see in what follows, the questions put to me, and the answers I gave, were not something I could have treated lightly. I pitied us if I farted inside this sealed 1.2 meter x 1.2 meter x 1.7 meter rectangular enclosure; even more pitiful would be if Ōno farted into the stifling air mass created by the tile-like stone of the heating source + the mass of the bench + the volume of our two bodies—or so I worried as I fidgeted on my edge of the bench, ha, ha. Boy, eighteen is an unmanageable age, isn't it?

Q. It is said that in the past several years you have received a certain amount of monetary aid—more than your compensation from the power plant—for supplying a nuclear intelligence report to Big Shot A. The anonymous informant who passed us this piece of information has also offered to furnish further details upon request. For fairness' sake, I'll ask this question: Is it or is it not your contention that this informant bears a grudge against you?

A. Correct. I believe the informant in question to be the younger brother of my wife/ex-wife, who ran away the day before yesterday after she wounded me in the cheek (if you're not able to see any gash now on my cheek, that's because I have been switched over).

Q. If that is the case, then given that the informant's vicious intent has possibly clouded his judgment, how would you respond to the basic facts in his statement? Is it true that you have regularly supplied the Big Shot with nuclear intelligence briefs in return for financial compensation?

A. I would question calling it intelligence work. All I did was translate and summarize articles that appeared mostly in European and American journals on nuclear power development and armaments in various countries, and then submitted the results in a monthly report.

Q. According to the informant, you usually spent one to two hours talking with the Big Shot to elaborate on the reports. If that is the case, you cannot deny the probability, or the possibility, of presenting unwittingly, or wittingly, other material not directly involved with compiling your reports. Also, according to the informant, it is understood that you call the Big Shot "Patron." You would not call him Patron unless you have something more than a business relationship with him.

A. To me, *patron* means something like a big brother. Therefore, it should not necessarily be translated as protector or guardian angel. Furthermore, the name is not my invention. I simply inherited it from a now dead friend of mine. We met in college. He had been studying international relations at Princeton for a long time. It was there that he fell in love with a fellow student from France, whom he eventually married in Paris. He then switched his foreign language concentration from English to French; he wanted to continue his studies in international relations at the University of Paris; his sole income came from working for the Paris bureau of a Japanese newspaper, with an occasional job as an interpreter for Japanese delegations. By abandoning his research in the States, he had also cut off his ties with his sponsoring university in Japan and this left him unable to return to Japan—let alone secure a position that would adequately support family life with a French woman in Tokyo. In the midst of all this trouble and worry, he happened to meet the Patron in his capacity as an interpreter. From that time on, the Patron gave him the job of gathering intelligence on Eastern European and Middle Eastern countries. All he had to do was collect French journal articles on politics and economics, translate and submit them in summary form. It so happened that when he was preparing one on the nuclear situation in the Middle East, I was at a nuclear research center in California, and he requested my cooperation as an old friend. After this, the Patron himself contacted me and asked for a position paper on my research speciality. For this reason, I began to call him the Patron.

Q. The informant reported that, having been charged with doctoring his intelligence report, your friend was executed by the Big Shot's organization. How do you react to that?

A. It is ridiculous to use the word *execution*. During the Cuban Missile Crisis, he continued to closely monitor the possibility of a global thermonuclear war from Paris, the center of European intelligence-gathering. A week after the crisis was over, he hanged himself. His wife found his body dangling beside their bed when she came back to the apartment for lunch from the Renault factory where she worked as a secretary.

Q. Is it not true that the day before he hanged himself he went to pick up the Big Shot at Orly Airport, where he was subjected to a reprimand for his negligence in collecting and reporting data? Why do you continue to conceal that fact?

While pursuing this pointed line of questioning vigorously, the scriptwriter-to-be slipped off the bench, her body dripping with sweat, as though the thought of making an emergency telephone call had just hit her. She gathered up the perspiration-soaked towel with one hand right below her navel, and marched, knees bent, between the scorching unpainted boards: what a gallant sight to behold! She had to push open the tightly closed spring-mounted door—it was burning hot, you see. She removed the towel, wrapped it around her arm, and pushed the door open bringing her weight to bear down on her bright red buttocks and thighs. I thought she was getting out, but no. She brought in a pail and a ladle which were right outside the door. Quickly gulping in a breath of cool air like a goldfish, I felt a vague sense of imminent danger, but there was no time to do anything. The scriptwriter-to-be ladled up water from the pail and poured it over the stone tiles that were the heat source! In a flash, a *solid* heat blast assaulted us as the water sizzled and evaporated with a crackle. She threw the ladle up in the air, and, spreading her fingers like a rake, clawed at her mons veneris and stamped her feet. Did she think her pubic hair had undergone some sort of spontaneous combustion? Ha, ha. Even as I swooned in the heat, I somehow managed to get her outside. Although a reckless act for a grown woman, her feat was a decisive one, wouldn't you say?

She leaned against a bathtub right outside the sauna, on her knees, her head hung low, panting. After I had grabbed the detachable rubber hose and run the water over my own thighs to make sure the temperature was just right, I poured warm water on her red swollen neck and shoulders with the reverence of a young devotee. Exhausted, she let out a pathetic *Aaahhh*, hardly moving a muscle. However, before she had fully recouped her strength—although she had rallied a bit from the shock of the heat blast—she expressed a desire to continue the cross-examination.

——How long are you going to keep pouring that cold water on me? My nervous system'll go haywire, she said in an angry voice. Is that the way saunas stimulate the skin?

——You got it! I aimed the now useless shower hose at my penis— she might turn around any moment, I thought, so I tucked it away between my legs—just when it was beginning to resist, ha, ha.

2

Q. In summation: Have you ever, up to this point in time, submitted any information or data about foreign countries to the Big Shot?

A. As I said before, it was only information on nuclear armaments, nuclear power for peace, or the potential for nuclear arms development in underdeveloped nations, all of which appeared in European and American popular magazines and scholarly journals. Of course, in recent years scholarly publications on nuclear issues have begun to appear in our own country. Therefore, topics on which I was to do extensive research were narrowed down to various nuclear accidents, thermal environmental pollution, and nuclear thefts—one of which I was involved in.

Q. Did your investigation and research take the course it did as the result of the Big Shot's instructions or because of your own personal interests?

A. The latter. However, I believe that my interests, rooted as they are in my own personal experience, in the end closely parallel the general development of the global nuclear situation.

Q. How would you characterize the conversation you had with the Big Shot, when you presented your summaries? Give me specific examples.

A. During these last years in particular, I collected a series of absurdly fantastic true stories which I used as the basis for our conversations. The Patron actually looked forward to listening to them, always with a wry smile on his face. They may have been absurd, fantastic, and yet true events, but he still insisted on connecting additional substantiating facts with them. Once he took interest in a mysterious episode, he demanded elaborations, and if there were any ambiguous points in my research, he openly expressed his displeasure. For example: in the summer of 1966, a U.S. B-52 carrying four nuclear bombs crashed while refueling in midair. Jose Lopez Florence, a grocer in Palmarez on the Spanish coast of the Mediterranean who saw a smoldering nuclear bomb drop into his tomato patch, gave the bomb a kick. The Patron requested further investigation of the man's current physical condition. I had actually already read a supplementary document which said that the report on the man kicking the nuclear bomb was unreliable, but I had deliberately withheld this bit of information for comical effect. The Patron was blunt in his display of displeasure.

Q. If you had collected tall tales for your conversations with the Patron, did you not go beyond the printed sources available from overseas and tell him about your job at the power plant, or your involvement in the anti-nuclear movement? . . . I record that you have nothing to say on this point.

I kept silent for a moment—desperately trying to recall something, or anything. But the scriptwriter-to-be immediately fished out a notebook—which she always carried with her to scribble down important script ideas—and began to jot down what she had just said. Writing was now possible where we were. Placing two pillows behind her back, with a towel wrapped around her chest and thighs, she sprawled on the bed comfortably; I, on the other hand, more self-conscious about the "cross-examination," sat down next to her—also with a towel also around my waist.

Her notebook out, she began to write down our exchanges in minute detail, going back over all the questions and answers up to that point. Watching her like this gave me a very settled feeling. What I had told the Patron about the general incompetence regarding power plant accidents, as well as the weird, but equally primitive nature of the antinuke movement, did come rushing back to me. Those tall tales were meant just for laughs, but of course every one of them was based on fact. When I told him about the Tin Men attack that had exposed me to radiation, the Patron appeared to be overwhelmed alternately with compassion and then with a sense of the absurd. Which reminds me; early in our relationship, I used to entertain him with the story of the "Yamame Corps."

——Isn't it possible that the Patron, with the ulterior motive of playing you for a sucker, could have passed on to other informants some of those things you inadvertently told him? And what if he turned right around and slapped you in the face with that; for instance, if he blackmailed you, saying he'd squeal on you because you'd spilled the beans about top secret information, that he'd inform power plant officials or the antinuke headquarters about you? Isn't it possible that you'd buckle under and deliberately pass on sensitive information bit by bit.

——**WHERE DO YOU COME OFF MAKING CONJECTURES LIKE THAT**?! I refuted her remarks aggressively, spurred on by the rising insecurity inside me. The power plant incident aside, there's no need for me to supply inside stories on the antinuke movement! Let's suppose the civilian antinuke movement is linked to an illegal underground network; I bet that intelligence would be passed on directly to the Patron from the Revs' Executive Committee, or from its opposition party. Both are supposedly revolutionary, but maybe one of them is a Counterrev faction of thugs? Ha, ha, or is it **VICE VERSA**? Isn't it common knowledge that both parties are receiving money from the Patron?

——**IS THAT POSSIBLE? HUH?**

——**SURE IS!** He could've set up an arrangement with the Revs in charge of bookkeeping where he channels funds to the party, and gets info in return on a regular basis; a real gentlemen's agreement.

——**THAT'S YOUR OWN WILD FANTASY!**

——**NARRATIVE DISCOURSE BASED ON FACTS!**

——**IMPOSSIBLE SLANDER!**

——I remember you moaning and groaning about how left out you felt by your own groupies. You must feel more left out by the Executive Committee, right? Is there a possibility those party executives are doing what you say is unthinkable?

A turtle-like cubic shape thrust itself forward and watched me intently: her face! Talk about squaring the circle! Could your sudden transformation be the effect of the sauna bath, or is it the dim light in the room? I said this flippantly to diffuse the new tension, but the ploy didn't work.

——**I'LL DOUBLE-CHECK BY PHONE,** she said in a *muffled* voice. Unable to stop her, I tried at least to run interference by pushing some of the toggle switches lined up on a panel at the side of the bed.

But my good intentions turned against me. While the adjoining room remained in darkness, five colored lights showered gaudy illumination on the bed, the smoked-glass ceiling transformed itself into a sparkling mirror, and the bed itself began to move! Standing with one foot on the bed, the other just about to touch the floor, she was smack center on the gyrating platform. I got a real clear shot, not only of the dark bush between those two bowling-pin pillars suspended in midair, but what in Western lore is called the gash gouged by the devil's claw—an apt description! And I saw it all with my butt rocking and bouncing in the hellish illumination of the pentacle of colored mirrors. She crash-landed on the tatami floor in the next room, but didn't curse, You fascist! like in yesterday's landing. She just groaned, *Umph!* skewering me with a look full of indignation and contempt, as I was left alone to bounce and roll on the bed. . . . You have to go through the hotel operator to call out; someone apparently picked up the phone, and a quarrel broke out between the operator and whoever was at the other end, and then between Ōno and the operator. As the number she requested belonged to Revs headquarters, no executive committee member would come to the phone to speak to her unless she properly identified herself. Being a famous television personality, she must have felt hesitant about revealing her name to the operator at the sleazy love hotel. But she made up her mind and quickly gave her full name. At the other end they conducted a terse exchange of words and hung up. At least she had managed to keep her dignity, so by the time she turned back to me, the earlier force of indignation and contempt was nowhere to be found; she was reduced now to being an overgrown infant girl at a loss over what to do next.

——Those kids're really blunt, always *putting* people *down.* But they're never irrational about it either, and that *puts* me *down* even more.

——An operator-assisted call is like authorizing your own bugging. You can't talk about anything serious.

——I can't blame them for being frustrated. It looks like somebody else got some results. Apparently thugs in the Counterrevs suicide squad have attacked the Big Shot. They didn't succeed in killing him. Just an impulsive act that looks justified on the surface. . . .

This time it was my turn to leap off the gadget-ridden bed and almost sprain my back. If I had not been switched over, I would have slipped a disk! News time was about over, but I crawled over to the television set anyway and punched the power button. Channel 1. Up popped a short, obese woman straddling the shriveled belly of a man, with her head thrown back, vigorously kneading her breasts, whinnying loudly. The picture from her waist down was a blur in a milky, umbrella-shaped blob. The camera then moved to zoom in on the man with a glum face, whose line was: *Don't neigh so loud!*

——That's what they call a *soft-core porno flick*. The assault had occurred only a half hour or so ago, there's no way it would be picked up on the TV yet. So we've got to go to the source.

When we went down to the lobby, the women employees, six or seven of them, were standing around, some beside the elevator, some behind the hemp-palm plant at the front, and others in the linen closet where the door was slightly ajar, all looking as though they'd smelled a rat—the phone call had done it. Without turning her face away from them, the scriptwriter-to-be took in all their gazes. Challenged by her impudent behavior, one of the women said in a low, indignant voice,

——With a young man.

——If you slander us, you'll cheapen yourself as well as your job, Ōno countered in return, ha, ha.

3

I parted with Ōno, the civil rights activist, my rock and fortress. Now alone, although there had been an attempt on the Patron's life and my relationship with him had been denounced, I gave no more thought to the fact that I was in immediate danger. I figured neither the Opposition Police nor the Yamame Corps would see any sense in making me their target at present. One of them had successfully injured the Big Shot, so they wouldn't consider a small fry like me worth their time. But, you see, if the Patron dies from his injuries, my monthly paychecks for the preparation of briefing papers will stop, and I'll have to worry about how to make a living. Since every paycheck from the power company now goes straight to my wife/*ex*-wife, I'd have to find some other way to feed my voracious adolescent appetite, not to mention that supporting my adult son, and probably his lover, would also become my job. The pressing problem is that there's enough money to tide me over for two weeks or so, but then what? Although I wanted to just hop in a cab and get home quickly—Mori and the girl should have been back by then—I took a train because I was so shaken by the impending financial crisis, and after several transfers, finally made it home. But the pair hadn't returned yet.

I got in just in time to watch the late news report on the Big Shot attack. It seems that one of the assailants, who had short-circuited the secretary's phone line, contacted the Big Shot on his private line, and paid him a visit while the secretary was out on lunch break. A half an hour later the secretary returned to find the Big Shot unconscious, with a blow to his head. A climbing pick—possibly the assailant's weapon—and blood not matching the victim's were found at the scene.

A pick? My mind raced. The pre-switchover Mori sometimes accompanied me when I presented my briefings—I don't remember the exact scheduled time. As you know, *our children* never interfere with adults' conversation. Every time I set up a time and date with the Big Shot, I arranged it on a private line, just like the one mentioned on the TV. A loud voice swelled within me, flatly rejecting my suspicion that the assailants might have been Mori and the girl. *If our switchover was meant to be part of the fulfillment of a mission given us by the Cosmic Will, why couldn't Mori take me along with him? Even if my role was merely to stand by him as a witness? Yes. That would be the reason! In the days when I lived with the presentiment of the switchover to come, I often dreamed that Mori and I would overthrow the Patron on the very day celebrating the consolidation of his political power. That's it, the dream is proof, Mori and I were together! How could he fail to fulfill the mission entrusted to him? If that ever happened, the switchover would just be a cruel joke on us. They're reporting that the Patron is still alive, and the assailant's blood stains were everywhere. Let's suppose that Mori failed in his mission, and was severely beaten while trying to avenge a loss. I, the survivor of the switched-over pair, must complete the mission. But what can I do? I've never regarded the Patron as my enemy. Besides, the Cosmic Will has never told us why we must overthrow the Patron. So, how can I carry out the mission? In other words, if this mission is real, Mori and the girl could not have committed the assault. I'm just getting paranoid about Mori's coming home late, that's all. Why do we have to overthrow the Patron especially since I feel such awe and affection for that giant of a man?*

I was caught completely off guard by this voice within me, powerfully, willfully rationalizing away. Although it's true I received monetary support from the Patron over a long period of time, our relationship was nothing more than that of an employer and a supplier of data; I certainly had never felt awe or affection for him. . . . But with my defenses down, once I yielded to that internal voice, I was powerless to reject its ruinous negation of all I believed. Astounding. Scribe, I'm sure you've been thrown off balance by my sudden outburst. To set things straight, I'll start first off with what I think of this Patron, the man I've known for so many years. Who knows, while you're transcribing this, you might bring to light something I haven't been aware of, how I came to feel awe and affection for him. At least you might manage to set down a readable account for the third party. Unless this is too much of a bother for you, now that everything's been shoved off onto you, ha, ha.

Come to think of it, I did find the tone and intonation of the Patron's voice utterly charming, even inspirational. Old as he is, he speaks in a clear, vibrant voice. He reminds you of those foreign language teachers who, in their efforts to distinguish each and every sound and accent, enunciate every word to the point of exaggeration. There's also a humorous side to his personality that makes the nickname Patron very suitable, you know, the kind of name students pick. Well, at any rate, he told me he had once taught Japanese in Shanghai, right before Japan's defeat in the war. It was a job that required him to teach Japanese to Chinese youths at the same time as he gathered intelligence information from them. The Patron, in his prime, was an agent attached to the invasion forces, assigned to infiltrate Chinese intellectual circles; the young Chinese he taught knew what was going on, but seemed to look the other way. Instead of concealing their rather complex personal histories from him, the Patron got the impression that each of them was going out of his way to let him know about his background, but at the same time expected the Patron to feign ignorance, or so he told me. As the Patron told it, he ended up protecting the youths from each other, preventing security leaks among them. By then the post-defeat timetable for the takeover of China had already been set up by the Japanese military. It made a big difference whether you came from, say, Yanan or Chongqing. Considering the life and death significance of personal data at that time and place, leaks were lethal on many levels. The Chinese who attended the Patron's private school were mostly newspaper reporters, teachers, poets, and novelists, who were well aware that the information they divulged was passed on to the enemy. At the same time, the Chinese were using the school as a cover for their own intelligence gathering. This school was well stocked with periodicals from all over the world, and the Chinese had every opportunity to pick up information they needed. The Patron's personal objective was not to control the enemy but to observe them, allowing them free movement so that ultimately he personally would be effectively positioned in the aftermath of the defeat—in fact he did fully succeed in laying the groundwork for his status as the postwar Big Shot. And isn't this somewhat similar to the way he's handled the funding of the feuding revolutionary parties?

To describe his appearance: the Patron has a humongous head, and unless its prominence is somehow allowed for in a photograph, his appeal is destroyed. Before I met him I remember once seeing his godawful picture accompanying an article that appeared in connection with some political scandal. He looked like an abomination, and that touch of the childish prankster he has about him only further exaggerated his repulsiveness. In that particular picture, the Patron wore a kind of hood or a brimless hat which, the story said, hid scars he'd gotten when gangsters shot him. Rumor had it that at that time of the sniper incident, individuals on the lowest rung of the ladder at X-affiliated trading company—which had underworld connections—took revenge on the Patron, who had transferred certain concessions in Taiwan and Korea from X-affiliated trading company to Y-affiliated trading company. His picture caricatured this shady rumor.

However, in the flesh, the Patron's broad-beamed forehead and capacious jaw, the scale of every feature of his face, totally canceled out the impression of repulsiveness captured in photographs, especially since that face came as a package deal with a beefy, good-sized body! Or consider his eyes: in the photo they had a criminal look about them, each eye gleaming in its own fishy way. In real life they looked nothing like that. Like an iguana, his left eye was immured in deep wrinkles, sightless. But even if the good eye glared out in anger or suspicion, right next to it was the other eye permanently sunk in deep shadow. It felt as if your body and spirit could be easily sized up by this pair of eyes, yet that those eyes would never confront you with their findings.

Do I sound as if I'm in awe of the Patron, and full of affection for him? Assuming you're recording my narration exactly as I tell it, the written word attests to that, doesn't it?

At midnight, I prepared rice in the rice cooker and stir-fried a can of some cured beef with some onions while I waited for Mori and the girl. As I began to munch away, I realized the canned beef was what that *zombie* secretary—ha, ha, he was enjoying his lunch during today's attack on his boss—parceled out to me, as well as to all the other informants, from among the end-of-the year *oseibo** gifts given to the Patron. In light of this, I must say, the Patron certainly casts a long and multi-layered shadow over my daily life. But it's natural, don't you think, on a night when his life was threatened, he'd constantly be on my mind? The way things were going, his influence, unbeknownst to me, might have already extended into the emotional part of my switched-over life. At that thought, and after having put a third of the meal under my belt, I felt a

---

*An "obligatory" custom of giving gifts at the end of the year to express appreciation.

disgusting churning motion in my stomach. I began dwelling on how unconscious I actually am of the extent of the Patron's influence over me, and how ignorant I am about the resulting subjugation of my psyche. This immediately brought to mind the image of my friend's dead body in an apartment in Paris where he'd climbed onto his bed, the highest point in his apartment, and hanged himself. *In the beginning, didn't he too fail to grasp the totality of the Patron's plan, and despise his boss, who had, after all, just a layman's knowledge of international relations? But without realizing it, didn't he harbor totally contradictory feelings, didn't he also feel awe and affection for the man? And worse, out of financial need, didn't he decide to gather, summarize, and submit intelligence reports to please the boss? My friend got himself mired deeper and deeper into the interstices of the Patron's overall plan—a plan still unknown to me. During the Cuban Missile Crisis, he must have figured out for the first time the real motive behind the scheme, and the kind of man he was assisting all along; he must have realized it was already too late for atonement. He couldn't even confide any of this to his French wife, also a student in international relations at Princeton University. So he must have made up his mind to put an end to his relationship with the Patron. Rather than tamper with the data collection process, he sabotaged the summaries and even their presentation instead. The Patron then came to Paris. A direct confrontation ensued. However, this showdown was nothing more than the Patron issuing a one-sided reprimand. Exhausted, with no energy left to look for an alternative solution, he hanged himself above his bed, knowing full well that the apartment would be the only asset left to his wife, who would have to continue to sleep in that very bed!*

The phone rang at two in the morning. Mori's girlfriend gave me a rather *ambiguous* message, in language that sounded more like that of a spaced-out college kid than a militant activist, the role she was good at. I was impressed by her cautiousness—she must have suspected that my phone was bugged—the same girl who had offhandedly flashed her butt, and given me a peek at her crack and more.

——Hello, hello? Mom and Pop're on the watch, and we can't get anywhere near the garage. So for the moment I don't think we can meet at your house as we planned. Are you pissed off that **WE DID IT ON OUR OWN?** Well, we can't blame you. How should I say it, he says that **IT WAS SOMETHING OF A COURTESY CALL. WHEN THE REAL THING COMES AROUND, HE'LL DO IT WITH YOU**. It must be your fate. Can't do anything about it. I hear Mom coming, so bye now. He sends regards, **SAYS HE'S FINE!**

So, the pair, Mori and the girl, had attacked the Patron! Here I was, supposedly unable to accept the fact that I was left out, but at the same time persuaded otherwise right then and there by Sayoko's message.

*How should I say it, he says that **IT WAS SOMETHING OF A COURTESY CALL. WHEN THE REAL THING COMES AROUND, HE'LL DO IT WITH YOU.*** *It must be your fate.* So today Mori and the girl went to warn the Patron. When the mission actually comes about, Mori and I are fated to go together as a switch*ed*-over collective body. Therefore, there's no problem with me being left behind today! Why this instruction from the Cosmic Will to attack the Patron? Again, though, there's no problem as long as Mori leads the mission!

According to the phone caller, the police have my house under surveillance. The neighbor's garage is almost at my front gate. The girl's words are an accurate reflection of what any passerby would observe. After she hung up on me, I almost switched the light off in the living room, but I suddenly froze, controlling my urge to look outside through the curtains. I didn't want those in the stakeout to know that I had been contacted by phone.

Of course I knew that their reason for watching me was not because they had somehow found out the identities of the pair, Mori and the girl. If that had been the case, they would have showed up in no time at all with search and arrest warrants. Somebody had squealed on me personally, not on the pair. They must have half-believed their source because they decided to stake out my house. Luckily, either Mori and the girl, or those who escorted them home, smelled a rat, and made a clean getaway.

Who squealed on me? My wife/*ex*-wife, of course! She saw the news of the attack on the Patron and immediately made the connection. A natural deduction, wouldn't you say? The Mori-girl pair or their escort had perceived, and dodged, the trap set up by my wife/*ex*-wife, I figured. Whatever secrets she might divulge about me from now on would serve effectively to divert the police chase from the pair. I felt pretty encouraged. Suddenly, now that I'd substantiated that Mori and the girl had attacked the Patron, for the first time in ten years I felt that I'd stumbled onto a way of reconciling myself to the body of my friend dangling there from a high, high place in the streets of Paris. The image in my mind of the Patron as the object of awe and affection quickly crumbled, transmogrifying into the odious face in the photograph; I even relished envisioning him lying on the floor in a pool of blood. Boy, how quickly an eighteen-year-old changes his tune, ha, ha. The only thing that bothered now me was Mori's injury. Well, didn't the girl say, in a singsong voice, *He sends regards, **SAYS HE'S FINE!***

I waited twenty minutes before I turned off the light and went to sleep—not in my own bed, but in Mori's, with my feet sticking off the end. I woke several times before dawn; I sensed the presence of the police out in the street in front of the house, on the prowl for sure. When I was asleep, there was always the danger of a surprise attack: from the upper echelon of the Ōno group, who suspect me of being a spy; from their opposites, the Counterrevs, who think I'm an Ōno group sympathizer; from my wife/*ex*-wife and her gargantuan brothers who are out to get me. But then, with the police stakeout on my house, I had the best protection in the world. Life has so many different facets, and unless you see things with the compound eye of an insect, you novelists can never capture life in its entirety, can you? What is there to say, after all, without the construct of the me *insisting on talking,* and the you writing it all down, ha, ha.

4

Brimming over with an excess of reverence for human rights, the police at least gave the switched-over eighteen-year-old plenty of sleep time before they made their appearance, as two gentlemenly law officers. So, the only one who seemed to be tearing about with no consideration for human rights was probably my informant, my wife/*ex*-wife, ha, ha.

The minute I awoke I was all fired up to set the stage for the struggle against the authorities. I, Mori's comrade in the struggle, couldn't afford to get out of shape when he'd already begun to carry out the mission given him by the Cosmic Will. First, house cleaning. As I opened up all the windows, I noticed a car parked four, five houses down, on a street where no parking is allowed. From my vantage point, my eyes took in a long-haired guy, just beyond the neighbor's garage roof, in dirty boots, with time on his hands, walking into the early spring wind; he looked chilled to the bone. His boots and clothes showed the wear-and-tear of life, but still held a stylishness uncommon to the run-of-the-mill long-hairs on the streets, ha, ha. The doorbell rang; I went out to find two uniformed policemen standing in the hallway—definitely not plainclothesmen on a stakeout. One was a Hercules, a winner of police kendo tournaments; the other, a pale-faced guy, probably had been on leave till the end of last year to recuperate from a bout of TB, recently back on the active force, and just starting to work into the routine this spring. Their silence spoke of a dual set of tactics, one conciliatory, one coercive; each was clearly prepared to play his role. Lo and behold, Coercive stated my name and added the question "Is he away?" This immediately restored my confidence in the switched-over me.

——My aunt and uncle went out last night and haven't come home since. Well, my aunt has been gone since the day before yesterday, I think. They have a son—my uncle took him. Three days ago, in the evening, there was a family spat and they asked me to housesit for them. What's happened this time? Tell me, I'm a relative. Did my aunt or one of her brothers take a knife to my uncle again?

——You his nephew? . . . Housesitting? Why was your uncle knifed? And twice?

——Huhnn!? A leading question!

——We're talking serious. Coercive leaned forward. You say he didn't come home last night! He's still out, right? Has he contacted you?

——Nope. Nothing. Tell me what's happened! I'm his blood relative.

——You've been watching too much TV, haven't you? said Conciliatory with a look in his eyes that said he had formed a certain opinion of me; for a moment I flinched under his penetrating gaze, but apparently all he saw was a dumb kid. We've found a man who got lost looking for your uncle, so we offered to bring him here. Well, if your aunt, uncle, or whoever gets slashed, or slashes someone, report it to us immediately, hahaha. I'm not trying to trick you with a leading question, simply requesting cooperation from an upright, law-abiding citizen, hahaha.

There's a scene in an old comedy where two policemen are stepping back as the door behind them swings open, and a fireman rushes past them. That was exactly the way the Mediator burst in on the scene.

Seeing him at close range, his face battered black and blue, almost compelled me to ask, Are you alive? But the overall effect of his face wasn't morbid; in fact, it was quite the opposite of a dead man's. Although swathed in black-and-blue skin, his broad forehead, triangular nose, mustache and all, endeared him to me as soon as our eyes met. A gleam of what looked like admiration shone in his serious eyes as he adjusted his black-framed specs. That was all the encouragement I needed: he had come to contact me at the behest of Mori and the girl, and, although Mori had already explained our switchover, on beholding me, the other switched-over person, the Mediator was positively captivated.

——In your azalea bushes, he began without greeting, a cat is giving birth. Glad it's a warm day. . . .

Naturally the policemen mistook his statement as a coded message. Coercive stationed himself at the Mediator's side to hold him in check for the rest of the message. Conciliatory betook his experienced self out to examine the azalea bushes. I felt sorry for him as he stumbled backwards from an angry growl, **WHAAHH**, and the orange-spotted forepaw that clawed at him.

——Better not scare her. Once she senses danger, she'll eat the kittens. Probably she already has. There's only one kitten left. Were there some prowlers messing around last night, scaring the mother cat out of her wits?

——**I'M THE ONE** who's been scared witless.

Conciliatory said this panting heavily, and in obviously bad humor. Well, maybe my initial classification of the two policemen as passive-aggressive should have been the other way around. . . . The Mediator grabbed his chance to break in on the policemen, who seemed to have lost the thread of their conversation and were unable to find it again. He faced them at an angle with half of his nose and moustache lined up like a three-blade propeller, and greeted them in an uncompromising tone of voice.

——**MY GOODNESS**, I must apologize for all the trouble! **GOODNESS GRACIOUS**, Officers! Thanks a lot for all your help!

Clearly forced to withdraw due to the linguistic pressures of the situation, the two officers left with the usual farewells. They slammed the gate shut so violently that I thought the latch would rattle off; the cat confined in the bush let out another **WHAAHH!** Or, was Coercive growling? Ha, ha.

——Should we give her water or some food? I hadn't thought about that before, any more than the policemen had. . . .

——They're not trained to arrest cats, you know, the Mediator observed with a dourness that almost bordered on neutrality. If the mommy cat isn't yours, leave her alone. . . . At least she has a full stomach now.

——Are you some sort of feline psychosis specialist?

——Specialist? Feline psychosis? They are usually much older. . . . May I come in?

Of course there was no reason for me to say no. We sat opposite each other in the living room with him staring me full in the face. Motes of charcoal gray danced in his eyes behind thick spectacles, cheerfully expressing the marvelousness and humor of it all. Out came an astoundingly childish voice,

——Good God! You actually did it! **THIS IS FANTASTIC!**

I felt my young switched-over face redden, all the way down to the throat.

——. . . Mori did tell me about you . . . but what a *transformation*!

——A **SWITCHOVER.**

——Right, a switchover. You must have been through a lot; it's so total, so fantastic! Yesterday I didn't notice it at all. I would never have guessed it, even though I did see you at the meetings before the switchover. **FANTASTIC! YOU REALLY DID IT!**

——Is Mori with you? His exuberance was too much for me, so I decided to try to dampen some of his fervor. I heard he was injured.

——He's at my martial arts rehab center! The injury isn't that bad! The girl's unharmed, and is even arguing with the center staff; Mori's taking it calmly, and his character and accomplishments have earned him a lot of respect. . . . I just wanted you to know. . . . I also came here because I'm interested in your switchover, something to do with the research I used to do. . . . I was on my way to becoming a molecular biologist, but I gave it up, so you can't really call me a full-fledged researcher!

Then for the first time, fine vertical wrinkles appeared, as if carved by unhappiness, on the darkish skin between his eyebrows. I felt those wrinkles cut right into my soul. I had also abandoned my research halfway, so we shared a common regret, didn't we?

——About the switchover. . . . When Mori attempted to communicate with you, did he speak directly, or did he use some other method? At any rate, did you believe in the switchover? Do you still believe in it?

——**DEFINITELY! NOW MORE THAN EVER, DEFINITELY!**

He let himself go in one big burst, his body convulsed in a laugh he had suppressed until now. He tried to continue between the painful gasps and belly laughs,

——**THIS . . . NOT TO BELIEVE THIS . . . AHAHA . . . AHAHA . . . IT'S IMPOSSIBLE!**

Dejected, I watched him finally bring his convulsions under control, and wipe his tears and saliva away.

——Where did Mori get injured?

——His head. . . .

——**HIS HEAD?!**

——Woops. . . . He told me to keep quiet about it. Now I've betrayed his confidence, just like that!

——Is it serious? Is that why he told you to keep your mouth shut?

——Not serious at all. He made double sure that I wouldn't reveal where he was wounded. . . . I sure betrayed his confidence. He trusted me to give him first aid.

——Is the wound at the back of the head? Or . . . ? How did you take care of it?

——I'm no professional, I sterilized the area around the wound and bandaged it. Yes, it's at the back of his head. The bleeding had already stopped by the time I tended to the wound, but I had to touch the blood clot just to make sure—it looked to me like an old wound had been reopened. Mori confirmed that, so no one got really worried. I did get a bit shook up, though, when I heard the skin was torn open by a pick.

——A pick? Wasn't that the weapon Mori took with him?

——**EXACTLY!** Mori struck Big Shot A on the head with the pick. The girl thought they'd retreat immediately afterward, but instead Mori handed the pick back to the bloodied, staggering victim who, although his vision was blurred, seized hold of the weapon. Mori stood waiting for him to strike back, she said. Big Shot A swung the pick around as he collapsed onto his backside; the pick, still in his hands, caught Mori on the head and tore the skin. **MORI'S QUITE A CHARACTER!** Now that I've met him and know of his exploits, *I swear* I will protect him, do anything he wants me to do! My martial arts rehab center retrains political dropouts, dropouts from the two warring parties, to reconcile their barbarism and to help them start anew. . . . The militant nonviolence that leads to true reconciliation is already manifested in Mori's action!

——While we're on the subject, do you think the attack was a final act on Mori's part? Or was it the warning of a different, decisive act to follow? The girl thinks it's the latter. That concerns me.

——**WHY DO YOU ASK?** Now that you know the whole picture, how could you say that his action is conclusive? Are you scared of participating in what will follow? Then don't take part in it! Keep your mouth shut and stay out of sight! **ARE YOU INSULTING MORI?**

——Huh? What kind of question is that? **ME, INSULT MORI?**

Like two fighting cocks right after their first bout, we glared at each other from the middle of the room, half rising, as though gathering every ounce of energy for the next decisive assault. But I'm one cock who easily loses his fighting spirit; I felt awkward, sat down, and apologized to the opponent, who likewise sat down, also looking embarrassed.

——I clearly see it all now. Big Shot A tried to enslave me at the time of Mori's abnormal birth, taking advantage of my confusion and weaker position. He meant to kill Mori in the intensive care unit, and enslave me for life. . . . The way I see it now, therefore, is Mori's attack was the natural consequence of his plan. In the end, although Mori survived and I did escape from slavery, Big Shot A's plan of oppression remained in force, so according to a sort of debt-collection list of reality, he was struck unfairly. That's why Mori handed the guy the pick. But Mori must also have had another reason for his action beyond the logical formula of the real world. . . . When I try to reconstruct the logic, I feel there is some symbolic meaning in the fact that the pick again tore open the stitched-up spot in his skull. Now that I'm on to the real significance of Big Shot A's scheme, I might as well tell you more about how he tyrannized me when Mori was born. By the way, I always call the guy the Patron. . . . Hey, do you really believe I'd insult Mori even though I may be a rash, inane, egocentric, switched-over brat?

——**WELL, SORRY ABOUT THAT!** the Mediator apologized, the ferrous cast of his black-and-blue skin verging on maroon. Still, the way he continued on emphasized his insolent tone toward me; I was clearly not someone he admired. Don't we sometimes make mistakes against our will and insult someone we really think the world of? Do you think we'll ever be able to make up for it, even if we have two, three lives?— even someone like you who's been fired up by the switchover?

7

A Multifaceted Study of the Patron

1

On the day Mori was born with a defective cranium, I told the Mediator, I moved him to a university hospital, where I sat waiting on a bench for nine hours. What was I waiting for? Someone to announce to me, The tiny monster you brought us breathed his last, just the way you wanted. Ha, ha. Next morning I picked up the red phone in the waiting room. Who was I dialing? It wasn't my family or friends, it was none other than the Patron. I reported the incident of the abnormal birth in a translation/summary style, as if what had befallen me were one of those strange stories I'd unearthed from foreign magazines and newspapers. To my surprise, he displayed intense curiosity. After a few volleys of questions and answers, I realized that the Patron had gotten it into his head that the new infant's abnormality was the result of my exposure to plutonium. I was stunned by the fact that such a bond of suspicion could tie the baby's abnormality to me. Later on, this grew into the deliberate lie I told my wife/*ex*-wife, typical of the nuclear age. This is what I mean by the Patron casting his shadow over every aspect of my life. A neurosurgeon had already explained that what happened to my baby was a freak of nature. When I passed this on to the Patron, he immediately lost interest in the baby except for what he instructed me to do.

He ordered me to copy down the telephone number of a certain hospital, and said, Transfer the kid there by this afternoon. I'll arrange everything. What did I do? Showed no resistance, accepted it right on the spot. But in another corner of my mind, I was thinking: I'm having my baby killed by a total stranger, and, what's more, I'll be at the mercy of the Patron for all of this. From now on, he can wrap me around his little finger; I'm his, body and soul. I felt as though a storm cloud were hanging above my head, but at the same time sensed that this cloud had a silver lining, that I could take solace in the fact that I was safe in the arms of a huge, reliable man! All that afternoon I was depressed, withdrawn, I could do nothing. I was already half an hour late, yet I still felt pressed to find a cab. At the taxi stand I got in without the baby and ended up at a Turkish bath in Ikebukuro, near the hospital.

Regardless of sex, when people of my generation are in a funk, do they have a tendency to hole up somewhere in a sauna or a Turkish bath? Ha, ha. Even at that stage, however, I hadn't forgotten to calculate the time needed to return to the baby's hospital. I lay on the low massage table and watched indifferently as a masseuse devoted her rubbing to the area near my crotch; with the same apathy I also looked down toward my penis. In the meantime the young woman who had been seated on the table lifted herself; her hips twitched once, twice, and down came her panties. She placed one of her feet next to my head, almost squatting with one knee drawn up. I rather shamelessly shifted my head toward her, and, there before my eyes was the most arousing sight I've ever beheld in my life! Although her underbelly was a pitiful pile of skin and bones, the pitch-black pubic hair clung helter-skelter to it like a thick entangled mass of sheep hair. Beyond in the shadows lay her half-open genitals, dark and menacing. These organs are mine, out of all the female sexual organs in the world, they're mine. Resigning myself to my fate, I wasted no time at all and stretched my tongue out to lick at them. The woman ceased all activity, and said, in a hoarse yet audacious voice—as if it was a lot of bother, *I'll lie on my back, easier, I'm sure, for you to lick me.* I kept on licking, duty-bound, I should say, until she grunted, Unnh! Just like a suckling baby whose attention has just been piqued, I glanced up with one eye from between her thighs and saw sweat, like fly's eggs, dotting her body from throat to chest. I felt something, so I shifted my eyes down to her clitoris; as though it had a life of its own, it quivered with orgasm. After this, with my head now between her knees, I nudged her, teasing her, *Let me in,* because the hands which had once restrained me began to lose their strength in a post-orgasmic rush. Her bloodshot eyes, set in a childish face with a pointed chin, took in the bristling penis. She said, *I don't want it, there's milk on it.* Without hesitation I wiped it off with a bath towel on the table and mounted her. I didn't think twice about doing it even though I saw another masseuse in a room across the hallway peeping through the beaded curtain.

And . . . that was it. I spent some more time with her, lounging around, and then returned to the baby's hospital. It was a long time after the appointment set up by the Patron, and I was told by the head nurse at the intensive care unit that my baby was well, vigorously sucking his bottle. I found a surgery resident and immediately requested that they operate on the baby. If anyone asked me how I mustered my courage to do that, I would reply. *Because I've been through something I'd never dreamed could happen to me! I'm suffering from a plutonium poisoning which has its origins in twentieth-century America, and now I'm about to become a V.D. victim, a disease originating in sixteenth-century America. From these actions I learned this:* **IT'S BETTER TO DO IT THAN NOT TO!** *I pulled one over on the Patron, with his plan to kill the baby, and on me who went along with this plan up to eighty percent of the way, and will take upon myself for the rest of my life the job of raising a child with a defective cranium. Because I've never thought myself capable of doing anything like that!*

Keeping this story of Mori's birth and the Patron in mind, you can better understand now why Mori, granted freedom of movement and with enhanced physical strength because of the switchover, went straight to the Patron to turn the tables on him, to strike back at the murderous conspirator who slated him for death when a lump sticking out of Mori's cranium kept him from tossing or turning in the crib. I was finished with my tale when the Mediator responded, justifiably.

——I think I have an explanation for the counterattack. Since consciousness functions even in actions which do not jibe with the logic of reality, after Mori dealt the Big Shot a blow, he docilely waited for the latter to strike back. Mori handed the pick to the bloodied and reeling old man, and voluntarily invited a counterblow to his head. What courage! What's more, he's got a head lined with plastic. Now that I've heard you out, I think there's a clear reason why Mori didn't take you along on this particular assault. And it was only the first in a series of assaults. . . .

2

——Why do you respect the switched-over Mori? Why do you place your trust in him, and in my switchover as well? Why do you believe it all? I put these questions to the Mediator in lieu of thanking him.

——How can we doubt Mori? Did you doubt his switchover? . . . I believe that switchovers, while rare, are steadily happening all over the world. And I've been lucky to run into two of them by accident. . . .

I must have directed quite an incredulous look at him because of his unusually soft-spoken manner. He responded by trying to convey to me a reason why he thought grave calamities like the switchover were taking place all over the world.

To sum it up, according to him, Earth's orbit is presently contiguous with the outer waves of a dying cosmos, and the prodigious force of the vortex sucking the cosmos into obliteration is causing bizarre stresses and warps on Earth's surface. These perturbations in turn are creating phenomena that appear abnormal to the everyday observer.

——Kurt Vonnegut and other sci-fi writers often quip that the history of this earth, and that of humankind—chronologically speaking, tacked on at the tail end of Earth history—are nothing more than a step to complete the whimsical program of the Cosmic Will. I believe every individual's imagination is rooted in humankind's collective consciousness. We should take note of the fact that this collective imagination captivates every sci-fi writer. I myself once came up with a story along those lines, and in the process of creating it became increasingly convinced of the common fate of all humankind, ahaha. My personal speculation is this: Earth is part of a gigantic cosmic construct, and it is being pulled along, like on a conveyor belt, toward its proper place in that construct! And our Milky Way is the conveyor belt carrying Earth to its designated point on the blueprint; at the last stage of this journey, the Milky Way functions both as the launch pad, and as the energy source providing the correct vector and thrust for Earth's liftoff. This near-perfect spherical unit, humankind's abode for so long, will fit into place with a snap, and complete the preplanned cosmic construct! However, back in the preparatory stages, when all the units for assembling *were first being created,* a minute defect was found on the sphere called Earth. In the end, to correct that defect, beasts, birds, fish, and insects, as well as humans—all infinitesimal on the cosmic scale—had to be introduced. . . . I think those nuclear explosions that have occurred—on deserts or coral atolls—are Earth's finishing touches, the polishing up or corrections of the defect—whatever you want to call it. The next targets are big cities, excluding of course the two already devastated. When Earth is a perfectly sized sphere meeting cosmic specs, it will blast off from the Milky Way launch pad, and snap into its proper place in the ultimate structure! This gigantic structure, it should be remembered, was already reflected in the Ptolemaic system of the universe, or in Dante's celestial map. Of course, I don't have the ability to elaborate further on this wondrous cosmic construct, ahaha. But once this cosmic project is realized, Galileo will be reassessed—provided humankind has time left to reevaluate him, ahaha. He was a pioneer who based his experiments on a revolutionary view of the cosmos, but, as is clear from the records of the Inquisition, as a Catholic he did not reject Dante's consummate spiritual atlas. That means there was no contradiction in what he said and did! *The earth still moves.* And the Milky Way moves continuously at supersonic speed. That very motion allows the constituent parts of the enormous cosmic construct—which extends from heaven on high to the depths of hell—to snap into place. So, if you think about it, Galileo the conformist, who renounced his apostasy can be at one with Galileo, the innovator who held a revolutionary view of the cosmos. I think his soul must have ultimately attained the sublime solace of release into the cosmos. He once wrote: *No matter who it is, if one experiences even once what it is to comprehend something in its totality, if one tastes of how knowledge can be gained, one will know one understands absolutely nothing of the infinitely numerous other conclusions that can exist.* Ahaha.

I kept silent. It may have been a crazy story, but for someone who has studied physics all the way through college, how can I laugh off a guy who quotes Galileo? The Mediator continued in this vein as though flustered by my silence.

——I'm infuriated by this polishing-up project that calls for rubbing away Earth's rough edges and surface imperfections to suit a blueprint of the Cosmic Will, and then launches the perfected unit, bingo, to slot into some gigantic structure. You and Mori's switchover has come about, I feel, as elemental resistance against that rub-out process. The base of resistance is the switched-over people. But then, the switchover itself is caused by the warp and stress of Earth's zooming toward the end of time. So isn't a switchover too an expression of yet another Cosmic Will, just as every action has its reaction? Isn't that so, Mori-father?

The question was not one I could readily respond to, but the switched-over eighteen-year-old in me leapt to answer on the spot as though that were exactly the type of question I'd been waiting for.

——We'll get to the bottom of this. We may have been switched over just for that purpose. **WE'LL GET TO THE BOTTOM OF THIS!**

——It's really heartwarming to see you so full of spirit after the switchover—to say nothing of the impact of Mori's presence! said the Mediator. Then he abandoned his dreamy tone of voice, increasing its volume to activist level. Tough cookies, aren't they? Even though they made their exit rather quietly a while ago, he continued, I can tell you for sure, if your wife squealed on you, and her info jibes with what they know about what went down with Big Shot A, the stakeout will still be on. No lie, the phone's bugged, and if we go out, they'll tail us for sure.

Until they get a change in orders, *our police* are such that once they begin to shadow you, they'll never let up.

I mentally reassessed my situation vis-à-vis the switchover. Provided my wife/*ex*-wife's story is about a pre-switchover middle-aged man who attacked the Patron, I shouldn't fear being arrested at home or out walking the streets . . . at least so long as *our police*—to use the Mediator's phrase—have no daringly imaginative men on the force who might arrest a boy still wet behind the ears on the hunch that he actually is their thirty-eight-year-old suspect, ha, ha.

However, if, as a consequence of the stakeout, they happen to find a man in his prime with a head wound, they'd be sure to take him down to the police station. I'm the only one who can prove he's my son, and that I'm not what I appear to be; but unless I can make the police believe Mori's and my switchover, I won't be able to persuade them to release him.

——It's risky for me to check on Mori's wound. What should I do for now?

——The logical thing to do is contact the Big Shot's secretary, and offer your condolences. . . . Tactically, I think it's the best move to make. From now on, to aid Mori in his fight, we've got to conduct a multifaceted study of the Big Shot. . . . Your phone's out of the question. It's bugged. Why don't we go to the nearest public telephone and call him up?

The Mediator, obviously a TB patient from the way he spat a glob of phlegm into a tissue, stood up with a velocity that took no account of my reaction, and urged me on with a look so intense that his specs seemed to fog up.

3

So we went downtown. As the air was neither hot nor cold, and the buds in the trees were visibly gorging themselves in anticipation of the coming spring, I'd say the life of a tail wouldn't be that dreary, either. At the first intersection, the Mediator waved me on, whispering, *You go straight!* which meant either that he was splitting off in another direction, or that he was going somewhere to get a pack of cigarettes. He turned right. This area was once farm country and the streets meander every which way; once you make a turn, things get complicated. You can't simply go back the way you came, and expect to find yourself on the street at which you started. There wasn't time to explain all that to the eager beaver as he darted down the lane with his arm slightly raised. I couldn't very well call after him, If you turn left there, you'll hit a dead end!

After a while, the man who had taken up the challenge of losing *our police* tail came running after me, his flat feet in oversized shoes slapping the pavement. For a second, I thought I had to run, too, ha, ha. Out of breath, the Mediator caught up with me, his face a dappled black and blue, his bespeckled eyes smiling quietly yet triumphantly.

——Two big ones, ahaha! After I shook them the first time, they must have done some sort of tactical reevaluation, because I heard them loudly discussing whether they should split up to chase me. That was when I ran past them. Did they panic. It was as if I'd taken control of the operation, ahaha!

Isn't he innocent? I pulled out some change in front of the telephone booth and suddenly, for no particular reason, felt scared. The Mediator, his ingenuousness gone, was now into goading me.

——. . . You've got to call the Big Shot's secretary. There's no way you can pretend to know nothing about the incident! Even though we don't know how much they know about your connection to the Mori-Sayoko pair, it's a nuisance to feign ignorance to them. That is, if you really mean business to work for Mori. After all he's the one who made the first move and got injured. . . .

I dialed the same number which the pair had used to make their appointment with the Patron. The secretary picked up the receiver after the first ring, as if he had been waiting for this call. What's more, I didn't even have to impersonate my pre-switchover voice; he obviously knew that the call was from me. I didn't just imagine this. He gave me a prearranged message.

—— . . . Oh, it's you. The Patron says he wants to see you in a couple of days. . . . No, it's not that serious, the guy who did it was just a punk. If the Patron is up to it, you can see him anytime. Do you want to set up an appointment with him now?

——I'll go visit him in the hospital, but I'd rather not schedule an appointment now. . . .

——Well, go see the Patron, the sooner, the better. I'm leaving for his room right now, and I'll stay there for twenty-four hours. If you ask for me at the front desk, you won't have to go through security. . . . I appreciate it.

——The way he hung up might indicate that the police standing right next to him began to show an interest in the conversation, said the Mediator with the dour look of a tactician analyzing a situation not necessarily to his advantage.

——Does it mean that the Patron and his secretary are protecting me from the police?

——That's my guess, especially judging by what the police gave out to the mass media. Unless the police and the secretary are in cahoots to set you up. . . . But the Patron is a *big shot;* he's unlikely to conspire with low-level functionaries. He must really want to get in touch with you. I think he must have made the connection between you and Mori's attack.

——Right. . . . So it's all the more urgent that I speak to Mori before I see the Patron! I can't make the right moves to back Mori up unless I find out for myself the significance of the attack!

As we carried on our rather intense conversation, the Mediator and I kept walking on the street leading to the train station—in the aimless sort of way my classmates and I did when I was eighteen, the first time. Preoccupied with some new problem, his entire face looking like a big *stain,* he became meditative. He gave several tosses of his large head, and suddenly looked over his shoulder. It appeared to me that he was not so much on the lookout for tails, as he was exaggerating his gesture to intimidate them. How can a gesture intimidate *our police?* I'm sometimes baffled, because I can't fathom the true intentions behind the Mediator's no-nonsense conduct. When it comes to his desire to save humankind, this man who missed a chance to become a biologist is not to be compared to your everyday biologist. Apparently, quick sudden movements and slow meditative thinking can coexist in this man, younger than the pre-switchover me, yet much older than the post-switchover me. . . . What he said next made it clear that his mind was working furiously on the problem of linking the Patron, Mori and me.

——If you find out the real purpose of Mori's assault on the Big Shot, you'll know he didn't do it just to avenge the Big Shot's attempted infanticide. Of course, it's just speculation, but I'm almost sure the attack was a warning of things to come. Your visit will take on a special significance only after you consult with Mori. We have to make sure nobody interrupts or blocks what Mori's begun, although that could never happen anyway, could it?

——That's true, I said, hearing in my voice the sound of a child running to the base as a pinch runner after a hit unexpectedly early in the game.

We had arrived at the front of the station, where a horde of tardy students slowed us down and jostled us. Fear took hold. Those tailing us might be right behind us, close enough to grab us by the scruffs of our necks. I was just about to ask, *Where shall we go if we can't see Mori right away?* when, as if he had just finished debating with himself on what action to take next, the Mediator spoke in an exaggeratedly muffled voice that was surely meant for spies or passersby!

——With both of the feuding revolutionary parties funded by the

Big Shot, it probably doesn't make any difference which one we talk to, but let's find out what they have to say about the current situation. My rehab center's full of dropouts from both parties; but it looks as though they were expected to drop out, and they're pretty much in the dark. Do you know anyone we can talk to?

——I know Sakurao Ōno, through the antinuke movement. . . . If she'd heard anything from the Executive Committee, I am sure she'd share it with us.

——Sakurao Ōno! She'll do perfect! The passion of the Mediator's consent took me aback. She's an activist to the core!

——Hard-core? She doesn't look it. Besides, she has no influence over anybody in the Executive Committee of the party.

——She's really hard-core. A walking record of the movement's past! One could detect his obvious admiration, even through the thick Shikoku accent. In the days before the Six College Coalition she was the only delegate from a prestigious girl's high school. She was thought to be the party leader's lover or something, and an opposing faction kidnapped her. They tortured her to tell them the whereabouts of her lover's hideout. In those days even green Rev activists had some sense of ethics; they'd never use rape to torture a woman, heeheehee. Or at least they felt they had to somehow maintain their own prudishness. So, the story has it, she was forced to masturbate with a Coke bottle, until she came, *eeheehee*.

——Won't work.

——*Hmmmh!?* Not even with a jumbo-size Coke bottle? . . . Her emotional trauma was so great that she took off to Europe. Once back in Japan, she started up a civil rights movement. She's one tough cookie. . . . I'm sure there are lots of people in every party who respect her. The weird misrepresentation about the Coke bottle, his own laughter, his flushed blue-black cheeks, all seemed to be forgotten as he stood awe-struck, subdued, shivering.

I also found myself in a rather formal mood as I rang up the script-writer-to-be. A melancholy voice answered as though she had been eavesdropping on our conversation. She had just packed off the "kids" released from police custody and their rescue team for a rest at her parents' mountain villa—she's an heiress. When I explained that the Mediator and I would bring along two policemen, our shadows, she immediately agreed to meet us. She specified a Korean restaurant in Shinjuku as our rendezvous. I went along with her plan, hoping that, even if I had to look her straight in the eye, there'd be enough of a smoke screen from the barbecue grill to shield me. How powerfully a cruel anecdote such as the one about the Coke bottle could actually affect the mind of an eighteen-year-old. Such naivete, isn't it? At any rate, a veteran activist never makes impractical or illogical choices: she picked the restaurant to give a quick fix of protein to the Righteous Man (?). That was how she called the Shikoku antinuke leader accompanying her. That puzzled me, so I questioned her further. She told me that this man of righteousness was staying at her house, and that meeting with him would probably be more beneficial than what we would get from today's morning newspapers. Since neither the Mediator nor I had read any of the morning editions, we felt left out of Ōno's intelligence briefings; we grabbed whatever was still on the newsstands before we stepped onto the train.

None of the articles on the Patron assault went beyond the TV coverage of the previous night. The extent of his injuries, his present condition, were hushed up. In briefing the reporters, the Patron's secretary hadn't even told them what he revealed to me on the phone.

The reason the Patron is called Big Shot A is clear not so much from what the newspapers say but from what they leave out. I learned from an article on the editorial page of a business paper that the power behind a conglomerate which owns a third of Japan and Korea's nuclear industry and development concessions is none other than the Patron. Embarrassed, I felt as if someone had lied to me. *This tells it like it is—what a letdown! If the Patron owns all these nuclear power concessions, domestic and foreign, it means I've merely been management's errand boy. When Canada opened negotiations for the sale of nuclear reactors to Korea with a Japanese conglomerate as an intermediary, I collected data from European sources that criticized the deal. When all is said and done, doesn't it mean that, in handling the Patron's request for intelligence on profit potential, I worked for a pittance? . . . Even though the pay was low, I had been full of gratitude because I believed the Patron, for totally unselfish reasons, was doing me a big favor by putting me on the monthly payroll—that was why I faithfully submitted intelligence summaries upon request. But it turns out that I was just temporary help doing an important job for dirt cheap wages.*

My emotions exploded in a fireball of anger, although I did feel petty, reduced to thinking only of what I had gained and lost. Frankly, I could barely control my outrage, which I suspect was probably identical to what my friend in Paris felt as he hanged himself: a fleeting moment of petty-minded yet total indignation, his life at a dead end.

——Once Ōno learned the Big Shot was deeply involved in the nuclear industry for profit, she immediately set up a meeting with the antinuke leader. It really shows her mindset! The Mediator's admiration was quite evident.

——The Shikoku leader came all this way to attend the meeting—

where you happened to be giving a speech at the hall entrance. He must have been pitching in with the rescue operation ever since. . . . There's no reason for you to credit Ōno with any of that.

——An attack on the Big Shot occurred when we least expected it. He's deeply involved with the inner workings of the nuclear industry. Now, all we're doing is passively accepting an unforeseen event, right? However, for her part, Ōno is playing an active role, bringing the anti-nuke leader to meet with you. She lives to create the conditions that will allow her to act meaningfully like that every day. And her very life is rooted in the situation. That's no ordinary task!

——As a "volunteer mediator," you deliver rousing speeches, you manage a rehab center, and you even give shelter to those who carried out the assault on the Patron, the outcome of that unforeseen event. That's what I'd call living rooted in a situation. . . . So, aren't you and Ōno two peas in a pod?

His blue-black cheeks flushed! He was about to meet Sakurao Ōno and something inside him had taken shape.

Ōno swaggered into the restaurant, kicking at the hem of a hyacinth-yellow floor-length coat, squared at the shoulders like medieval armor. The antinuke leader was properly turned out in a trim khaki tunic. He acted as if nothing had happened, as if the fight with his denture-weapon, so courageous yet showing his years, had never taken place, ha, ha.

——Sitting around swilling beer when we've got urgent matters to tend to? By way of greeting, the scriptwriter-to-be bawled us out. Look at you, chewing on radish pickles as if guzzling beer was the sole purpose of your lives!

Guzzling beer over pickled radishes? Actually we were merely having a nip; I could no longer hold my liquor well after the switchover, and the Mediator's tolerance level was equally low due to circumstances beyond his control. But we couldn't just walk in, sit down, and go over all the newspapers we'd brought in without ordering at least beer, because a man with the look of an agitated stinkbug stood at the partition between the kitchen and the restaurant, glaring out into the dining room where we were the only customers!

——How about you, Mori-father? You're a pitiful sight even though the switchover has taken years off you. Why don't you at least shave!

——I'll lend you my razor.

——Hmm, do you always carry a shaving kit?

——I have to keep close by you as long as Mori's at the Rehab Center. That probably means I may not be able to go back there for a while. Makes sense, doesn't it? The Mediator said this to me, but it was meant for Ōno to hear. The Righteous Man sat palming his freshly shaved chin. The entire group suddenly fell under the spell of Ōno, the star, ha, ha.

I shaved, groping in a tiny room with a faucet and a drainpipe that served as a sink. If I did an about-face, a mirror, over which hung an artificial flower heavily scented with room deodorant, would be available; I wasn't particularly interested in staring at my own *pitiful sight.*

By the time I returned, the three had already formed a bond and were immersed in a heated discussion. Smoke from burning grease coiled above the gas burner on the table. The owner of the restaurant, who had been on edge a while ago, now seemed freed from the fetters of his earlier self-alienation, and was cheerfully doling out beer, and showing reverence to the TV personality, the scriptwriter-to-be.

4

The Shikoku antinuke leader had launched himself into an eloquent oration. His outsized eyes and nose were crowded onto a small face, elated in a self-possessed sort of way. He spoke the quasi-Kansai dialect, typical of a man from Shikoku.

——I said to myself, Now, one big hole's been blasted through, and it's in the direction of the Imperial *Family*! There are plenty of big shots, string pullers, and what have you, in Tokyo, and you know the boonies are full of these same types! They've always got their paws in something, although our common sense can't see why! Shortsighted self-interest and greed—that we can understand. Most of the time you can look the other way. They don't amount to much! But, sometimes a strange mirage, bulging with hot air, is suspended above the heap of self-interest and greed. When you stare at it for a while, you can see a big hole being blasted through it —sometimes twisting and turning—in the direction of the *Family*! It doesn't do any good for us to try to figure out its logic. We'd simply be repeating *wasteful* official strictures. Stricture or no stricture, this is a real issue; a big hole has already been blasted through toward the *Family*! That's why, as a matter of principle, if we decide to have a showdown with the big shots, string pullers, monsters, and what have you, if we don't want to get taken in by their black magic, we've got to look at what's above their heads, check out the conditions of the hole that has blasted its way toward the *Family*!

Thereupon, he turned his eyes and nose skyward, and indeed it did look as though a superhole had been blasted through the thick smoke swirling from the grilled meat.

——. . . Take this incident. One of the few lines we've read says that

Big Shot A is the real power behind the nuclear industry. That's enough to show me what's hovering up there, what he's kept us in the dark about; there's a hole blasted through right above this influence peddler's head! Probing into how business concessions are acquired is not as easy as it seems, and putting pressure on local opposition Diet members will get us nowhere. Once we know a string puller like him is involved with the nuclear power project, then it's a foregone conclusion that our movement will disintegrate and Shikoku's largest power plant ever will spring up—that is, if we take a peek through this huge hole of his. When the plant starts operating, never mine the hot waste water, the *Family* will be there in no time at all for an inspection tour! What then? All of Japan will kneel in worship, bowing in the direction of the southern tip of Shikoku! What a super display: The power of nuclear energy combined with that of the *Family*—120 million Japanese will kneel and worship in front of their TV sets!

——An activist like you, pessimistic about something as insignificant as the Emperor System?! The Mediator broke in, the tone of his interruption underscoring his neutrality so as to sound out what Ōno felt about the subject.

——Why's the Righteous Man a pessimist? He always assesses the content and extent of an impending difficulty, and continues his normal activities without building up too much hope or despairing too much. . . . Isn't it the same when you mediate a dispute, probing into the basic problem at hand in a factional confrontation?

Feeling myself shut out of this tight-knit group as they carried on their intense discussion, and also irritated at the way the Karubi, Tan, and Hatsu were shriveling up and burning on the grease-laden wire mesh over the gas burner, I couldn't help but draw their attention away from the profound discussion at hand and turn it to a more mundane topic: the pitiful condition of the broiled meat.

——Aren't you going to eat? The meat's burnt. It's not nice. The chef will feel bad.

——Right now, eating is of secondary importance! Vexation was in her voice as she said it, but she reached for five, no, six pieces of smoking meat—she had a unique way of handling chopsticks, what you might call the grand style or even rough-and-ready—and plopped them on the Righteous Man's plate.

Each of us followed her lead, and as soon as I hurriedly reached over with my chopsticks to snatch up pieces of Karubi and Tan, Ōno immediately began picking up a large amount of meat from a platter, shoveling it onto the wire mesh. In trying to broil a whole bunch of meat at one time, she'd burn it again. You always eat Korean roast beef rare, making sure that what you've eaten is replaced on the wire mesh. This principle of Korean cooking never entered Ōno's mind, although she'd come here with me more than ten times. I resented that. I quickly averted my eyes from the smoking wire mesh as I ate my dried-up Karubi and cardboard Tan. With a haughty air she gave a command,

——Waiter, please. I wonder if you'd mind turning up the fan. It's getting stuffy in here! The owner was reduced to bowing and scraping to meet her demand.

Sublime in his thoroughness in ignoring the principle of Korean table manners, the Righteous Man ate the roast beef totally in violation of the rules; it moved me greatly. Set in front of each of us were two small dishes, one with sauce for the meat, the other with spicy bean paste for the pickled pig's feet. The small middle-aged man bunched several slices of meat in his chopsticks, dunked them in both dishes, and popped them into his mouth. He slowly chewed the contents, always looking straight at whoever was speaking, grinding away with his dentures firmly in place. Although we were a little disturbed by the indiscriminate way he had mixed together the sauce and the bean paste, the gravity of the man's eating was so overwhelming that the rest of us couldn't bring ourselves to correct him. Besides, we couldn't slight the dignity of someone who considered eating of secondary importance. . . .

——You were saying I was a pessimist? the Righteous Man said calmly, obviously enjoying the meal as he savored the roast beef still in his mouth. When you look at the global nuclear arms race and the development of the nuclear power industry, I'm convinced pessimism is quite a realistic option for humans. But, of course, humans are generally optimistic. You see that waiter who takes so much pride in adjusting the fan? He'll be dead in twenty, thirty years, and he's standing there oblivious to this simple inevitable fate. What guarantee is there that the general public will worry about the fact that they will die from the radiation emitted by nuclear bombs and nuclear waste, that they won't be able to give their offspring even a chance at survival? Well, how about us, the ones who're fretting about the future? Do we have any trouble getting our food down? NO, we sit here chomping away!

Exactly. But, something about the Righteous Man's story made Ōno somewhat meditative as she continued to gnaw—that's all she'd been doing— the joint of a pig's foot on which there was hardly any meat. In lieu of eating, she had maintained the wire mesh for the rest of us. In the meantime, the discussion had taken an abrupt nosedive and now centered on me. Apparently the Righteous Man had heard about my switchover in great detail from Ōno.

——A person like Mori-father cannot take his eyes off his present condition, and all of its ramifications, can he?

——True, the switched-over Mori and Mori-father are the most biting examples of the negation of the natural order, the Mediator agreed. I still don't quite understand the relationship that the Righteous Man says exists between the *Family* and Mori-father.

——Have you ever thought of the possibility of a switchover inside the *Family*, a family whose unbroken lineage goes back to the Sun Goddess herself? There would be no way to deal with it! Mori-father and the *Family* inhabit different dimensions, occupy different levels of meaning—that is to say, from a nonmilitant stance.

——Now, Old Man, speaking as a militant, do you mean Mori and I have to flaunt our switchover at the *Family*, march right into the Imperial Palace and contaminate it with the switchover?

——I didn't mean to get you mad, Mori-father. Take the problem of nuclear waste water. I, for one, think that the natural order's gone haywire because of it. The amount of waste water we're talking about is astronomical. Really. Once things go haywire like this, it's no wonder that a switchover occurs. Believe me. . . . But those promoting the nuclear industry are pressing ahead with the view that the natural order as manifest in the unbroken lineage of the *Family* won't go haywire! To top it all off, as the pro-nuke camp continues its hard-sell, the *Family* will be brought in to inspect the plant, and by this connection the nuclear industry will be accepted as a marvel of natural development. With one relay broadcast, 120 million or so will accept all of this just like that. That's why a hole has been blasted through to the *Family*!

——Old Man, are you going to invite us switched-overs, Mori and me, to the anti-nuke demo during the power plant's opening ceremony? ha, ha.

——Your use of "old man" is nothing more than boastful speech, simply the desire to tell yourself and the world that you've been switched over in mind and body. The phrase would definitely make for awkward dialogue in a film script. . . . We're all in this together, aren't we? Drop the "old man" bit, and call him the "Righteous Man." Why don't we keep it all functional?

——You see, once I get a little beer under my belt, I start to shoot my mouth off—I can turn a good phrase, make sure you know I'm here, what I'm thinking. That's all I do, yak away! Shame on me! If I tell that to my antinuke buddies back home, they'll say, *There you go again, the same old routine!*

——Wait a minute. To act as a unit, we must get to know each other. This is an indisputable prerequisite. The Mediator had said this hoping that Ōno would nod her approval, but was ignored.

She appeared eager to lay out a plan of action to which she'd given much thought. You should know that this is what I call the axiom of a civil rights activist's life; if you sit down to talk with them, they'll never let up till you've promised to take some supposedly effective action (even if its preposterousness blows your mind, ha, ha). The plan of action that Sakurao Ōno wanted to present to me and the Mediator by bringing the Righteous Man with her went something like the following. She said she wanted an explanation directly from the leadership of her party concerning an almost open secret, namely, that certain high-level members of the Revs were accepting funds from the Big Shot. As the top representative of the Ōno group, she felt she's entitled to an explanation from them. She'd made innumerable fruitless efforts to contact the leadership—what an injustice!

Therefore, what she and her supporters should do now is drive into the Revs headquarters (of course, I don't mean with an armored car, but in a VW which the scriptwriter-to-be already had borrowed from a great fan of hers), since the only way to get the low-down out of the Executive Committee members about the Big Shot issue would be to question them directly. The Righteous Man would accompany her, as an activist from the front lines of the antinuke movement. The Mediator and I should participate in this effort, bringing along with us a pair of distinguished representatives of the national police force—the two flatfoots. Surely this would reinforce the effectiveness of the whole strategy because the Revs wouldn't dare detain or interrogate us as long as the two tails were there to keep the heat on.

The way Ōno comes up with her ideas, those soaring leaps of logic— and so superrealistic to boot—proves she once worked for Luis Buñuel as a scriptwriter's assistant. She insists that it would be unfair not to seek the opinions of the Counterrev thugs. Furthermore, the one who carried out the attack on the Big Shot—the thugs of course think one of theirs did it—is being sheltered at the rehab center. Therefore, if his switched-over younger father and the Mediator join forces and ask for a meeting with the Counterrevs, they can't possibly get turned down, can they? Besides, if things get out of hand, Ōno will be at the ready to appeal to our faithful flatfoots to rescue us from the violence of the unjust Counterrevs thugs in the name of citizens' rights. For the Party's sake, according to her scenario, the Counterrevs will, of course, put up no resistance.

——We do need to rig up flags or banners on the car to announce our intentions, but I didn't have time to make anything yet. . . . As soon as Ōno said this, the Mediator, who seemed to have been in the doldrums for some time, suddenly became animated.

He pulled out a white banner from the shoulder bag in which he also carried the aforementioned shaving kit. On a table spread with newspapers he wrote on the banner, **"FORUM FOR THE ELIMINATION OF OBSTACLES TO RECONCILIATION,"** then went out and attached it to the car. The owner of the restaurant, who'd been watching the whole affair, came over with a piece of fancy traditional *shikishi* paper to get Ōno's autograph. Using a magic marker, she wrote, **"WE OPPOSE ALL GOVERNMENT INVOLVEMENT IN NUCLEAR POWER! WE REJECT ALL NUCLEAR POWER PLANTS!"** in a kind of calligraphy that was totally unpretentious, unadorned. She never does anything halfway, does she?

——The Big Shot has been supporting you all along, so it's only right that you should use his dirty money, and she handed me the bill, ha, ha.

No choice but to shell out. As I rushed to catch up with Ōno, who had left for the front kicking the hem of her coat, I turned on the Righteous Man and began to taunt him in teen slang.

——Hey, Old Man! Lookinngg ggoood. Did Ōno help you pick it out at the Young Men's Shop?

——I was sent by Osaka University on a faculty exchange program to MIT and I bought this outfit there. It's living proof of my shame, for those days when I worked with my American colleagues on computing missile trajectories. . . .

Boy, that antinuke leader with his hick Righteous Man demeanor sure put one over on me, just your basic inexperienced eighteen-year-old, ha, ha.

5

The Korean restaurant was situated down a narrow alley that fed into a wide avenue, and at that intersection sat a bright green VW. The banner-rigged body of the car was a perfect match for Ōno, who stood nearby like a temple guardian. The Mediator looked prim and proper, with a smaller version of the banner draped diagonally over his chest. Wasn't this a cutesy demonstration of his intention to sit next to Ōno who was going to drive? Surveying the area carefully as though on a reconnaissance mission, he made no move to enter the car until the Righteous Man and I had taken the back seat, but once the car was in motion, he quickly took on the role of the driver's devoted assistant.

——Our friendly neighborhood flatfoots have had plenty of time to arrange for a car. Really, I tipped those two off early on by putting the banner on the VW! By now, they must have a detailed plan to tail us in a car of their own. Leave that to *our police*!

——Where to first? My associates? They've left me in the dark about a lot of things. . . . I had to squeeze my kids to get them to tell me that the Big Shot's contribution is only to be used for the Revs' production of their own A-bomb! It's been agreed that, when production goes into its final phase, the Big Shot will contribute an unspecified sum, surpassing anything received so far. And ditto for the Counterrev thugs, the kids said. What's the Big Shot's motive for doing all this? And are the leaders of the two parties revolutionary or counterrevolutionary? On what sort of outlook do they base their actions? My political experience tells me that such unruly conduct is unbelievable. I want to know the logic behind it.

——Let me clarify your use of the word "unruly": Do you mean A, the Revs making their own A-bomb, or B, the Big Shot paying for the bomb?

——Huhh? A and B? Don't complicate things, or I won't be able to drive. . . . Well, let me see, I'd say B.

——Things like B happen all the time! There's nothing a big shot or any other monster cannot do! Giving money to two warring parties intent on killing each other—that's classic. Unruly? What an absurdity! . . . When I heard you talking about being unruly, I thought you meant A. I was invited to Tokyo to attend the antinuke meeting, where people took wonderfully good care of me. But on the other hand, those same young people are trying to make an A-bomb. If that's not unruly, I don't know what is! They most certainly do want to produce that bomb—indeed, are very committed to producing it—yet they're activists in an antinuke movement. Now, how's that for being unruly!?

——Righteous Man, I really can't blame you for the way you feel. . . . But you can't wish those kids away, and what's more, they're actually following the party leadership's general line. I understand that it is possible for private individuals to make a bomb. Isn't that right, Mori-father?

——Just as I told you before, if you keep it where it's assembled, and don't worry about the problem of transport, yes, you can.

——Do you think those young bombmakers really exist? What's their *excuse* for doing it? They're all screwed up!

——Why screwed up? The Mediator's attitude was now defiant. How can you say that? As long as the superpowers hold a monopoly on nuclear arms, then weaker and smaller nations have a right to go nuclear and make the political situation more fluid, right? When the State uses its monopoly of nuclear arms to hold the masses hostage, there's nothing strange about a political party or an individual developing nuclear arms as a protest, is there?

——If you mean that, then I'm totally pessimistic. If there's such absolutely absurd relativistic thinking on the nuclear arms race circulating even among antinuke activists, things're even worse than I thought! I'm flabbergasted. You say an A-bomb is actually being built!? . . . Who are they, where!?

The Mediator didn't reply, but kept silent. The interior workings of a silent man are best seen from behind. I sensed that, like it or not, he had picked up certain kinds of information in the course of his everyday activities. But if he gave us the inside dope on the parties, he'd lose his position as the Mediator.

——Righteous Man, if you want to know what those kids are doing, you should ask Mori-father. He was the victim of some youngsters who thought they could build an A-bomb overnight.

——Victim?

——That's an exaggeration. . . . I still don't know which of the parties was involved; I was almost robbed by some characters in tin armor of some nuclear material we were hauling from the retreatment plant. That's all.

——The incident in which a researcher resisted the nuclear hijacking and was exposed to radiation—**THAT WAS YOU!?** I was at MIT when I read about it in the *Christian Science Monitor!* I was really moved! That incident braced me up, morally, to continue my antinuke activities! **THAT WAS YOU!**

——What a heartwarming story, don't you think? the scriptwriter-to-be said coldly, which really ticked me off.

——Are you trying to pick a fight?

——It's not so much a matter of picking a fight. I'm sure what she meant was that every action has room for criticism, the Mediator interrupted in Ōno's defense. Let's suppose some young men from the Revs try to recapture the nuclear material from the authorities. Since the authorities monopolize the material, you can justify the Revs' action by my previous argument. A researcher-technician—who's not necessarily a watchdog for the power company—does everything he can to protect the nuclear material, oblivious to the danger of radiation exposure. Doesn't that mean that all the employees at power plants, including the low men on the totem pole, are doing their part to help the nuclear establishment accomplish its goal? That's what the young men who attacked Mori-father think. The problem is the victim does not represent the nuclear establishment in any way, and they can't commit cold-blooded murder just to steal the material. So, they had to abort the attack, and yet Mori-father was irradiated. From the Revs' point of view, they were up against the wall that time. . . .

——Did you participate in the hijacking? The question I put to the Mediator was not entirely a joke.

——Are you kidding? He denied it immediately. However, the quickness of his denial made me suspect that he was one of the Tin Men after all, that radiation exposure was the source of his black-and-blue skin.

——Let's suppose that somewhere in a corner of Tokyo, there exists a group with sufficient political imagination, morality, and a fundamental love for humankind. . . . (So began Sakurao Ōno's theme for an imaginary film project, probably never to be completed, ha, ha.) If, one day, this group declares that they have developed an A-bomb, our country will be transformed. At least one thing is sure. The typical man-on-the-street enjoying his meal who never gave a thought to someday dying will be less carefree. Wouldn't this be a useful antidote to the Righteous Man's pessimism?

——**NO WAY!** No matter what your intentions are, when you try to evaluate the bomb in a positive light, nothing but depravity comes out of it!

——That's absolutism. Aren't you being a bit naive? . . . My basic stance when I talk with the party leader we're going to meet will be, if the Revs develop the bomb on their own, there's no reason for me to oppose their acting on principles. That's the first point. The other is I criticize their acceptance of contributions from the Big Shot to carry out their plan to develop the bomb. I want you to accept these two points in the name of freedom of thought.

I stole a sidelong glance at the Righteous Man as he pursed his lips like two narrow persimmon leaves, his eyes widening but seeing nothing, and all his appearance issuing a sense of total repugnance toward the real world. I couldn't help but say something to him.

——Old Man, you said a hole's already been blasted through toward the *Family* above the Big Shot's head. But if some group in Tokyo decides to develop the bomb to blackmail the government or the financial community, they won't be able to accomplish that by cuddling up to the *Family*, will they? Don't tell me that both parties the Patron has been funding intend to use what they've taken such great pains to produce, just to end up supporting the *Family*. Given all these conditions, how is the Patron going to control use of such a bomb in the hole above his head that's directed toward the *Family?* I don't get it, Old Man.

Whereupon the sense of disgust he held for reality evaporated, and he looked at me with large, clear eyes. He was once again an invincible activist, fired up with a sense of mission.

——Without a shadow of doubt, a hole has been blasted through toward the *Family* above the head of the Big Shot! But that the hole there above him was taken into consideration by him as a major premise! He eggs on the young revolutionaries to make their A-bombs! Not just one, mind you, but two warring factions! I call that deja vu, **DEJA VU!** All he needs to do is bring a terrifying source of superenergy into the social situation—in the form of an A-bomb—and he'll be able to manipulate things at will! One bomb will do the job; two would be even better. The supertension the bomb will cause among the people will consume the society, which will be sucked in all at once through his hole! Picture it: a gigantic tornado that strikes with a roar and lifts the *Family* higher than ever before, to the absolute apex of creation! I bet those young revolutionaries are fully confident of outsmarting the Big Shot at the very last moment. But it won't work that way. From the perspective of all preceding cultural history, it's never worked!

——If you're such a seasoned activist, why are your conclusions so pessimistic? The Mediator's remarks were meant to be critical, but the Righteous Man ignored him.

——**AS I SAID EARLIER,** the Righteous Man's wrinkled throat trembled as he continued, the Big Shot is trying to divert all that supercharged tension into his own hole. To resist him, someone must confront him with equal energy and tension, and it must be someone who won't be dazzled by his power. That's the kind of man we've got to find! . . . Wouldn't you say Mori's and your switchover is a **CLUE TO THE RIDDLE?**

——If that's the case, what Mori's done makes sense. I take Mori to be a man of great vision.

Thereupon, those voices of the past, shouting, *GO, GO, GO,* began to swallow up my young body as well as my spirit—although whether it was young or still middle-aged, I wasn't sure. . . .

8

A Sequel to the Multifaceted Study of the Patron

1

We were stuck in a traffic jam in downtown Oji, and I was trying to shake myself out of boredom when a joke came to me. *The Revs' headquarters are around here somewhere. I wonder if they'd like to conduct a little A-bomb test at Asukayama.* * I didn't repeat it aloud because of the mounting tension in the car. But the Righteous Man, who'd certainly object to my cracking a joke about an A-bomb, was deep asleep, looking half-dead in his khaki tunic. The toll of the years showed in his face as it drooped over his chest. Ever see those shrunken heads kept by witch doctors in South America? The Righteous Man looked like one of them, a tiny face on a tiny head, with a nose and ears sticking out. But then it hit me, he'd taken out his dentures. The shrunken face was really spooky, ha, ha.

We slowed the VW as we entered a narrower, more crowded street, and were stopped by two cops. We parked the car in front of a branch office of some investment company. One of the cops poked his head into the car. Everything happened so quickly. I scrunched down in the

---

*Asuka is the place-name associated with the rise of imperial rule around the sixth century A.D. Asukayama, literally Mt. Asuka, refers to a hill in Kita Ward in Tokyo, famous for the beauty of its cherry blossoms since the Edo Period (1603–1868).

159

back seat, knowing I had no satisfactory ID. The Righteous Man woke with a start, a little rattled but still in control of himself. With his bloodshot eyes wide open, he stuck his dentures back in, restoring his shrunken face to normalcy.

But there was no need for him to open his mouth. Quick as a wink, before the cop could say a word, Ōno had thrust out her driver's license and network ID, leaning forward aggressively, as a star is wont to do.

——Would you like to check with the police car behind us? So began the negotiations in which the Mediator insinuated that we were driving with a police escort. We're with the media and we want to talk with someone from the movement. We're not politically affiliated with any of their organizations. And the last thing we want to do is get ourselves involved in any kind of violence!

The two cops must have gotten the word from the car tailing us. They exchanged shouts over the low roof of the VW, and the IDs were gently returned to Ōno's lap. I sensed they were responding to her acting ability. She sure has a director's talent. The VW immediately moved on.

——The headquarters' bodyguards, the "Opposition Police," must have recognized our car. Besides, a report should have reached them by now about how the police had given us preferential treatment. I'm sure they no longer think we're some Counterrev creeps raiding them with hand grenades or something.

____I hope those young activists guarding the place don't believe what they read in the faction newsletter about the opposition always getting the upper hand by forming an alliance with the police. If they take that seriously, we've just endangered our position!

——The watchman will see the banner across my chest and catch on that this is a variation on what I, as a Volunteer Mediator, have been doing all along. They won't bomb our car. The quiet confidence he exuded was most convincing.

——Are you saying you've been here before with a banner on your car, giving speeches to win them over? . . . You are courageous! Ōno said.

——I've been in the business so long, it's just a matter of getting used to it, he said with shyness.

Our car crawled through the crowds of passersby, the air heavy with antagonism. When we turned at the first intersection, a no man's land stretched before us. Fifty meters beyond stood a row of wood and mortar buildings that had escaped bombing raids during the war and apparently withstood all that nature threw at them. A three-story building, some sort of clinic, occupied the middle of the block. Except for the iron fire-escape, all the entrances and windows were boarded up. When we looked up at the rooftop where a pigeon coop had been added on, we saw a group of helmeted people with towels over their faces staring at us.

——They might think we're a car-bomb squad if we park right in front. Let's go on and park over there, said the Righteous Man.

——Let me off here. Park it at the end of this clearing. Keep an eye on me, and if you see something weird going on, well, can't be helped, contact the car shadowing us!

The scriptwriter-to-be dragged her oversized body out of the VW and walked toward the "stronghold," kicking the hem of her coat, upstaging everyone in sight with her dark purple sunglasses and matching purse. Perhaps feeling the hostile vibes of his surroundings, the Mediator slammed the accelerator to the floor and the car took off at breakneck speed. The Righteous Man stayed glued to the rear window and intently watched the building, whereas I fixed my gaze straight ahead, trying hard not to think about the ordeal Ōno had to go through as a high school girl at the hands of the party gang.

She's survived many a bloodletting, a real seasoned activist. She sure fought well in that free-for-all, didn't she? Less than ten minutes later, she stepped out of the broken-down battleship of a building, which had been cleverly camouflaged with gray-brown boards, with one of the Revs members.

Breathless with excitement and joy, the Righteous Man whooped for our attention from his vantage point, and as I turned my head twisting my neck in the process, I saw a pigeon-toed man tripping along with Ōno, who with dauntless strides was closing the distance to the car. Except for his shades, he looked like a petty civil service bureaucrat. His rather subdued clothing contrasted eerily with the work coveralls and helmets of the young men who followed four or five steps behind him. The metal pipes stuffed underneath their bulky coats were just too obvious to go unnoticed.

——We've decided to go to a coffee shop the Revs frequent. I'm told I can bring only one person. Mori-father, you'll be the one. The Righteous Man finds it impossible to carry on a dialogue on nuclear issues, and I want the Mediator to take over the driving. . . . Drive around the block a few times and be back here in an hour, will you?

——Hey, wait a minute! I said thirty minutes, man, the shades said in a patently false voice, the tone of it familiar to the point of rudeness.

——Come on, hurry up, Mori-father. To obey her was our only option.

I'll recount to you the dialogue between Ōno and the party functionary in the question-answer format that I recorded at the time in her notebook. Put this party member—actually one of the leaders—down as "L." He wouldn't remove his shades even in the coffee shop. Were they meant to hide those ridiculous eyes of his, always roving, unfocused? He spoke fast and indistinctly through his upper lip. He must have been thirty or so. He said his pharmacist wife was supporting him—he certainly dressed like it with his expensive tie and gold cufflinks. I wonder if this was part of a PR campaign targeting the general public.

With no other customers or even a waitress to disturb them, L and Ōno drank coffee, seated near the door of the shop which was clearly visible from the pigeon coop. The young men placed themselves strategically on both sides of the door, quietly ate the sweet rolls they had snuck in their coats, and sipped from their glasses of milk. So I decided to have milk. At my age you easily get influenced by cool-looking guys, ha, ha.

O. *We have intelligence reports that say the Revs have been receiving funds from the Big Shot. Even the television news has picked it up. Its also said that the Counterrev thugs are receiving funds from him as well. Now I don't belong to the Revs, but I've been active on the periphery with its issues. The people I lead, high school students, those preparing for the college entrance exams, college students, all of them are quite upset by these reports. If you aren't on the Big Shot's payroll, you should immediately make that fact public, protest to the media. I need something I can tell my people, so I'm requesting that you tell us the executive committee's official view on this matter. I've tried repeatedly to contact your headquarters, but you wouldn't have anything to do with me. Now, aren't you resorting to fascistic tactics?*

L. *If you call us fascists in public, we'll make life difficult for you. Our view of your individual case is that your movement is under the party's domain and guidance. But on countless occasions your public statements and conduct in the media seem to deviate from our basic line—not that I personally watch television, of course. So, why don't you come to one of the party's self-criticism sessions?*

Anyway, everyone knows media news coverage is meaningless and basically irresponsible, so there's no need to mount a protest. What we do is use the media from time to time—for strategic purposes, of course.

We haven't as yet announced our official position in regard to the Big Shot so what I'm about to say is only in the realm of speculation, mind you. But let's say he wants to contribute some money to us. What's wrong with using that money for political activities based on scientific analysis of the world situation? It goes without saying that the Big Shot is scum from the right-wing international mob—actually, more likely a small shot. (Laugh.) But, money is money. Regardless of where it comes from, if one acts according to revolutionary principles, if one uses the money for political activities based on the Revs' correct situational analysis, the funds will be used correctly, and in the end purified. People in the corrupt money-politics structure may accuse us of being on the Big Shot's payroll, but to criticize us for it, from a logical or phenomenological point of view, is what you'd call the pot calling the kettle black.

If the Big Shot is also funding the Counterrev thugs, that's none of our business. We deal only with the fact that he gives us money. Besides, it's too much to expect that he's not giving any to anybody else. After all, he's one of the biggest wheeler-dealers in corrupt money-politics. As I said earlier, he's just scum, a right-wing international mobster. How can anyone expect revolutionary morality from a guy like that?

O. *I'd like to know what the leadership thinks revolutionary morality is.*

L. *A revolutionary movement based on a scientific analysis of the world situation that is rooted in Leninism creates revolutionary morality. Morality is not something you can create on your own, as you please. Well, since speculation has a habit of going in circles and is inefficient, I'll move on. To summarize: Whether it's the Big Shot or someone else, if someone offers to give us money, we'll use those funds, basing our strategy on revolutionary principles and scientific situational analysis.*

O. *When the rumor hit the streets that the Counterrev thugs were receiving money from the Big Shot, a sympathizer group or possibly one of their own party members attacked him. The Counterrevs have jumped the gun on you. You've been smeared with the stigma of taking the "Big Shot's money and now it's all over the media.*

L. *I've explained to you that we have no reason to attack him. Don't you think it's counterproductive to keep rehashing the same things over and over again, ignoring the logical direction of your own questioning?*

Domestic-variety scum like the Counterrevs, attacking right-wing international mobster scum, failed to kill him, and even left the assault weapon behind. We leave it to the Counterrev bunch to orchestrate such farces. But there's a clear, possible motive behind the assault. The Big Shot may have cut off funds to them, disappointed when he learned what they're really like. Their attack was probably a desperate attempt to get back at him. In fact, our revolutionary intelligence network has substantiated this. The party paper will eventually disclose all the facts.

As the dialogue continued, it became clear that Ōno had begun to consider this leader a "family" disgrace, and her irritation and embarrassment at this realization were even more obvious. The thirty-year-old man's confidence soared as he warmed to his subject, effectively displaying what he believed to be his intelligence. He didn't even notice the changes in Ōno's attitude. My enthusiastic attempt at being a scribe seemed to heighten his eloquence still further. What a farce! On the other hand, after they consumed their sweet rolls, the young security boys listened quietly to his oration with bowed heads. It was rather moving.

O. *Deliver nuclear power back into the hands of the masses!—that's our movement's slogan. As long as I'm participating in that movement, I don't object to the Revs making an A-bomb. However, if, as is being reported, A-bomb production funds are being supplied by the Big Shot, and data on the manufacturing process is being reported back to him in exchange for the money, then I am really concerned. Isn't it possible when everything's ready, the Big Shot will take advantage of the Revs, A-bomb and all?*

L. *I'm not in a position to state my opinions on official tactics and strategies, including those on the nuclear arms issue. There is no chance at any level of political activity for international right-wing deviationist mobster scum to take advantage of the Revs. Which party, us or those bastards, is acting in accord with revolutionary principles based on a scientific situational analysis? Isn't it obvious?*

O. *I'll dare to ask you this question. What happens if the Counterrev thugs make the bomb first?*

L. *We're not fascists, so we won't threaten them. I find your lack of faith hard to forgive. This may sound like a fable, but I'll tell you a true story. It has to do with the Counterrev thugs, and how they can never decide on what tactics or strategies to pursue, as a result of which they can't accomplish anything. Almost ten years ago they put together a weird, ridiculous group called the Yamame Corps. They were already receiving money from the Big Shot. They carried out what they called the Long March—isn't that ridiculous?—prowling the deep mountains of the Tohoku region, careful to avoid any human contact. Over time some died in gun accidents, some dropped out, many were executed for desertion, while the rest finally got too old to serve as soldiers. Humidity ruined all the guns they had. The group died out without a chance to engage a real enemy. Now we don't take unproductive detours. We behave according to our revolutionary principles, basing our action on a true scientific analysis of the world situation, so we never miss the mark in our tactics or strategies. What makes you think we would ever lag behind a group like that?*

I had kept my side of the bargain Ōno had made with the party leader and had raised no objections to any of his comments up to the point when he referred to the Yamame Corps. I was so angry that I felt my head start to spin (of course, you should also remember I was writing with my head down in a dimly lit coffee shop in order to record the dialogue, ha, ha).

——The Yamame Corps was able to stay active for a long time. Neither the police nor the Self-Defense Corps could catch them. I don't believe that the group just died out. Obviously they've aged, but I'm sure they've kept themselves in training and are waiting for the right day to take action. After all, they're only ten years older!

——That's it. He's broken the agreement. **BRAT, WHAT THE HELL ARE YOU YELLING ABOUT?** The leader made threatening gestures, and his eyes rolled behind the sunglasses, but with no hint of aggressiveness.

In no time at all, the two young stalwarts in jumpsuits stood at the ready beside him, right hands clutching something inside their coats, glaring at me with bright eyes full of burning hostility. My spirits withered. I tried to hasten after Ōno as she strode to the door.

——You have to pay for your own drinks, and also the 3,000 yen fee for the interview! The leader said throwing his head back as he shifted one leg over the other in his chair. It was hard to tell whether he was serious or just ridiculing me; in any case I put whatever cash I still had left over from the Korean restaurant down on the table.

I stepped out into weak sunlight illuminating a vividly bizarre scene. Piles of feces on the street, yet not a single dog in sight, an apartment complex, a factory, and the "stronghold" lined up in a row on the street. I felt as though countless irradiated eyes were watching me, and that the pavement was part of a large octopus skin; I could feel all the pigment of that skin about to gush, forming rapids, while all the muscles that lay below the surface were *swelling,* and that the whole facade was about to transform itself. I felt the moment of transition had come. I had a gut feeling that the switchover was making rapid progress inside me, and I was gripped with fear, a fear that I might revert back to infancy. On the pavement, soft and undulating, Ōno bent herself forward and pushed on. Gone were her usual long, haughty strides, replaced by the small running steps of a broken-hearted girl scurrying for cover under dark clouds. All of a sudden, I felt that she too had reverted in flesh and spirit, back to a high school girl under torture, that I was following her, holding the disposed jumbo-size Coke bottle in my hand. I automatically stretched my arms upward. . . .

2

The Mediator reported to Ōno that while they were driving around, they had spotted *our police* once again, hot on our trail. The scriptwriter-to-be turned a deaf ear to this. Broken-hearted melancholia was so obvious on her face that even the Righteous Man, who had a keen interest in the Rev Executive Committee's nuclear policy, simply puckered up his thick lips and stared at her profile, refraining from putting any questions to her. As I stole glances at each one of them in turn, I wondered what sort of experiences had mellowed them out like that.

However, Ōno just needed a brief "grace period." In no time at all she managed to subdue all the demons that had welled up so evidently inside her. Restored to preeminence was the temperament and attitude appropriate to a civil rights activist. She steered the car onto the freeway as if to signal that we were moving into the next phase of our plan, and began to relate the content of the interview. I wondered again what mix of experiences had served to build up her voluntarily selfless spirit.

—— . . . How can a bastard like that be on the Executive Committee of the Revs? He can't be, said the Righteous Man. I'm pretty good at predetermining which college students will turn into political leaders; in fact, I have met some fairly decent young politicos.

——Of course he's not one of the higher-ranking cadres, although he works in the Party Secretariat. I know him personally because he was in charge of liaison work with intellectuals and used to attend film-related union meetings. As far as I've seen, the real leadership's nothing like that. There's something more to them, something steady, ardent, and open. Their perseverance is really marvelous. And it's those young people who are being killed in the struggle against the Counterrev thugs and the authorities.

She fell silent as though tasting something bitter and cruel, and seemed to be reorganizing her overall plan, using the unproductive interview as a springboard. The VW convulsed, leaping forward in fits and starts as if her brain waves were connected directly with the gear box. We were frightened half out of our wits. The car on our tail must have had some difficulty as well. *Our police* must have pretty good driving techniques, because we didn't shake them, ha, ha.

The occupants of the car remained silent as it sped along,

——PSSSUUU, the Mediator burst out laughing hysterically, the scarlet of his face spreading even to his neck. Taken completely by surprise, the Righteous Man and I stared him full in the face. Ōno kept a poker face throughout the laughing fit, her eyes glued to the road ahead. The Mediator's eyeballs turned upward in his desperate attempts to suppress his fits of laughter—it must have been painful—and with the back of his hand wiped away tears from the sides of his triangle of a nose as his head collapsed forward.

——He must be dead tired! The Righteous Man tried in vain to intercede on his behalf, but Ōno's features remained frozen.

We got off the expressway near our destination, and she broke her silence to present her new strategies.

——It's no use wasting our time with a petty party bureaucrat like him. Imagine having to listen to his sophistry—not one iota of concern for ethics. . . . Since we still need to find out what they think, how about going to a meeting of rank-and-file activists? They're having a meeting at a university where the Counterrevs hold power and there'll be a report on the Big Shot attack. Look, I see a poster announcing the meeting. Let's go. If we tell them that the Mediator is sheltering the brave warrior who attacked the Big Shot, they won't keep us out.

——I'm all for it, the Mediator announced with obvious fervor—I guess it was his chance to make up for his earlier disgrace. More to the point, since he was a practical man of action, he didn't forget to warn us. Just to be safe, I want you to remember that once we get inside the university, we can no longer rely on *our police* tailing us. . . . We're going to run into guys who were in that brawl—do you think they'll take Ms. Ōno and the Righteous Man for spies?

——They might gang up on us to settle the score, said the Righteous Man with a sidelong glance at Ōno and me. He was probably a bit concerned that we might have witnessed his own peculiar fighting style, ha, ha.

——I'll try to get in first so I can initiate contact with the steering committee of this meeting. As a Volunteer Mediator, I've put in appearances at plenty of meetings of both parties, so I shouldn't trigger an automatic rejection. I'm sure the worst they'd give me would be a diplomatic brush-off. If I run into someone who knows Mori's actually at the rehab center, then you can all march in.

——All right, Ōno said, we'll proceed on to the university at Ochanomizu.

——I've got to get inside before those plainclothesmen catch on. But if we just drive onto campus, *our police* won't be able to follow us, and might interpret that as an attempt to shake them. They could take more drastic measures against us.

The moment we signaled to turn at the Surugadai traffic light, indicating that we were going to the Ochanomizu Station, a dirt-encrusted subcompact Toyota conspicuously ran the red light and easily shot past us! Inside: the passive-aggressive pair who had visited my house this morning; Conciliatory at the wheel. And glaring at me from the rear window—my wife/*ex*-wife!

All I could see was the look of disbelief on her face as she turned around to say something to Coercive. The car tailing us cut sharply in front of us, forcing Ōno to brake as she tried to make the turn. That killed the engine. Three or four cars appeared out of nowhere, and almost smashed into us.

——Can't we just forget about turning here and get out?! I yelled.

But with the traffic jam and policemen nearby, there was no way we could change direction.

——The riot squad's crawling all over the place, and three police vans are parked over there. Do you expect me to commit a moving violation right in front of those bastards? Ōno yelled back at me. I wondered if the engine going dead on her had so thrown her that she actually believed the riot squad would handle a routine traffic violation.

——This meeting about the Big Shot must be quite sizable. The Mediator made this on-the-spot assessment at the very same moment that I informed Ōno,

——My wife was in that car with the two policemen.

She seemed to go blank for a split second; then, as if grasping the significance of my words—from what she already knew about my wife/ex-wife's threats—she realized we were in for a pretty sticky situation.

——What's she doing around here? What's she going to do?

——With or without the switchover, if my wife makes a scene, insisting that I'm her husband, the police will take me in for questioning for sure. I can't repeat in front of her the story I told those policemen at my house—you know, that I'm just a relative, and so on. I have a feeling she'll rant and rave that even though I may look like an eighteen-year-old, I'm the one she's after, that I've disguised myself. She may even try to pull my face off thinking it's a mask!

I'd hardly finished my sentence when we saw the police form a wide circle, surrounding the university's front gate. They were in battle formation. Even though our car was moving at a crawl, we were quickly closing the distance between ourselves and the police.

——Even if we break through, they'll catch us at the bridge ahead, the scriptwriter-to-be said with resignation.

However, the Righteous Man, who'd been holding his peace all this time, made the following suggestion.

——Stop the car right in front of the main gate. I'll get out and start a ruckus, protesting against those students who're handing out leaflets for the meeting! They totally disrupted our antinuke meeting, so if I get rough with them, they really can't say I'm provoking them for nothing! Once the commotion begins, the riot squad will move in, right? Grab the chance and get inside. . . .

——I'll go with you! You can't create a proper diversion all by yourself.

——No, no. I'll do it myself. I've got a reason to protest. Someone like you, who's a staunch practitioner of nonviolence and conciliation, what would you be doing resorting to violence without provocation? You're a Volunteer Mediator—don't you practice what you preach?

I watched the Righteous Man deliberately take his dentures out and,

perhaps as a precaution, put them in his khaki jacket. The car stopped
and the Mediator got out first. When he pushed the front seat forward,
the Righteous Man turned to me, his deep-set eyes peering back at me
with a strange expression, and mumbled something through his tooth-
less, shriveled mouth. He smiled at Ōno with a smile neither innocent
nor sheepish. Then, suddenly, he bent his body in a runner's crouch,
thrust his head forward, and took off at full tilt. I was still watching him
when the Mediator rushed up to me,

——What are you waiting for—you want your wife to catch you?

I felt something was about to happen. My mind in a whirl, I struggled
to get out of the car. A building stood beyond the gate, and next to its
open door a group of masked and helmeted people were assembled.
The Righteous Man must have shouted something at the top of his
lungs for they turned toward him almost as one. He stopped abruptly in
front of them, and, continuing to shout, began to hop and prance, his
arms flapping in the air. The Mediator ran toward the crowd and I
followed suit. We grabbed the gate post, the force of inertia spinning us
halfway around as we made an abrupt left toward a nearby courtyard.
The two policemen and my wife/*ex*-wife, who were on the lookout for
us, fell for the Righteous Man's trick, and moved a few steps in his
direction. That allowed us to slip into the campus unnoticed, smooth as
silk. But our running away from him made me feel a deep sense of
betrayal: there he was, hopping around, this time to avoid the blows of
the Counterrevs' security squad who overwhelmed him once they'd
caught on to his illegal entry into the campus, and were bludgeoning
him with iron pipes! As an escape artist, I'm unsurpassed, so I wasn't
outrun by the Mediator. However, that pair of policemen, the passive-
aggressive dyad, and my wife/*ex*-wife tried to block my way. I remembered the characteristic look in her eyes, a suggestion of something that
was weird and revolting, yet laughable—and it spurred me on to run
even faster. Overall, though, I noticed she looked distinctly wasted; the
black dress and gaudy scarf around her neck were sure, if sorry, evidence that she had at least resolved to start a new life.

I ran into the courtyard and hoped to cut through what I took to be
indifferent student bystanders. But one of them turned on me, and
before I knew it, I was on my back screaming with fear. It was as if my
wife/*ex*-wife's stony gaze had dealt me a punishing blow. The Mediator,
who also had wound up on the ground, turned his head toward me,
alarmed by my screams. There was only a split second to gauge the
intensity of that look before the big man who'd first tackled me began
kicking, first my head, then my abdomen, and even my testicles. Soon
his comrades, the helmeted, masked students at the gate, joined in a

throng around me. At this point, I would have taken anyone's help, even my wife/*ex*-wife's, ha, ha.

3

Now in captivity, the Mediator and I were dragged to a room occupied—legally or illegally, I never found out which—by the Student Council. All the kicks and blows must have done damage to my eyes because I had difficulty adjusting to whatever light was in the room. Sometimes it was the glare that hurt, sometimes it was the dimness. This condition intensified the weirdness of the room: not only the walls but the ceiling and floor were covered with writing. But first let me enumerate my physical impressions at becoming a captive, and then tell you what happened afterwards.

1. I was lying huddled up on the pavement of the courtyard as they kicked at me; my temples, stomach, and testes were especially good targets for their hard-rimmed tennis shoes. Even the roughnecks I fought off in my first teenage brawl had avoided going for the soft parts. This time it was different—I had to focus entirely on protecting myself. The way they were assaulting me triggered a memory of something very *graphic*. It was a scene from a Vietnam War newsreel. Physical violence is also a means of conveying a message, some scholar once observed with unnerving nonchalance. Is a certain level of violence to be expected then, according to this theory? Is it the "in thing" in this mass media age? The newsreel I was remembering showed a captured NLF soldier being savagely kicked by a South Vietnamese soldier; the prisoner's hands were tied behind his head, and he was forced to his knees. Whenever he moved his body forward to protect the side under assault, the South Vietnamese would quickly respond with a kick to that side. The victim knew how useless it was to curse or show any anger. The close-up of his face displayed clearly that he had no intention of appealing to anyone, and only felt disgust at the fact that his pain was visible. I'm sure my face must have mirrored that same pained expression, with my whole body numb from the shock of being thrown to the stone pavement as I waged my clumsy defense. If the perpetrator of such a situation is influenced by the prevailing level of accepted violence, mustn't the victim respond accordingly? With my dirty cheek pressed to the stone pavement, from the corner of my eye I caught sight of the Mediator being kicked by several people surrounding him. He bore the same expression as I did—and he's supposed to be used to such treatment.

2. As the Mediator and I were being dragged away, after our faces had been worked over and our bodies thoroughly kicked from head to toe, I wondered aloud, Wasn't this all just some weird, painful dream? What finally did me in was the fact that students standing around by the entrance of the building that bounded the courtyard went about their business as though nothing were happening. Some continued their stroll, others stopped to chat with friends. They all showed a total lack of interest in what was happening to us. This brought out another particularly vivid *visual* memory I had. Since hitting the pavement, the only thing I seemed able to use at will was my mind's eye. Was it taking the lead over other parts of my consciousness? What I remembered was a scene from a movie by Cocteau*—maybe the one with the screenplay written by Sartre? Anyway, a movie from *that* era. In a bucolic country-side setting, a motorcyclist from hell collects fresh dead bodies to take back to the underworld with him. How that matched the present scene, with those attractive students going about their mundane business in their multicolored outfits. This was all the more striking because compared with their technicolor existence, the attackers' and my world was monochromatic. We were "invisible humans." My tormentors who were trying to smash my testes were so confident of their own invisibility that they could proceed without batting an eye: I was terrified.

We were dragged into the aforementioned room covered floor to ceiling with writing. Thank God, my young eighteen-year-old testicles were still intact, ha, ha. The window latches were wired shut, the window panes covered over with plywood, and all other nooks and crannies sealed with duct tape. They made us sit down on two wooden chairs placed side by side in the center of the room. When had they ever found the time to set up such a secure detention cell?! Maybe it was a room for routine interrogations, but thinking about that was too depressing. We sat submissively in the chairs, barely able to breathe through our swollen noses. People kept traipsing in to gawk at us captives; the room got so crowded that twenty or thirty iron pipes propped up against one wall fell crashing to the floor. I heard myself and the Mediator scream simultaneously, **WWAAH!** My ears were bleeding. They say that in Renaissance Italy *they tortured you by simply showing you the instruments of torture;* our captors certainly *tortured us by simply showing the iron pipes.* We didn't even have enough energy left to stifle our **WWAAAH!**

---

*Jean Cocteau (1889–1963), French poet, playwright, graphic artist, and film director, was master of the enigmatic, dreamlike, poetic/political film. His movies dealt with the eternal, mythic role of the poet in a murderous society. He used the myth of Orpheus emblematically, setting the ancient legend in contemporary contexts, and building his powerful scene-imagery by combining and juxtaposing modern horrors—especially the Nazi variety—with primitive mythic terrors.

But evidently once they knew they had us in their clutches, their rough handling eased up a bit, and we were spared a high-class torture session; you know, where they poke you with iron pipes a few hundred times until your innards feel like shredded wheat but the outer skin shows no bruises. In other words, we were not ordinary prisoners, just suspects. This lucky break came about thanks to the words of the Mediator, which he conveyed through his "iron will" while being knocked around. Under the onslaught of blunt-edged soles to his temple, sides, and testes, he had somehow managed to say that I was a relative of the Big Shot's brave assailant, whom the Mediator was sheltering. Quite a guy. Watched intently by onlookers eagerly anticipating the next violence to be perpetrated on us, we were clearly prisoners, but at the same time we could pass for guests at a Big Shot Near-Annihilation Memorial Meeting.

Our silent audience hardly looked like Rev activists; rather, they seemed to have regressed to their infancy, full of passive anticipation of things to come. They all wore helmets and their faces were hidden under towels, leaving only their eyes and noses exposed. I couldn't tell which one of them had kicked me. After all, if you put thirty babies together, you really can't tell them apart, can you? Unless, of course, they're babies like *our children,* ha, ha. While I was rolling to and fro trying to dodge their kicks, I vowed that sooner or later they would get theirs. They may claim that they committed violence as members of an organization, but, I told myself, violence is perpetrated by the hand of an individual, so I'll even the score with that individual. I was burning with hatred to get back at them but I couldn't even remember the faces. A feeling of sadness fueled the pain in my numbed body.

Once the Mediator had communicated what he wanted to say, he seemed to have made up his mind not to utter another sound until his message had been properly passed on to the leadership and acknowledged with their reply: the roles had been reversed. He no longer persistently said what he had to say even while being kicked around. Once again I had to take my hat off to him for his prescience. I, too, had no intention of letting one word pass my cut, swollen lips. Silence was also the rule with the onlookers, who were prepared for any kind of festivity, be it a party to lynch a captured spy—that might begin any moment—or a celebration of brave warriors. Our captors looked pretty childish with their silent intensity, but I imagined that inside they must have felt smug over what they'd accomplished.

That doesn't mean this mute collection was not giving out a silent message: and what a stench, ha, ha. The cold late-afternoon air of an early spring wafted the atrocious odor through the enormous building.

Still, I couldn't help admiring them. With what feverish desire they are driven to wear themselves out, with no time even to wash their stinking bodies!

One Executive Committee member, who had elbowed his way through to us, was clearly turned off by the stench and didn't bother to hide his disgust. He was minus the towel and helmet get-up of the activist. He was pretty much a carbon copy of L, the low-level apparatchik, except he was a bit on the heavy side and of average height, and was soberly dressed in a coat. He sat down on a chair which had been placed in front of the Mediator and me, and, when he removed his specs to carefully wipe them off, his face took on a meditative look complete with knit eyebrows and a squint. And then, in a slow, measured, but husky voice, he spoke to the "Mediator."

——You, we know about. But, how about this young man? What is he to you? A disciple? . . . I should put the question to him directly. . . . Who are you? What have you got to do with *our fighters?*

The group behind us broke their silence with hoots (they had not even grunted while they kicked us!), as though his question was meant to be humorous. Their outrageously idiotic guffaws did it: I immediately made up my mind on what to do next. I'd keep on insisting that I was Mori's father, that the switched-over Mori was my comrade, and that I'd teamed up with him in his enterprise. I had a premonition that, if I couldn't manage to tell the truth about the switchover convincingly even to this petty official, if I made up a story that I was Mori's cousin or something just to get by, I'd never be able to fulfill the mission entrusted to the pair of us. How could I let those bastards get away with saying that Mori was *one of their fighters?* I was ready to tough it out.

——It's inappropriate for you to use the phrase *our fighter.* You don't have a clue as to who the Big Shot's assailant is, do you? Mori's and my whole life revolves around him. That's why I've named myself Mori-father. I've constantly relied on him. After all, I'm his father.

——Of course he's using father in the metaphoric sense, the Mediator broke in, his swollen lips clumsily forming the words. He sure likes to mediate. It must be in his blood.

——I'm not being metaphoric at all, I dismissed him brusquely. At this stage in our lives, Mori and I can't afford to use metaphoric language. We're in the post-switchover phase! In this new word, *switchover,* lies a prophecy that will spread the world over, for in it one can read the future of humankind! You who talk of revolution, take heed of this word. . . . Are you aware that the Big Shot's assailant is a twenty-eight-year-old man?

——You're talking gibberish. The interrogator, feigning befuddlement, paused long enough for those behind him to burst out laughing, and then continued. . . . After the successful attack on the Big Shot, we received a full report.

——You should know then that Mori was a twenty-eight-year-old man. I'm Mori's father in the body of an eighteen-year-old! And unless you understand those facts about the switchover, there can be no constructive dialogue!

——No thanks. We don't want any constructive dialogue. I'm just asking who you are. *Who are you?* We have other methods of finding out, but I'm sure you've seen enough shoe leather for the day, haven't you? Let's be *reasonable.* Who are you?

Rather than questioning me, the bastard was provoking the docile troops behind him, who would burst out laughing every time he paused.

——I'll repeat myself again. I'm Mori's father, and the one who attacked the Big Shot—with a girl friend whom I assume is a member of your party—is my son. I've meant to be *reasonable* from the start.

——You have to help us out. We're not too bright, you know. Let's go over the basics. You're eighteen, and your son twenty-eight? That means you were born when your son was ten; then how were you born? Did he have a hernia operation and you came out of one of his testes?

Unexpectedly something in my unconsciousness was thrilled by his comments. At that moment, I judged my interrogator, this thick-set, rather ordinary-looking man, to be playing the fool; he wasn't really thick-headed. I waited for the soldiers to quiet down from their outburst.

——I was once thirty-eight, the father of eight-year-old Mori. If you want to get the basics right, start with that. Then we had a switchover: I lost twenty years and Mori gained twenty. Simple arithmetic, right?

——Revolutionaries oppose all forms of discrimination, so far be it from me to show any prejudice. An "epileptic fit"?* You're not quite yourself? Naturally, as revolutionaries, we don't discriminate against mental cases, either. . . .

——Prejudice in this instance is not semantics, or some subconscious error in the choice of words, but the way one's active consciousness works. Take it from me, I've had some experience with discrimination. . . . What I want to clarify is very simple, if you have an open mind! Mori took a girl with him, one of your party members, on his first adventure. The attack on the Big Shot makes sense only in the context of carrying out the mission of the switchover. It has nothing to do with your aspiration to take a lead over the Counterrevs. Mori is not

*A pun on *tenkan,* "switchover," which is written with different characters.

one of your fighters! . . . You've never really been able to figure out the Big Shot, have you? You've announced that you're going to hold a celebration in honor of his assailant, but the truth of the matter is, even now you really don't know him. What is he to you and why did he have to be attacked? If you know it all, **WHY DIDN'T YOU TRY TO BEAT MORI TO IT?**

While I hammered at the interrogator with my opinions, I looked him straight in the eye—if you want to control a dog, don't move your eyes off his, they say, ha, ha. At first, the interrogator's pudgy little nostrils flared, but then, before I knew it, an icy indifference spread across his face as though he'd used polarized glass to sever the controlling contact of my eyes. It was an indifference to the brutality that could visit me any moment. With that silent cue, the easy laughter of those behind him transformed into a monolith of enmity, a rigid mass of tensed muscle reeking of an atrocious stench. They looked as though they were about to go for the iron pipes and inflict as much internal damage to our bodies as possible. At that moment the Mediator began to ply his talents.

——Don't provoke Mori-father, and quit working up these young-sters. It's true, Mori-father is a relative of the Big Shot's assailant. It doesn't matter if he has it in his head that he's something more, does it? Who cares as long as he'll be of use to the movement? . . . Yes, he'll be very useful. What's more, even if you somehow manage to bring Mori onto campus, you'll need Mori-father to interpret when Mori speaks at the meeting. He's the only one who can do it!

——Warrior-Mori has already arrived, the interrogator replied casu-ally. It does seem to affect the wound in his head when he tries to speak—I guess he needs someone to help him, to interpret for him. . . . Warrior-Mori carried out his duty and in the process overcame many difficulties, but he's very reticent about it all.

——**NO OBJECTION!** A thundering chorus arose from behind the interrogator, rattling the glass windows boarded over with plywood.

It struck me that this chorus of exhausted-looking soldiers was yelling much too loudly, in voices that were at once raucous and overbearing, yet somehow at the exact same time reluctant—the effect was unforgiva-bly vulgar! Besides, I couldn't stand the petty bureaucrat orchestrating these young people and using Mori so vulgarly; so——what eighteen-year-old impetuousness—although I was quite unsteady on my feet, I lunged for him!

——**GIVE BACK MY MORI!** I kept screeching. I won't let you call him *your fighter!* **GIVE MORI BACK!**

Where did I muster the energy to yell like that? The obnoxious bureaucrat's head, the target of my fist, suddenly dropped out of sight, and in its stead two identical-looking automatons instantaneously materialized on the spot, and knocked me across the room! The back of my head hit the plywood that covered one of the windows. I had just enough time to prove its effectiveness as a barrier before I crumpled to the floor. I didn't black out. I was still conscious enough to feel the pain, but I played possum just the same. The violence of these bastards had something prodigious in it, some powerful energy at its very source that allowed for no resistance other than a display of disgust, just as in the film footage of the Viet Cong prisoner in the Mekong Delta.

4

I maintained my mock state of unconsciousness. . . . I guess to an outsider it appeared exactly as though I was really out cold. Otherwise, I'm sure I'd have been forcibly revived by some rather cruel and persistent means, then put back under—beaten to death for real this time. But the Mediator's negotiations with the Revs made my little subterfuge possible. He accurately sized up the situation and immediately set to work. First he decided I was best left lying on the floor. Then he demanded that, as someone who had sheltered Warrior-Mori for a time, he be allowed to see him. He was escorted out of the detention room with the rest of the Rev group, who left only a babysitter behind.

Fresh blood from my ears and nose oozed over the caked blood of past wounds, making my head look like a heavily layered painting. My head lay on the floor, on soiled agitprop posters which stunk of ink and benzene. Without the posters, my babysitter would have noticed that I was paying close attention to where my battered head touched the floor. As if my physical pain were not enough, a fundamental doubt kept gnawing at my soul, a vision painted in dark red, a memory, albeit revised, of a biblical passage. "Before the cock crows, you will deny your switched-over self three times." The *you* refers to Mori, not me. I doubted him; he and the girl might have become buddy-buddy with that crowd who called him *our fighter,* and forgotten all about our switched-over mission!

My thinking up till now had been that Mori's attack on the Patron was his first step toward the fulfillment of our mission, and, to follow in his footsteps, I had proceeded to certain actions which landed me here on the floor, a beaten wreck. Wasn't everything I'd done just a one-man show? Did he attack the Patron as instructed only because in the girl he'd discovered a good sexual partner who could meet the needs of a switched-over twenty-eight-year-old body, and she expected something in return for her sexual favors? If, therefore, she then reported every-thing to her superiors immediately after the attack, it explained a lot of things.

If that's the case, we're way off track, diverging from the main plot of the switchover; Mori is injured, the subject of a police manhunt, and to make things worse, in blindly trying to keep up with Mori's *action*, I've fallen into a truly sad state of affairs. The way things're going, the switched-over pair might well break up without carrying out the man-date of the Cosmic Will.

The terror that I was hopelessly lost, suspended somewhere in utter darkness, was too much to bear, and I slowly blacked out. . . . Some-thing similar had happened to me once before. In the year following Mori's birth, on a scorching hot summer day, my wife/*ex*-wife was brief-ing me—I lay inert on the bed with my face buried in the spread—on what was in store for the infant, just as she'd heard it from the doctor. I had gradually passed out while listening to her. She realized something had gone wrong and repeatedly called my name, but I could not even move my sweaty arms, let alone turn my head toward her. I felt I was sinking deeper into a state of being more dead than death itself. When I think about it now, what forced my acceptance of that state—rather than surrender to death—was that tremendous sense of loss, the dread terror of dangling helplessly in the darkness. . . .

When I managed to open my eyes, I forced the rest of my facial muscles to rouse themselves although they still preferred to play dead and resist—I was now flat on my back; the bandaged head of a teary-faced Mori loomed before me. . . . My brain-computer, overloaded with impatience to regain consciousness, flashed a message in a beam of purplish light: "I remember the words you said to me, 'Before the cock crows today, you will deny your switched-over self three times.' I went outside and wept bitterly." Mori is so racked with tears, did he deny his switched-over self three times? Before the cock crowed?

Once my body and spirit passed beyond their comatose condition of deader-than-death, the neural pathways like newly repaired telephone lines resumed their normal communication, and I began to perceive in the tear-soaked face fixing its gaze on me that a fundamental act of purification was in process. That expunged the earlier suspicion gnaw-ing at me, clearing away the residue of its dross. Mori's switched-over body and spirit, now accustomed to their new condition, had taken on a gentle calmness. His gaze expressed the essence of both tranquility and clarity, yet at the same time could be interpreted as sorrow, pity, or even an attempt to placate. In the meantime I began to feel the infant me fighting back tears after a lonely, punishing walk in the night, now safely out of harm's way, and clutching the knees of my protector. I took a few deep breaths before those tears could become sobs and somehow kept myself under control.

When I'd regained enough presence of mind to be able to look around, I found myself sprawled on my back on a desk with Mori's girl friend, who wore a distressed look on her face, wiping off the blood and dirt from my body. The Mediator—it was obvious from his demeanor that *he was no longer a captive*—poked his head out from behind the vigilant Mori.

——The Righteous Man is dead! Whether it was murder or some sort of accident, we don't know, but **HE IS DEAD**! he informed me bluntly.

——You don't know whether he was murdered or died in an accident? **YOU'RE BEING SO VAGUE!** I immediately shot back; I meant to sound forceful but my voice, still suffering from the effects of its deader-than-death coma, sounded like a six-year-old brat's.

——But . . . that's the only way I can put it! . . . They let him out to go to the bathroom and he bolted. Detention had weakened him but he was still the old pro of one hundred antinuke demos. The guards chased him but they never even got close, he just kept on running. And then, they told me, there was this beam of light shining right on him as he clambered up the concrete wall at the back of the university. The party chasing him—by then it had ballooned to fifty—tried to yell a warning to him **AAAHHH!** because it's an eight-meter drop to the JNR* tracks on the other side of the wall. As though pressed to go on by the voices yelling **AAAHHH**, he crossed the barbed wire, glancing back over his shoulder as he did so, and with a shout of **AAAHHH**, he just disappeared.

The Mediator stopped short; his eyes narrowed to slits, mist swirling in the vortex behind his specs, the tip of the triangle of his nose trembling, he sobbed as if in a coughing fit. At that moment I knew that Mori's tears were also meant for the Righteous Man.

——**WHAT A SCREW-UP!** I shouted as I began weeping bitterly. *The Shikoku antinuke leader fell to his death off that wall in some back alley of a university. It wouldn't make any sense to his people back home! What he tried to accomplish blew up in his face. All screwed up,* **WHAT A SCREW-UP!** I croaked once, twice, like a frog with a coughing fit.

——No use crying like that. What a dead person screws up, the survivors have to undo, right? The girl sounded cool, but it was obvious

*The Japanese National Railroad (recently renamed JR).

from her militant statement that the Righteous Man's death had frightened her.

As I lay with my eyes closed, I could feel reverberating through my innards the unspoken words Mori sent out in response to her via the hand that touched my side. It was just like way back when the pre-switchover Mori used to groan sounds that never formed words, but when his fat little fingers danced over my body they sent out electromagnetic waves, and I understood everything he was saying to me. *That's it, screwing things up is no good. But why's it no good? Because the survivors are forced to live with an icy loneliness and terror. It's like being struck by gale-force winds howling and whipping by the hill separating the netherworld from the world of the living. There is a Shinto prayer about a woman who dies, and when she reaches the boundary hill of the nether world, she thinks back on a troublesome child she left behind; soul-freezing loneliness and terror assault her, forcing her to turn back to look at the world of the living. When I think about the ancient poet who composed that prayer, I recognize that soul-freezing cold whipped through the world in those times as well. But we don't live in his historic time, when a communal society existed. We live in a world which is fragmented, alienated, disintegrating. This is our number one problem. We can't keep on screwing things up. We've got to rebuild, restore, reintegrate the world. Shouldn't we strive to do just that?*

——How long do you want to play dead, Mori-father? the girl said laying a clean shirt upon my chest. You can't communicate with the dead that way.

But I had communicated with a live Mori right beside me, via the hand that touched my body. As I sat up to get off the desk, I felt a sharp pain in my head, as if it were about to be torn off at the base of the neck, but the aching in my joints was beginning to ease up. Remember, I've got the body of an eighteen-year-old, ha, ha. While I put on the shirt, I kept an eye on the open door and saw several soldiers leaning against a wall in the hallway, dimly lit by a single naked bulb. There they were, two-dimensional paper dolls stuck to the wall. I blinked hard at the light. My battered left eyelid was swollen completely shut, so I could only see with my right eye, depriving me of any depth perception.

——So, what are we going to do? What am I expected to do? Stay here, a hostage without purpose?

——Mori's going to report on the Big Shot attack, and we want you to relay his message!

——You mean I'm going to interpret Mori's words on stage for the same bastards who've beaten me up? What a thrill!? . . . However, I'll do it under two conditions. Make sure my wife/*ex*-wife won't sneak into the meeting. If we don't keep her out, she'll raise hell. There'll be no trouble picking her out. She'd look out of place at any party meeting.

——That was the woman at the front gate, the one with the police, right? I'll inform the Organizing Committee right away, the girl said and stepped into the hallway. She was flaunting the fact that she was the only one who could come and go as she pleased.

——What's the other condition? the Mediator said with concern in his voice.

——Before relaying Mori's ideas to those murderers, I want to tell them what the mathematician-activist Righteous Man was really like.

The Mediator, who'd been overcome with grief as he reported the death of the antinuke leader, objected immediately when I said this.

——If you start with something like that, they won't listen to Mori's story. Then they'll move in on us and we'll both be put up before a kangaroo court. . . . And why do you have to talk about the Righteous Man? Do you think you'll be able to convince them that he was a great man, that they shouldn't have killed him? Besides it's their meeting. . . . Now, whatever I've done so far may seem fanatical, but it's my job to argue that every activist's life is irreplaceable. So, based on many failures. . . .

How could an inexperienced eighteen-year-old resist all that? I pledged myself to follow his counsel. But don't think that my feelings toward the Righteous Man were diminished by my fit of weeping either. By dying in such a screwed-up way, he'd been borne aloft into the sky above our heads like some visionary kite! He'd often spoken ideologically of the holes that blast through toward the *Family*. I wasn't quite sure what he meant then, but it makes more sense now when I superimpose his ideas on the vision of him as a flying kite. Couldn't I say that he risked his life for that bizarre ideology? It would be some time, I felt, before I broke free from all that the kite signified. And I trembled with a strange thrill, as though I'd just discovered yet another meaning to the switchover. All because his death was a ridiculous screw-up.

9

The Switchover Pair
Analyzes the Future

1

The speech that night, made with my body serving as a combo amplifier/speaker, reproduced and even boosted the static which Mori's spirit broadcast. In return, **THEIR** voices creeping forward in unison like an earth tremor, alternating **NO OBJECTION** with **BULL-SHIT**, assaulted Mori and me. Resisting them with all his might, the near-silent Mori transmitted hardly perceptible signals to me; yet his are the real speaker's words to be recorded, and you, the ever-silent one, will write them all down. And I—alone on that stage, shouting at the top of my lungs till my throat turns raw and all the joints in my body throb with pain—will vanish along with the disappearing sound waves of my voice.

Well, it doesn't matter. I'm the one who created this ghostwriter set-up. Still, just for the record, as far as my speech goes, capture the characteristic bombast of an eighteen-year-old; I want my real voice to ring out loud and clear. I'll reproduce the speech here on tape, and send you the cassette. You know the rest: Just transcribe the speech as we've agreed.

* * *

I, the ghostwriter, have transcribed here the contents of the tape mailed to me by Mori-father. All I cut were the undecipherable asides,

181

repetitions, rewordings, mistakes, and self-corrections on the tape—in other words, the obvious coping and compensation mechanisms for someone embarrassed at recording himself. A ghostwriter's style might influence this pruning process. If Mori-father, who is preoccupied with capturing *his real voice that night*, objects that accuracy is sacrificed when the scribe's style is merged with that of the taped speech, my response is this: Isn't the anticipation of the ghostwriter's style and presence equally distorting to Mori-father's own speech? Doesn't he read each installment of the tape transcripts with that in mind, and on that basis move along in his narration? If so, that tendency should show up in this taped speech. Conversely, as I put Mori-father's words on paper, I detect his influence on my scribbling hand, the extension of my body and spirit.

The voice reproduced on the tape was no doubt that of the post-switchover Mori-father; it had a disconcertingly squeaky, childish quality about it as though he really had become a young teenager. I had a suspicion that as the switchover continued to progress, he was regressing in age to the time when one's voice cracks. But, it turned out the squeak had something to do with a bad motor in the tape recorder. How could he, an engineer, overlook such a noticeable problem? Wasn't it just a scheme of his to use a squeaky voice to shock the ghostwriter? What's more, the speaker taped two different voices on his recording. I'll distinguish Mori's speech from Mori-father's.

* * *

Greetings, ladies, gentlemen, and all of you struggling resolutely at your party's work. In the cosmic view of humankind, those who don't give their all to the struggle are nothing more than empty shells. Now you can't hold a lifeless shell in high regard, can you? We do not wish to venerate emptiness. We can only truly esteem the living. So it is only natural that, from every corner of the universe, the Cosmic Will focuses attention on this planet. Because this is where the struggles of the living are sustained. We salute you! Unfortunately, however, we're not yet able to exchange greetings with others in the universe. We are still sadly incapable of recognizing messages from another struggling being in the universe. It's a tragedy that we are unable to reciprocate!

We also send greetings to all of you in the opposition party who are struggling resolutely to carry out your party's work. We salute you!

BULLSHIT? Why? If greeting one party is sound practice, then it is just as sound to send salutations to the opposition party, isn't it? Well-grounded theory is common to both parties. And if our greetings to you are bullshit, then why get upset over our sending the same bull to your enemy? Why are you booing us? What idiotic heckling! You mean the **MEDIATOR'S ATTEMPTS AT CONCILIATION ARE BULLSHIT?** Actually, I would second the criticism of peace mongering. The only true advancement of struggle is continual radicalization! But dismissing him as merely a peace monger is rather shallow. You still have a lot to learn.

You must take up arms! All of you! Kill each other! Use what, in the cosmic view, are the most humane weapons available to men: the cudgel, the lead pipe, and the crowbar! Factional violence is a symbolic act that expresses the essence of the real revolution. As this phase of factional violence moves even closer to the moment of true revolution, you will be even more thorough in maiming and murdering each other! After you've killed your parents, what recourse is there but to turn on your brothers? Wouldn't it be more efficient to reverse the order and kill each other off first? From the cosmic view, it's perfectly transparent. After you've killed your brothers and sisters, you'll need an energy boost to finish off your parents. After all, if they beat off your attack before you can deliver the coup de grâce, how'll you proceed on to revolution? The fratricidal will of those killed in a revolution possesses those who survive! Revolution is the survivor's obligation to those he has struck down!

FRATRICIDE AND COUNTERREV HOOLIGANISM ARE TWO DIFFERENT THINGS, did you say? How different? How is killing your brother any different from killing an enemy? How is a party inquisition different from a lynch mob? They're both homicidal acts of petty bureaucratic violence. What Mori is talking about is a symbolic model, from the cosmic viewpoint, that penetrates through to the core truth of humankind's existence. Imagine a pair of incomparably brilliant brothers walking congruent paths toward the future of humankind. As long as the brothers are two separate beings, it's rather meaningless for them to *live exactly the same life,* isn't it? But what if a fusion of the two brothers could be achieved for the sake of improving the human model? All that has to occur is the division of each body and spirit in half, and then their recombination into one new being. Let's suppose medicine and biology reach a level where they can overcome every subtlety of tissue rejection and successfully reconstruct these brothers, such that the resultant "older brother fused with the younger brother" and the "older brother combined with the younger brother" are each able to live on their own. But, if they keep to earthly life's precepts, seriously, fratricide between these newly assembled brothers must follow. Is there another choice? What if these two brothers are actually "chosen ones"—constitutionally strong enough to survive the reconstructive surgery performed for the good of humankind's ultimate revolution. Even taking a cosmic perspective, you don't often find an act as obvious as fratricide signifying an opportunity to open up the future of humankind. Or do you? This mode of symbolic action can be traced back to antiquity. Remember the three legendary brothers, the Princes Hoderi, Hosuseri, and Hoori, and how the two truly revolutionary ones were pitted against each other in the roles of fisherman and hunter? Why did those two so vehemently oppose a reconciliation that only required them to exchange tools? Why did the younger of the two have to travel to the sea god's palace, there tearfully to recount the hapless loss at sea of a hook borrowed from his older brother? Why did the sea god then bestow on the younger brother great magical powers, causing the older brother such destitution and despair that he mounted a suicidally courageous attack against his more fortunate sibling? His defeat was terrible, and he was drowned. But why? And why must his descendants, the Hayato tribe, according to legend, be forever condemned to reenact that battle, defeat, and drowning, as a symbolic act carried over from antiquity to the present—and on into the future!

We must analyze the current conditions prevailing throughout the universe with a view to how to triumph in this ultimate revolution-as-fratricide, and how a revolutionary who has killed off his brothers, sisters, even his own father, can avoid becoming the next patricide in line. For us earthlings, eternity—that is to say, perpetually changing revolutionary time—has no reality! Nor is there a time now for a new revolution to arise and overthrow the new Stalinism! We have been living in history at a leisurely pace, one so slow, in fact, that we actually waited until Stalin's death before we even attempted the next phase in the revolutionary process. But there isn't time left now even for a Great Cultural Revolution. Becoming freed from an earth-bound revolutionary perspective is essential if the final phase of humankind's ultimate revolution is to be achieved within the next few years. Since we have been switched over by the Cosmic Will, we believe we have an obligation to talk about a cosmic revolutionary outlook!

If you really think about it, haven't you sometimes felt yourself in contact with something that stirs your body and soul in a cosmic direction? For instance, take the time when Americans stepped out of the lunar module onto the moon. Think of Nixon, later forced out of the presidency under intense pressure after his vile and ludicrous stonewalling, who stood mouthing high-sounding pronouncements about world peace and harmony as if the week of the lunar landing were the greatest seven days in world history since Creation. Weren't you caught up then in a sort of maddening premonition? What if the astronauts had set up a plastic dome on the moon's surface, and built a little bonfire using an oxygen canister. . . . Couldn't the tongues of that flame, shooting upwards, have set off respondent bonfires inside moon craters? Couldn't moon beings, little virus-sized lunar ticks, have mustered all the technology at their disposal into their minifires, "in reciprocation?" Couldn't that have been an opportunity to exchange cosmic good will, using bonfire diplomacy? Couldn't humankind have begun the process of understanding the secrets of the universe? After all, didn't earthlings launch their lunar mission in search of a connection with the cosmic order, some spark that might set off humankind's ultimate revolution? Was your maddening premonition on that day experienced in vain? Don't all of you have a soul, attuned to the real revolution . . . and the moon . . . ?

What? **QUIT YAMMERING ABOUT THE MOON?** You're knocking yourselves out screaming **BULLSHIT** or **NO OBJECTION**; this screechfest may have some meaning to you guys, but it communicates nothing to us. Except, one of you just yelled out a cry at the top of your lungs that is the most significant response since this speech began: **QUIT YAMMERING ABOUT THE MOON!?** That goes way beyond the consciousness of the individual who did the yelling! Don't you see that Mori talked about the moon to elicit just that kind of outcry? If all you can do is to let your body and spirit meander around the earth meaninglessly, like the sound of your **BULLSHIT** or **NO OBJECTION,** Mori's words will never reach you! But if your body and spirit are open to the cosmic flow, even the tiniest of anxieties buried inside you as a creature of the cosmos is bound to surface, much the way frost spires rise up off the warm earth. Have you forgotten that the planet called Earth is an integral part of the universe? Lift up your eyes! Lift your eyes to the heavens! Isn't **QUIT YAMMERING** the anxiety-ridden outpouring of one who actually wants to lift up his eyes? Come on, one more time, somebody, I wish you'd give me another **QUIT YAMMERING!** The meaning of what Mori's saying can only be bridged when the buds of a cosmic connection are engendered. Without those buds, no matter how hard I try as an intermediary, I can't convey his meaning. **QUIT YAMMERING ABOUT THE MOON!?** There, this time you were laughing when you shouted it, but a sheepish grin floated across your face, masking your own anxiety about being on the verge of cosmic connection.

What was the attack on the Big Shot all about? It was simply part of a larger, ongoing plan to confront him with a basic problem. The operation's first phase delivered a blow, in the hope that he would feel his encroaching death. If he gets rattled about his imminent death, he'll certainly try with one fell swoop to complete the project for which he has risked everything. That means we've reached the second phase of the struggle. If we can successfully maintain the fight, then we can foil his plan. What is his plan? It concerns the whole of humankind, and revolves around the type of leader who tries to rule everyone except himself. Every last vestige of the Big Shot's project must be eradicated!

Did you say, **YOU ARE SO SIMPLE-MINDED**? Do you regard the higher order of complex ideas as simple-minded just by virtue of their being expressed in simple terms? Even you revolutionaries!? When simple words distill a deeper complexity can they become powerful instruments? Do you mock Lenin or Mao for using words that are too simple? In the history of humankind, what more vital and complex subject is there than the relationship between the ruler and the ruled? To overthrow the institution of the rule of men by men—isn't that revolution? Are you trying to escape your own terror of the task by drastically reducing all that is implicit in the complex semantic structure of the word *revolution*? Isn't the truth of the matter that you are terrified of the power of the very word, *revolution*, precisely because it's so simple a concept? Mori expresses himself in truly simple terms which cut through the complexity of everyday life. And the straightforward meanings of his simple words convey the Cosmic Will's message to humankind!

Specifically, how does the Big Shot intend to implement his version of the rule of men by men? With A-bombs. Two A-bombs are to be secretly produced by two small political groups. The role you were given by him is to make one of the two bombs. The factional violence to which you all have so faithfully devoted yourselves was part of his plan.

Did you say, **NO, THAT WASN'T FACTIONAL VIOLENCE**? I'd say in making an A-bomb, in your efforts to eliminate your opposition, your role in his plan has definitely gone beyond the bounds of factional violence. Your party's secret task force—with some God-awful name or other—seeks out targets, tails them, corners them, and eliminates them, based on information provided by its own intelligence network, in accordance with its own code of behavior. The death toll has already climbed to thirty or forty. Three or four hundred have been severely injured. Since that's all a matter of revolutionary principled fratricide, I won't criticize you on that count. Sharpen your butchery all you want! But what did you—or, perhaps the opposition party—achieve going to such lengths to advertise rather than conceal the killings? The mass media just helped the violence snowball. It makes no difference which group spread the news. You advertised your justification for the killings, and promoted your meticulous planning and determination, and the Counterrevs denounced the brutality and tragedy of the murders. **AND VICE VERSA!** Meanwhile, all the general public actually absorbs is the tragedy and brutality, nothing else! The effect is terrorizing. And it has snowballed, settling over our society until it too may induce mass hysteria. I don't know what kind of headway you've made in manufacturing the bomb, but you and the Counterrevs have certainly accomplished the public's education in terror!

And it's the Big Shot who's seen your splendid accomplishments in this arena for what they are! Just think of it, in downtown Tokyo, one or two A-bombs will be manufactured by private individuals. Right away, they'll start advertising the fact that they have the bombs, and the blackmailing of the general public will commence. No matter whether you or the Counterrevs become the first A-bomb party, or both of you go nuclear, your nuclear strategy will inevitably require some sort of public announcement. The result? A demand for the total evacuation of Tokyo and its environs. And that intimidating course of action would sound even worse given the education of the public in your past brutality. In other words, your announcement would be received with the public's preconceived notion of your party's capacity to commit every kind of atrocity. The guaranteed escalation of prepackaged mass hysteria in the targeted areas would allow evacuations on a mass scale. In any case, I'm sure this part of the publicity campaign would have to be well rehearsed. Of course, not everyone will manage to leave before the final stage of the campaign, when detonation of the nuclear device will become unavoidable. Firefighters in particular must remain behind. And you can't cut off all the electricity in the city as long as there are seriously ill patients left behind; this will increase the potential for fires caused by short circuits in deserted houses. The police must also stay behind, because looters will be sure to break into abandoned houses. Evacuations on such a grand scale would require police patrols of the affected areas. But what kind of police force, what size? I'm sure your war council, when it moves in after the evacuation, will discuss that issue with the government crisis team. But one thing is sure: the government will use the same riot squads that have always carefully regulated your political demonstrations. If too many squad members refuse to follow orders, saying they don't want to do their job in a place where a handmade A-bomb may or may not explode, the situation could get quite complicated. The government crisis team would use this as an excuse to call out the Self-Defense Corps. How to negotiate, or even better, how to prevent this mobilization would be the first time you could really show your stuff. I strongly advise you to improve your rhetorical techniques for that moment.

Let's say the nuclear blackmailers were able to persuade the government to leave behind only a handful of people—the police force, plus the bare minimum for firefighting and medical transportation. That would probably be the opportune time for civilian suicide squads organized by the right, and various vigilante groups, to infiltrate the Metropolitan area. Chances are even apolitical teenage motorcycle gangs would show up for some action. Self-Defense Corps commando units would also probably pick this time to sneak in, either disguising themselves as part of the revolutionary blackmailing unit or the regular government forces. The so-called police would probably take care of some of those violators, but how would you handle the situation? That's when your reputation as combat-hardened street fighters could pay off!

I can just see it. A combat unit of the nuclear blackmailers, notorious for its ruthlessness, would patrol the city in commandeered cars. The Revs' flag and the registration numbers issued by your war council would be clearly on display. When they come across firefighters, police, or Red Cross vehicles, nothing will happen. But when they run into the suicide squads, street fighting will immediately erupt. During the ensuing firefight, the frightening reputation that you and the Counterrevs have built up about yourselves will precede you, shaking the enemy's morale and resolve. You and the Counterrevs will be the most formidable civilian fighting forces since Meiji times! Small-time gangsters and the Yakuza are just a big joke in comparison.

Three weeks into the occupation of the city, all the stray dogs and cats left behind, even the rats whose source of garbage has been cut off by the flight of the city dwellers, will feel emboldened enough to take over the streets. Terrible hunger together with their keen instinct to size up their prey would make them cocky; their well-chosen attacks would begin on those people remaining in the city. Then you, or a Counterrev attack unit, will have to launch a counterattack on these vermin. Remember in the old days how both of your assault units used to call anyone you attacked vermin; and not only that, the way you beat them up and even killed them was like torturing and killing small animals. I bet you'd find those past experiences extremely helpful in the mop-up operation against the street animals. Each of these scenarios, by the way, is anticipated and detailed in the Big Shot's plan.

2

Now, how in the world can we avoid a head-on collision with the Big Shot's quest for domination of his fellow man? As long as the main orientation of our switched-over body and spirit is geared toward his overthrow, a clash between his program and the whole structure of our switchover is bound to take place. He is planning to rule not just us, but the entire human race; how can a clash be avoided? No matter what, even if we end up dead, we must, as switched-over beings, become leaders in the destruction of Big Shot A's plan to rule all humankind. We will do it!

What did you just say? Did you say, **WE DID IT** . . . or did I hear, **IDIOT** . . . ? Your groaning sounded weird, and it sure came across like you said, **IDIOT.** That's the second meaningful message I've heard today in your chorus of groans. You know the symbol for the character *yurodivyi*,* Dostoevski's religious fanatic?! I thought that's what you were calling Mori and me. What a scare. But it sure woke me up! Not that I've been standing up here half asleep, shouting my lungs out. It's just that I've been punched and kicked so much today that, as I transmit Mori's words, I feel my body and spirit weakening by the minute, as if they were full of holes and every bit of energy was seeping out of me!

That term *idiot, yurodivyi*, jolted me awake, but right way I realized that I wasn't hearing you right, that instead I was receiving a message from the Cosmic Will! Psychologists—and their patients for that matter—are always making slips of the tongue, taking every opportunity to say what's really on their minds. Wait a minute, the Cosmic Will has just thrown some light on our special relationship with society, between our switched-over selves and the societal Other. Our switched-over state has revealed our innate fervor, which happens to converge with your own revolutionary goals. A word of warning. You've rejected what we've been yelling about as lunacy, but if you start denying us our passion about our beliefs, we'd find the course of your revolution very questionable indeed! Wouldn't you say our role as switchovers is the same as that of Dostoevski's religious fanatic? People treated him like a pariah, but they didn't eliminate him. So, if you're tempted to drag us off the stage and soften us up a bit with iron pipes, please take what you've heard only as the warnings of the Religious Fool. Control yourselves, ha, ha! Of course, I don't for a minute doubt Mori's sanity as I transmit what he's saying. We're only trying to put ourselves in your shoes!

In his plan to dominate all humankind, the Big Shot brought in an A-bomb, which he has hidden somewhere in the Metropolitan area to blackmail the government. Don't you think it's only fitting that his rather grandiose ambition has demanded nothing less than the most powerful weapon on earth? But, what's his reason for picking you, the Revs, and your opposition as surrogate blackmailers of the government and manufacturers of A-bombs? Have you ever given a thought to that, discussed it among yourselves? Why is it the Big Shot, whose ends always justify his means, has provided you funds for the production of an

---

*In the original Japanese, the author engages in wordplay on several levels, auditory and visual as well as literary/historic. He uses the word *yoroshii*, meaning "agreed" literally in Japanese, which resembles *yurodivyi*, the identification for a Dostoevsky character known in English by the title of Dostoevsky's novel *The Idiot*. Dostoevsky's "idiot" (Prince Lev Nikoalevich Mishkin, the central character of the novel) is not an "idiot" as we understand the word in modern American usage. He is more properly understood to be "God's fool"—a sweet, unhappy, saintly being who figures reverentially in the folk mind in many cultures. The term signifies a person of childlike innocence, often given to fits and seizures, sometimes exhibiting physical deformity, but sometimes very beautiful, incapable

A-bomb, and promises you even more money is forthcoming? First of all, it goes without saying that he rates your scientific know-how very highly. But that's all relative. You're not the first to develop a nuclear bomb. And besides, you're using nuclear fuel that's been refined elsewhere. What's more, you don't need a complex bomb. All that's needed is one simple bomb that can be made in an underground factory. I'm sure those of you who dropped out of physics during the demonstrations on college campuses, already have enough scientific and technical information to make one bomb. And with the kind of financial clout he has, it would be very easy for him to round up other ex-students outside the Party. The real reason behind his selection of the Revs and the Counterrevs over others is that, as Mori-father said earlier, through use of the mass media both parties have impressed the public with their commitment to resort to any means to achieve their goals. That's the quagmire you've created with all your assaults and murders. Let's take a look at the real potential for a group such as yours, or the Counterrevs to blackmail the government, and Tokyo's residents by the manufacture and possession of an A-bomb. Blackmail can become ineffective for the following reasons. Number one. The blackmailed targets harbor doubt over the blackmailer's resolve to detonate the bomb which will destroy themselves, the city, everything. Number two. The residents completely ignore the threat because they have no idea, or don't want to imagine, what a real A-bomb explosion is like, or they oppose the government's crisis team which has given in to the blackmailers. If these factors converge to create an opposition force, organizing a large-scale evacuation would be out of the question. Large-scale evacuation will only be possible if the latent energy of mass hysteria inside the residents triggers an avalanche. At this point the government, which was pretending to be in confusion, will try to capitalize on this situation to negotiate with the blackmailers.

But none of those potentialities for failure are operating with the two groups the Big Shot has picked for his plan. They've already proved themselves capable of anything in the long-standing murderous struggle for their political goals. Let's face it, for political gain you and the Counterrevs will do anything, maim or kill anyone, including detonating a nuclear blast! This information penetrates most effectively into the minds of those who don't use their imagination. The way such people see it, you and the Counterrevs set the stage for the Big Shot's project, assiduously applying yourselves day and night to killing or wounding each other, vacillating between extremes of terror and gallantry.

What do you mean **BE SERIOUS!?** I'm talking dead serious, no-nonsense stuff here, about casualties from your own party and the Counterrevs! And what's more, we've just today lost one of our own comrades. Do you think we'd kid around about something like that? The only reason

---

of sin of any kind, gifted with precognition and prophesy, and serving a community as a kind of human divining rod; the "idiot" or "fool" experiences natural, spontaneous commune with the supernatural through a pristine channel. The intended resonances with Mori-son are strong.

we're not denouncing you for his murder is that there's really nothing we can do but resign ourselves to his death, accept it as something which unavoidably came out of The Big Shot's larger plan. Isn't that true?!

Whichever of the blackmailers succeeds first in reaching stage one, that is, in developing and manufacturing an A-bomb, then that group assumes control of the blackmailing of the whole Metropolitan area. But how will the Big Shot's plan to dominate humankind unfold then? **SCRIPT NUMBER ONE**: *In case there is an accidental detonation of a bomb because of a blunder made by the blackmailers during negotiations with the government, or if there's a nuclear suicide blast, will his investment have been unprofitable? No. The social flux brought on by a colossal release of nuclear energy is not disadvantageous to him. He certainly knows and remembers how our country's defeat in the war produced conditions very advantageous to him! Besides, once the possession of a nuclear bomb is announced, and until the nuclear blast takes place—except perhaps for some minor foul-ups in the early stages of the blackmail campaign—there will be a moratorium on all action. Faced all of a sudden with a no-choice situation, how can the city residents and the government leaders—who by this time have inevitably grown* **TYRANNICAL**—*seize the initiative swiftly?*

But the Big Shot, who all along has been gathering the necessary intelligence, will be in a position to tackle the situation with speed and accuracy. First of all, he will pass his intelligence information to high government officials and inform them that the nuclear threat is for real, and that the manufactured bombs have enormous power. He will then recommend that a swift evacuation be carried out. The problems of how one maintains a functioning government and provides shelter for the evacuees, and so forth, will all have been carefully researched and planned for by his own intelligence gatherers, so he will become a very powerful consultant to the government. Then there's the question of how best to transfer the Imperial Family. The solution with the most effective public relations value for the Family would be to evacuate them together with the metro residents. And what about the nuclear blast itself? The third A-bomb explosion experienced by the Japanese. . . . In the midst of the chaos, just as after the defeat in the war, the Big Shot could easily assume the new title of Great Defender of the Family!

. . . As a middle-aged man prior to my switchover, I had a long association with the Big Shot. But the man who showed me what was really going on in the relationship between him and the *Family* was the man you murdered, the mathematician and antinuke leader from Shikoku. I wonder, do you ever think about what the person you're about to kill is thinking? Do you ever try to see through his eyes the real world that includes you as assailants? **BULLSHIT?** Is that all you can say?! Are you sure it's all right just to pay lip service to self-expression without giving a thought to what you're shouting about? **I SHOULDN'T CRY?** Fine, that's a lot better, it reflects what you really want to say. What do you mean, **KEEP MY MOUTH SHUT**? No way, man! I'm a transmitter of Mori's message. Haven't you all come here to receive his message? **WE DON'T NEED YOUR WORDS,** eh? Well, that's right, you don't need my words. It's Mori's words you need; that's why I'm serving as an intermediary!

SCRIPT NUMBER TWO: In case a settlement is reached between the nuclear blackmailers and the government, how will the Big Shot accommodate this with his plan? Let's take a look at two separate scenarios, one in which a single A-bomb is produced, and the other in which the two rival factions each produce a bomb. In reality the difference between the two cases would be evident only in the beginning because both cases ultimately achieve the same end. Suppose both of the rivals manage to have a bomb at the same time, each proclaiming that they've hidden them inside the city, and each proceeding with their blackmail operations. As they occupy the Metropolitan area, under the protection of "their" bombs—they wouldn't of course use them—they seize every conventional weapon they can get their hands on and attempt to annihilate their rivals. The form the ultimate revolution will take in its battle against counterrevolution—it's the same no matter what the party—will be an unprecedented level of street fighting, a super bloodbath, until one side completely destroys the other! Even in the event that only one of the parties succeeds in producing a bomb, as soon as that party breaks the news, the other party is sure to take to the streets anyway, to fight for the revolution against the counterrevolution. Whoever wins will continue the black-mail strategy with their own bombs or the one they've seized—or with both of them. **SCRIPT NUMBER ONE** *also allows for the possibility of one party getting cornered in the fighting and rather than surrendering to the counterrevo-lution and entrusting it with the future, will opt to blow themselves up with a bomb. The Big Shot's direct intervention will probably become evident only when, as provided for in* **SCRIPT NUMBER TWO**, *a bomb is controlled by the party which has succeeded in annihilating its opponent, and the blackmailing moves on to its next phase.*

You and your rival's strategy of fighting a revolutionary war by nuclear blackmail is no longer aimed against some local governor or even against the national Japanese government as a whole. It also targets America and Korea, who have a military alliance with Japan. It's natural for you to have picked the Japanese government to negotiate with, but you must admit that the nuclear blackmailers will stand to benefit as well by allowing the Big Shot who's got enormous influence in the American and Korean political worlds, to pull the strings. In other words, everybody will be expecting him to make his appearance. That is how the revolutionary war with nuclear blackmail will necessarily un-fold. But you must be prepared for the danger that at any moment he will turn the tables in his favor, accumulating even more political power in his hands with the explosion of an A-bomb or the shedding of your blood in the streets. And with the increased power he keeps accumulating, he will prepare to blast holes through toward the Family sitting atop the power structure of Japan. Rather than having a revolutionary plot gone nuclear, you'll have a counterrevolution which uses those same nuclear weapons as a lever to carry out a downright reactionary war of restoration. Once that's started, you have no idea how much easier it becomes to wrap things up over all of Japan! A revolutionary war should only be started after you've clearly seen what the relationship is between us and the Family!

I can hear genuine aspiration in your snarling **HOW ABOUT A RIOT, A PEOPLE'S UPRISING?** By conducting terrorist acts against your opposition, you have not only lost members but also severed ties with any organization that tried to team up with you in the struggle. None of the existing left-wing parties, let alone labor unions, will respond to your call for an uprising. Even if a faction of labor union members who're still allied to your party tries to launch a wildcat strike, as long as a nuclear-based revolutionary war is actually going on, every fat-ass executive will be on red alert, and no splinter group will have a chance to get anywhere. What about a spontaneous riot by the unorganized masses? We're talking over 15 million people in the Tokyo metropolitan area driven to a pitch of uncontrollable fear and rage, expecting to be annihilated at any minute by an A-bomb, picturing the assets they leave behind reduced to piles of radioactive ash. There's no way you can provide food and shelter for fifteen million people who have suddenly become homeless—no matter how comprehensive the Big Shot's advice may be. Has there ever been a refugee camp on such a gigantic scale? You'd say under these conditions, we should be anticipating **A PEOPLE'S UPRISING**? And assuming it does happen, would it be as revolutionary as you would like it to be?

Let's say that in the chaotic flux of a people's uprising, a spontaneous revolt spreads to the outlying areas. Once an uprising/riot becomes a movement, it immediately creates its own internal executive committee. Theoretically, such an executive could take half of the Self-Defense Corps under its command. Once the hegemonic groups of the rioters and the rebels within the Self-Defense Corps unite, they might even propose negotiations with the nuclear blackmailers, bypassing the government crisis team. But, the minute they gather around the negotiation table, the leadership of the blackmailers will notice that every one of the newly appointed negotiators who sits across from them is the Big Shot's puppet! In his program to dominate all humankind, he would have already taken the necessary precautions to deal with this type of situation, too.

3

He himself will never make an appearance at the negotiation table; instead he will conduct a series of prenegotiation conferences with his puppets. Once reach an agreement (and since he will have already laid the groundwork, it will no doubt be concluded quickly), a makeshift revolutionary government will be patched together. At the request of the nuclear blackmailers' HQ, representatives from the people's uprising/riot will instruct the masses to return to the city swiftly. At that point of course, the bombs will still remain hidden. Equally important, the masses will have been given assurances that, until calls for another evacuation are made, the blackmailers will take good care of the bomb and will not use it!

The masses' spontaneous return to the city after this demonstration of the political power behind a nuclear weapon will be an enormous victory for the blackmailers in two ways: First, it will show the world that they can hold 15 million people hostage. Second, they also will have succeeded in giving the revolutionary process international status.

THE REVOLUTION'S INTERNATIONAL STATUS? RIGHT ON! Is that what I hear? Mori's trying to convey something really serious. Tokyo occupied by a nuclear-armed group, and all the residents evacuated—how would you describe this phenomenon from an international geopolitical viewpoint? And then what would the Korean side of the Japan-U.S.-Korea Defense Alliance insist on? Remember, if the Tokyo blackmailers bring about a revolution, Korea could be caught in a vise between communists in the North and in the South. Given what's at stake in that crisis, don't you think the Korean representatives will call for a nuclear attack on Tokyo? By this time, Tokyo would be a gigantic ghost town, with the population density of a desert. Anyway, the fallout from the nuclear blast wouldn't reach Korea.

Think about it: potentially this crisis could put the blackmailers in the most precarious situation since they started the operation. The Big Shot knows this and when he determines that the Japan-U.S.-Korea Defense Alliance is ready to act, **SCRIPT NUMBER THREE** will go into effect. He will pass information about the bomb's exact hiding place to those Self-Defense Corps members still loyal to the government, and eliminate any chance of the revolutionaries using the bomb. One missile would be enough to take out the A-bomb factory, you see. In one stroke, he would be the savior of Tokyo!

What would he do next in the event that the conference between the blackmailers and the leadership of the people's uprising, which includes rebel elements of the Self-Defense Corps, actually succeeds in getting fifteen million Tokyoites to return? That's when he will complete blasting through toward the Family, tearing open the biggest atmospheric hole in Japanese history. This would all be done behind the scenes; all he'll have to do is lay the groundwork necessary for this complicated political operation. He wouldn't ever actually be seen in public. His preparations are such that although they now seem to be without visible results, when the plan is put in motion, he's set it up in such a way that people will view the outcome as the most natural thing in the world. And once the results of his behind-the-scenes maneuvering are a reality, the situation of social flux created by the bomb will no longer directed toward revolution, but instead will have been co-opted into his program.

Did you say **BULLSHIT, again?** You're denying everything even before Mori has time to give the specific why?! I don't understand you guys. Have you ever really thought about what new direction the revolution would take if you actually successfully manufactured an A-bomb? Did you ever give a thought to what sort of revolution you would want once the bomb is in your hands? Would you really rather leave that problem to your present leadership, and just follow orders as selfless fighters for the revolution? Do those leaders onto whom you'd shove everything, who've supposedly got everything planned out, do they really exist? At this very moment, the party is on the verge of assembling its bomb, right? Are you innocently going to sign up for lessons afterwards, concerning the correct post-A-bomb line? I want to throw your **NONSENSE** right back at you. I don't like the eerie feeling I get from hearing it. It leaves no room for humor.

The groundwork for the Big Shot's crowning effort will proceed something like this: It will be imperative that he let the Family return to the city when the blackmailers and the leaders of the mass uprising set up a provisional government. Putting aside whether or not the bomb shelter in the Imperial Palace will be used, his decision to let the Family return with the refugees will be the biggest gamble he's ever taken. How many enemies would he have to contend with to prepare the way for the Family's return? The preparations would have to be on a global scale. The Japanese government and every conservative in the world, no doubt, would be scheming to bring the Family to Kyushu or Shikoku, or even America. But he will win out in the end; and with the Family and 15 million refugees deciding to stay with the bomb, he will move on to SCRIPT NUMBER FOUR!

In the end things will proceed not as a materialization of some revolutionary fantasy you have in mind, but as a coup d'état borne aloft on an unimaginably powerful air current that blasts a hole through toward the Family! Only then will the Big Shot reveal himself as the master planner-promoter of the whole intricate structure ranging from blackmail, to mass evacuation and return, all the way to the finishing touches of a coup d'etat by the Self-Defense Corps's rebel army. He will inspect his troops after the coup, standing atop the wreckage of dream and practice which has hitherto befallen every revolutionary movement, with all the undisciplined rabble of the people's uprising in attendance, and the home-made bomb firmly under his control. Present arms! Ten thousand bugles will blare out for the Family. . . .

RIDICULOUS? Really? Is that how you sum up Mori's revelation? **RIDICULOUS**?!

* * *

The tape of the speech by the switchover pair, with Mori-father's dubbing, ends anticlimactically with him casting back this word, the echo of several hundred people crowded into the meeting hall. In other words, it was not that Mori/Mori-father's assertions were out-argued, but it simply appears that at the sound of the audience's one-word response, *RIDICULOUS!*, the pair lost the nerve to continue the speech. Or . . . ?

* * *

All hell broke loose. But it sure didn't start because Mori and I were given a coup de grâce, pushed to tears by their shouts of RIDICULOUS, ha. Nothing of the sort. The uproar was lying in abeyance from the first minute we began our speech, dauntlessly hurling our words out at the churning waves of frenzy! Besides, we didn't exactly remain standing upright all the while that we delivered our speech. We were repeatedly dragged offstage, with the audience jabbing, pushing, and pulling us every which way as we tried to continue.

But you see, the moment I shouted back **RIDICULOUS**?! something fundamentally shifted in the farcical scene of this kinematic oration against a heckling chorus, performed while immured inside a foul-smelling human fence. The scene began to turn undisguisedly cruel and violent. Up to that point, communication had been open, but suddenly the hecklers closed up, pores and all. The party's entire membership—you might call it the materialization of brute power—turned the hall into a towering wall of rejection. **SSHH, SSSHHH BANG!** There were no actual sounds, but I still felt I'd heard something.

. . . In the next instant, six middle-aged men made their appearance between us and the members-turned-weapon. I don't know whether they came up out of the floor, or fell from the sky. The six, similar in build, presented their backs to Mori and me, forming a circle of protection around us while they rebuked the glaring crowd, still pushing and shoving its way forward.

——You've killed one today! Is that all you guys know how to do?!

My eyes focused on one of them, his mouth twitching right under my nose, middle-aged, with an overly tanned skin displaying the obvious signs of degeneration. I was struck by the intuitive realization that they were all thinking one thing: it was they who'd committed a murder that day.

Our six seemingly powerless protectors escorted us safely out of the hall, carving a path through the angry mob of students, who screamed at the top of their lungs, **WHAA, WHAA**. Before I knew it, the Mediator had joined the six guarding Mori and me, and was trotting alongside us in the phalanx. Somehow I felt awkward about saying thank you in the presence of these rescuers, so I turned to Mori and said,

——Isn't the fact that we've had a narrow escape more or less a proof that the Cosmic Will who switched us over has been watching our every move?

Looking intent and self-absorbed, Mori also proceeded out of the hall at a trot—I was so close I could've bitten his earlobe—and gave only a sidelong glance at my teeth. The lips of his half-open mouth moved and I received an almost imperceptible electromagnetic signal from him like those I had during the speech.

——**OF COURSE, WE'RE ALWAYS WATCHED! THAT'S WHY HE SENT A RESCUE TEAM, THE YAMAME CORPS!**

10

The Odyssey of the Yamame Corps

1

Those visionaries, the Yamame Corps: I'm not saying that they constantly kept tabs on what I was doing, body and soul, but when I try to remember them, as when I think of death, I know now that they kept a vigil on me from the *depths* of unconsciousness.

While the Corps's rescue operation was getting under way, the burning fear I had of the mob we left behind was rekindled. I think it was the same for Mori and the Mediator. Likewise for the six Corps members! I'd say their labored breathing was like that of old men clutched by fear; it was almost infectious. I call them old men, but they looked to be in their late forties. The smell of death hung redolent in the air, though, as they wheezed and tottered along in small steps, holding to a circle around Mori and me. I wonder if the Long March in the Tohoku mountains somehow accelerated their aging.

The three of us weren't faring much better than our six near-decrepit escorts: nine old men on the run, gasping more than breathing, I should say. We must have passed by several buildings before we found ourselves in front of an arched entranceway. Once inside, we suddenly came upon an underground passageway. At the end several steps led us into the outdoor night. There we were, just within the iron gate bordering the pavement outside the campus. At this point, the Corps ran out of steam, and squatted on their haunches to catch their breath. Mori, the Mediator, and I followed suit.

A healthy eighteen-year-old, I was the first to recover—physically that is, but not psychologically—so I walked over to a pillar in the shadows of the closed gate. I peeped out at the deserted street through ivy-laced iron bars. The police, the Revs, the Counterrevs—any one of them might be on the lookout for us, you know.

At that instant, a beat-up Citroen on the verge of disintegrating altogether roared down the street. In the front seat sat my wife/*ex*-wife in a black racing helmet glaring straight ahead. At the wheel was the giant in combat fatigues. I suspect that after the police surveillance and the stakeouts by the Revs and the Counterrevs were withdrawn, my wife/*ex*-wife coaxed and tormented her brother into keeping a close watch on the campus. She had been running around all night on my account, driven by her hostility toward me. As soon as I began to pity her, I also suddenly realized the underlying meaning of the sexual entanglement that existed involving her, me, and Mori. Not that my new-found understanding would do any good after the switchover, though. For the last two years whenever we made love in the dark, she would solicitously inquire, *Is it good? Does your weenie feel good?* And in turn, like an infant, I would respond, *My weenie feels good, I want to come now, come with me.* And now I had unraveled this entangled web, saw it for what it was: my wife/*ex*-wife had superimposed Mori onto me and imagined she was making love to him, while I too had superimposed Mori onto me and imagined it was Mori-me making love to my wife/*ex*-wife!

Before the Citroen had time to make a U-turn and reappear, and after making sure that no one was on the street, we scrambled over the fence leaving four of the Yamame Corps behind. We crossed the pavement, and hurried down a side street. Two Corps members whose bodies so recently looked rather wasted now took the lead. The short break had made quite a difference. Noticeably agile and surefooted as they clambered over the fence, they couldn't help but remind me of their many, many years of training and discipline.

The taller of the two looked quite the dandy in a colorful, clean parka, even though his perfectly round head was bald. The stiff way he held his neck, straight up like a flag pole, brought back images of bureaucrats I'd often seen inspecting nuclear power plants—you know, the "Able Official" type. The other wore a dress shirt, tieless, under an old raincoat. He knew he looked good. With his lackluster hair, pale dry skin, a big slit of a mouth that cut across his face, he looked like a dog: in my mind he took on the name "Dog Face."

——Why trot, not run? What are we looking for? I said to him. Immediately,

——Huh? Dog Face turned toward me, but it was Able Official who replied. The top hemisphere of his head—the forehead around the area of his eyebrows—twitched; his neutral stare focused somewhere above me.

——We're not trying to find anything, we're trying to be found, that's why we're only trotting!

Dog Face smiled faintly at this answer. It was really quite an innocent smile, conveying how much he appreciated his comrade's verbal dexterity.

——We're waiting for some comrades to show up who'll feed us and give us a place to crash, the Mediator explained.

——Don't you think we'll end up caught by some pawn of the Big Shot?

——You sound afraid, like he's a demon in a nightmare, said Dog Face.

——**A DREAM**?! I cried out. **A DEMON IN A NIGHTMARE**. . . ?

The fact of the matter was I wanted to get something off my chest: *We, the switchover pair, just called your attention to the threat of the Big Shot, and your reaction is he's only a nightmare?* I could feel the frustration building; when even the Yamame Corps reacts this way, who in the world could challenge the Patron's potential mega-violence? I was stunned.

At that moment, Mori, a bronze-like face with cheekbones and chin gleaming in the street light, sent me a message. *That's why our switchover was needed. Without the recognition of the pair, the Big Shot is just a dream demon to everyone on Earth, and when they finally realize what his true self is like, it'll be too late—they'll be devoured by the dream demon. That's why we've been switched over; we've got to fight him tooth and nail!*

——Look! A car's coming! the Mediator shouted, mounting joy obvious in his voice. As a mini-van slowed behind us, we dashed toward its open doors and hopped in one by one. It immediately picked up speed, and continued its acceleration down a slope. The scriptwriter-to-be who's always one for adding a little drama to her driving, was at the wheel. Sayoko was perched on the seat right next to her.

——Hang on! We'll shake Mori-mother. We didn't even make it to our seats before the jostling and bumping started, and it took a hell of an effort just to hang on.

——Did you see that?! It just passed us in the other lane, like a bat out of hell! Looks as if they're turning around!

——. . . Boy, is it ever moving! What a car! That thing's really flying low, like a bullet hugging the ground! the girl student reported, body hunched forward intently, baring total fearlessness over the possibility of any kind of gruesome wreck

Ōno slowed down somewhat, and those of us who had been thrown to the floor managed to settle into our seats.

——Well, where to?

——For now, anywhere!

——OK, the scriptwriter-to-be said.

2

Our mini-van passed through the industrial zone on the coast to a port city, and onto a highway leading away from Tokyo. Even after we had safely buried ourselves in a convoy of long-haul trucks, every time a car came up behind us and then passed us, the image of my wife/*ex*-wife's black racing helmet came to mind and made me cringe. The Mediator was complimenting Ōno on her driving skills. She took it for granted. Besides, according to her, the mini-van's engine had extra horsepower because it had been built for use in Africa, and a regular passenger car would be no match for it, or so she said. Once again I was reminded that she had contacts in the film industry, that she was an expert in procuring things, whatever they may be.

I was pooped after the long, strenuous day, and although my stomach felt like a bottomless pit, food was the furthest thing from my mind. All I wanted was to remain perfectly still and let the van's vibrations massage my body and spirit worn out by the switchover. I was sure Mori felt the same way. The Mediator was also giving in to extreme fatigue, but seemed to be having a hard time keeping his eyes off Ōno. The two Yamame Corps members were quietly seated in the back of the van. With a famous activist of a Rev splinter group in front of them, they were very much on their guard.

I also kept to myself. The scriptwriter-to-be and I were staring up at the pitch-black sky when suddenly the tarry clouds above us parted and I saw their soaring thunderheads catch the glitter of the moonlight. Then the tear in the blackness was no more. . . . It was a sign that, just as Mori had said, we were being watched by the Cosmic Will, the prime mover of our switchover. Turning to Mori, I was just about to ask, Did you see that? when Ōno, her eyes fixed on the road ahead, called back to me.

——Mori-father, if you're not sleepy, there's something I want to talk about. . . . **O GOD**, you know the Righteous Man has been killed, don't you?. . . Why kill such a righteous, fervent, and gentle person? **FASCIST BASTARDS!** Even if they, as revolutionaries, justify mass murder, they can never, ever, justify this murder!

——It's sad about the death, but isn't that grossly simplifying the political situation? How can you make one person so all-important, so absolutely irreplaceable, and denounce the Revs as a bunch of fascists? the girl retorted.

——**SHUT UP, YOU LITTLE BITCH! SHUT YOUR TRAP!**

——You're shouting, that's what **FASCISTS** do. Change your attitude, or I'll retaliate and denounce you! Take all the people in this van; Mori's my comrade, the two from the Yamame Corps are my party's trusted fighters, and the Mediator is supposed to be neutral about everything, right? So, you'll have to fight off everyone with that nutsy boy of yours!

——**SHUT UP, BRAT! CAN'T YOU KEEP YOUR TRAP SHUT!** If you keep accusing us of siding with the fascists, I'll drive straight into the oncoming traffic—an honorable death! Now, which side of the road will produce more casualties, figure it out pea brain! **DO YOU WANT TO BE SNUFFED OUT? YOU BRAT!**

And then the girl student, who had been hollering full blast at the driver's seat as if she were going to verbally gut it, immediately scrunched back into her seat. In a barely audible voice,

——Fascist, she cursed. Ōno's control of the wheel, plus her shouting, had powerfully bested the girl, but the power to prevail was really rooted in genuine grief over the Righteous Man's death.

——. . . I knew about him. . . . But, how did you find out? Weren't you detained by the police, cut off from the outside?

Thereupon the scriptwriter-to-be made an official report of what she knew to the entire group in the van—not really as a reply to my question. Although she was obviously lost in the deepest doldrums of sorrow and depression, she looked a bit shaken, and began in a voice decidedly different from that of shortly before, one very familiar to daily TV viewers and frequenters of party meetings.

——As soon as you all ran inside the campus, I tried to drive away, but the car wouldn't move! And wouldn't you know it, of all the places to be, there I was, right smack in the middle of the same group of cops who were still stamping their feet in frustration after the Righteous Man had escaped. The car just wouldn't start, as though on cue, somehow, obeying the policemen who were signaling me to stay put! In the end it was all for the better. Since there was no escape, I opened the door, without giving the slightest hint that the only reason I was doing so was because the car went dead on me. And suddenly, Mori-mother's gaunt, tense, mask-like face leapt out at me from the side of a policeman. **HERE'S THE EVIL WOMAN!** In self-defense I slammed the door on the face. The door edge hit her lunging head with a bang and she passed out. The nearest policeman caught her limp body and handed it over to a giant of a man who glared at me with the same awful eyes of Mori-mother before he rushed away with his load to a police car. And that was the end of my personal showdown with her. I wonder why, at that particular moment, she was helmetless. . . . Anyway, a rookie cop standing nearby was more than a little uncomfortable, not knowing whether to keep a straight face; I burst out laughing as I got out of the car. Ahahahaha! That put him and the others in the group at ease; they roared with laughter. I played dumb, and I asked them what was going on; they in turn asked me who had run into the campus. So I gave it to them straight. The Righteous Man went in to protest, nonviolently, the assault made on the antinuke meeting, while the Mediator and the eighteen-year-old had joined him as bodyguards. But I told the police that I didn't know anything about the boy, that since lots of kids offer help in the struggle, I couldn't possibly keep track of all their names or schools. I took out my business card and handed it to the most inno-cent-looking cop of the group. Of course, of the three, they already knew about the Righteous Man and the Mediator. And as for the un-identified boy, well, they were satisfied with my explanation that he was a New Left sympathizer. I think it's because they've been after the middle-aged Mori-father as their third man, right? They've got nothing on the boy. They actually saw him running into the campus, but of course couldn't imagine him to be their thirty-eight-year-old target, and Mori-mother, who had been insisting that Mori-father had disguised himself as a young man, was now incapacitated, unable to speak. In the meantime, an undercover agent came from the campus and reported that the Righteous Man and his two companions had been caught by a student faction and were being tortured. This removed any suspicion the cops may still have harbored that the Righteous Man and the others had taken part in the Big Shot Report Meeting. So the atmosphere turned friendly: We'd like to ask you a few more questions for the record, why not have a cup of tea with us? I was concerned about the three of you having such a horrible time. But I did accept their invitation. Nothing much happened, though. The rookie who got my business card told me that he was a fan. By then, they had already developed and printed a telephoto shot of a runner taken on campus a few minutes earlier; the person we saw in the photo was not a middle-aged man but a teenager. To make sure I wouldn't bump into Mori-mother, I asked them to send a car around to the coffee shop. That was how I got off scot-free.

——Our party members remain silent whenever dealing with any kind of authority. Which means they'd have a much harder time of it and wouldn't be let off so easily.

——SHUT UP! YOU LITTLE BITCH, STILL FLAPPING YOUR JAWS!

Ōno shook her head wildly, cursing in fits and starts like some crude long-haul truckdriver, but of course with the physical expressiveness of someone who studied film direction in Europe. It was at this point that the Mediator, hoping to avoid the possibility of a car accident, came up with a strategy. His manner became more formal before he spoke to the girl.

——Do you mind sitting next to Mori and looking after him? He's gone through quite a lot with that head wound. . . .

——Don't you think it's unfair for me to put our private feelings above group needs just to be near Mori?

——SHUT UP, BRAT! STILL FLAPPING YOUR JAWS!?

After this round of verbal abuse, the girl just bit the bullet and moved over to Mori. As she passed me, trying to hold her own against the lurch and roll of the vibrating van, I noticed her skintight blue jeans, but what really grabbed my attention was her body odor. . . . It was not sensuous or enticing at all, but the same stench that had hung in my nostrils throughout my captivity.

——So, how did you learn about the Righteous Man's murder? Did the party throw a press conference to celebrate his murder while they had us detained?

——They did no such thing! Able Official answered in a loud voice from the back seat. Unlike me or the Mediator, he wasn't hindered by exhaustion and aching muscles—no wonder he could raise his voice as much as he liked. That was an accident, a real unfortunate one, but certainly not something they could boast about. Those at the student level must be held responsible because the accident was a strategic error on their part. No way they'd give a press conference if they hadn't yet found someone responsible for the mistake.

——Does that mean you accept such accidents as strategic errors?! That won't bring back the dead!

——EXCUSE ME? Both Yamame Corps members sucked in their breath and held it for a second, implying that they couldn't believe Ōno had even asked the question. Able Official continued, representing the two, On the contrary, we've always accepted all accidents as strategic errors and remained vigilant in our self-criticism. When our battle group was first organized, we had one small accident after another, with many members falling by the wayside, so, to find out what caused these accidents, a proper assessment of strategic errors was a sine qua non. . . .

——What you mean by "our group" is the Yamame Corps, right? I believe what you've said, but only so far as it concerns the Corps. I don't think the students will ever admit mistakes that involve all of the Revs.

I turned around meaning to check to see whether mentioning the Yamame Corps would disturb or anger them. Instead my eyes fell on the girl, her hand affectionately caressing Mori's head as he sat hunched down in his seat staring despondently into the distance. I immediately felt a tinge of embarrassment and looked away.

——. . . Yuupp. If you put it that way, you're bound to think specific- ally of the Yamame Corps, right? Able Official said with a straight face, betraying only a second's hesitation in his reply. Beginning with those accidents we had in the early days, up till now, we've been investigating how to properly assign responsibility for strategic errors. . . . The Revs may share our political orientation, but it would be difficult to impose our "approach" to self-criticism on the student level of the organization. . . . It's impossible to share the lived experience we've had today, phe- nomenologically speaking.

——How dare you act so indifferent?! We're talking about the death of the Righteous Man!. . . . What you're saying is, not just phenomeno- logically, but **IN ESSENCE,** untenable! Ōno's agitation only increased as she went on: How could those bright sincere kids, **HOW COULD ANYONE, BECOME FASCISTS SO EASILY?!** There it was again; I saw that the extreme abuse which she continued to hurl at Sayoko actually originated in the intense grief she was burying within her. . . . That night, the police telephoned me—they had my business card, you see. They told me that the Righteous Man had fallen off the cliff behind the university and was run over by a train. It was as though he had died twice. Can you come down to identify the body? they asked. I went wild at that point, and called up my kids who were doing some guerrilla training in the mountains, and told them that the Righteous Man had been killed by the fascists. And all I got in reply was: Don't ever go to the police, never go anywhere alone. Until the Party's Executive Com- mittee evaluates this incident with the proper situational analysis, they said, it will only make trouble for the Party for someone like me, acting solely out of instinct and emotion, to go to the police and blurt out something right off the top of my head. Just lay low and keep away from the authorities, especially the new bourgeois types. They were con- stantly clearing their throats, as if they were really not sure of what to say next. . . . Why all of a sudden does every party member, **EVERYONE BECOME A FASCIST?** Every youngster in this country!?. . . They took turns trying to talk me out of going to the police, but I went anyway and identified the body. . . . And I saw the Righteous Man's mutilated body, both arms neatly severed above the elbow, the hands tightly clasped together. You know the way a weightlifter, after a successful hoist, raises his locked hands above his head in response to the cheering crowd. Exactly like that. When I saw the locked hands, I just knew it was him. The muscles in my throat tightened and all I could say was, *Yahh, yahh,* and step back. Right before that meeting, he'd leafed through his memo book full of notes on appointments, demonstrations, and meetings until he found the figure he'd been looking for, and then proceeded to calculate the amount of hot water a ten-megawatt power plant produces per day. I remember the shape of his strong, square hand holding the stubby pencil. . . .

The voice was teary; she moved her head violently, shaking off the blinding tears that continued welling up in her eyes no matter how fast she wiped them away. Finally she could go no further and brought the van to a halt on the shoulder of the highway. Through her retelling of what she had seen, she had reexperienced the Righteous Man's death, and could no longer contain her sorrow as it reasserted itself. She rested her head against the steering wheel and began to wail, finally surrendering to total exhaustion. There was nothing we could do. It was only Able Official's forthright action that got us through the painful moment: he put an arm around her shoulder and helped her to the back seat. He then took the wheel and drove to a nearby truck stop. We left her behind in the van while we went to get something to eat—we had to survive, you know.

3

Let's face it, when we stepped into the diner, we all looked rather outlandish. Me, the Mediator and especially Mori with his bandages made a really weird-looking bunch, but given the circumstances, there was nothing we could do. The fear that our appearance might prompt the manager to call the police was overpowered and utterly consumed by a far stronger voice beyond reason: hunger. We'll think about that on a full stomach! All eyes fell on us the moment we entered. But the girl at the cash register acted as if she was accustomed to our sort, however bizarre we looked.

——Just come from an accident? First aid's in the restroom. Must have had a terrible time!

——*Were we in an accident? We sure were!* We've been through hell?! the Mediator said in a deep voice, knitting his eyebrows in pain—his fine gift for quickly sizing up a situation clearly operative. Probably made the late-night traffic report, did you see it on the tube? The other party in the accident lost a passenger, you know!

Now isn't he decisive?! Got to hand it to him, even if he got kicked and beaten from one end of town to the other because of some useless speech he made; an activist like him would survive no matter what. By cleverly engaging the cashier in chit-chat—or rather, by putting our abnormality to good use—the Mediator had allowed us to fit in with the rest of the clientele. There wasn't a single whistle or catcall from the group of truckers watching us as we took a table in the corner of the diner, sandwiching the girl between us. Their eyes kept following us, gauging the extent of our injuries. Their solemn yet amused gazes only thinly disguised their mocking attitude toward such weak, pitiful, and easy prey. They were young men with the red, shiny cheeks of kewpie dolls, who hadn't touched a drop of liquor even though the clock on the wall said it was well past three in the morning. . . .

Slowly, longingly, I opened the menu. At last we were within reach of food. But my bruised fingers were cold and numb; the menu felt like a ball of snow.

——Let's have Chinese, it's a safe choice in a place like this, Able Official urged.

——The Chinese and crab tempura with rice for me! Dog Face said with obvious excitement; the girl also felt the urge to follow suit,

——The same for me, too! Sayoko's really cute, isn't she?!

As we waited for the food at our round table the Able Official poured tea and skillfully passed it around, but after we had witnessed the depth of Ōno's grief, it was very difficult to keep up much of a conversation. A muzak station blasted out an *enka* ballad *(I couldn't tear myself away. . . the moonlight!)*. Able Official stared into space blinking, and said,

——Equivocal.

——Yuupp, *obscurantism* for sure, Dog Face agreed with dead seriousness. There's no end to intellectual gratification, is there, criticizing the verses of pop ballads? Ha, ha.

However, as if changing mental gears, Able Official lowered his blinking eyes to fix me and went straight to the essentials:

——How did you find out about the Yamame Corps?

——When the Corps commandeered those hunting guns at the Kuma River in Gunma, I happened to be in the area fishing for *yamame*, you see. That's how I ran into the Corps.

——Requisitioned from the Hunting Association, Able Official wrinkled the vast expanse of his cueball forehead, his eyes now wide and locked onto those of Dog Face. Both their faces broke out in innocent smiles.

After they exchanged a few yells and cheers—totally inappropriate one would think for men in their late forties—they quickly composed themselves, resuming their solemn expressions.

———Those guns we requisitioned, they were all in good condition, but a mixed bag, some antiques, some high-tech. That became a real problem. You may learn how to use one type of gun, but then you have to start all over again if you're given another type, right? That was one of the main reasons we suffered so many casualties. A tactical error's victims. It was really the worst of times for us.

———An old-fashioned gun's perfectly all right, as long as you take good care of it. If you can stick to a single pattern, that works best for any fighting group. It's a simple matter in principle—or, even in real life—but once you have to tackle a new pattern—say, a new gun in our case—things change dramatically. You get caught up in it, and you're never the same.

———From time to time I've thought about the name Yamame Corps. It's not true, what the kid just said about *yamame* fishing, is it? The girl's question betrayed cautious interest here. She was definitely ready to change her line of questioning if someone laughed her down; there was always the outside chance that the term was a household word, familiar jargon, among those in a rival political faction, or even in the army reserves.

———*Yamame*, a hard-boned fresh-water fish in the salmon family. Our group was active in the region all along the mountain rivers where anglers fished for *yamame*. Then a newspaper in Iwate called us the Yamame Corps, and the rest is history. . . . You see, the name sounded like a joke to everybody, so the authorities didn't take us seriously. It's a good thing, too. If they had conducted their usual thorough investigation, we'd have had a devil of a time, no doubt about it. . . .

———The official map used by the Corps is in a book called *Mountain Fishing Places*—you can find it at any bookstore. If the public security people had gotten hold of a copy, they'd have saved themselves a lot of time. Boy, they would have given us more than a devil of a time, I assure you.

Dog Face quickly finished his Chinese *table d'hôte* and began to work on the crab dish. No wonder his complexion's so poor and his eyes have lost their fire—he's been abusing his stomach the way he eats, I said to myself.

———A few people saw the direct connection between the route of our march and the name Yamame Corps. The Big Shot was one of them. He tried to establish contact with us through a grocer in an army town along the river.

The Big Shot again!

———Well, if what you say is true, I must have been the first one who told him about the Corps. . . . But what was the purpose of contacting the Corps?

——He uses everything that moves! He tries to dominate every living being on this earth! Dog Face said, lifting up his head with greasy bits of crab meat stuck all around his mouth.

——But what possible use could he have for an organization which was out marching around in the godforsaken mountains of Tōhoku?

——It's true that the Corps had placed its hardcore types along the river, but being a modern guerrilla force, some of us were also assigned to the cities, "swimming," if you will, among the people. Dog Face said this with some dignity, an honorable sort of speech. The fact that most of the Corps kept on the move, armed and politically active, and completely outside the domain of the national authorities, could have been a threat to those of us inside the power structure. But our Long March and that of its namesake, the Chinese revolution, were entirely different. Basically, ours was a ritual. As long as this rite was symbolic, there was no need for every soldier in the Corps to participate in the March. The actual number of marchers at any one moment was really quite small. But the ritual went on without interruption. So each soldier found his identity within the group. Everyone got off the mountain of his own accord, holed up in a safe house in the city, and at some predesignated site picked up information that would link him up with the rest of the Corps. It was relatively easy to avoid attention in the mountains if one posed as an angler. As long as you got back into the mountains before dawn or at dusk, no one would suspect a lone fisherman of anything. The Corps had no trouble financing itself because the soldiers came down from the mountain, worked in the cities, and then returned to the mountain with the funds they had collected. In other words, the Corps is an *open* guerrilla group, it has nothing to do with the detention mentality of psychologically closed groups.

——Well, then why doesn't every revolutionary party adopt the Corps's operational style? the girl said as though she couldn't hold herself back any longer. But Dog Face ignored her, at which point the Mediator responded on her behalf.

——Generally speaking, once you let members leave a guerrilla group which has holed itself up in the mountains, the suspicion immediately spreads that one of them might betray the group. The suspicion in turn gives fuel to the desire for escape which already exists in every member's mind, and slowly poisons him long before suspicion has a chance to grow. I've been engaged in political struggle all these years, demanding reflection and reconciliation from every radical group I've made contact with: the purpose of my work is nothing more than to find an antidote to the poison. Guerrillas must disperse among the masses and liberate themselves.

——Guerrillas liberating themselves through contact with the masses—come on, what sort of guerrilla tactic is that? Since Dog Face directed that question to Able Official, he showed he flatly repudiated the Mediator's statements. A guerrilla "swimming" among the masses should not be dispersed out like laundry detergent. If that's the case, the movement would die out! . . . It's the reverse. A centripetal force should always operate, drawing members back to the core guerrilla group; each and every one in the group must intrinsically feel that force, which would mean there'd be no need for tests of loyalty and precautions against betrayal. Wouldn't that be a superior quality to develop for a guerrilla movement? In the case of the Corps, the centripetal force was continually regenerated by the Long March, despite the small number of participants.

——But in the end, didn't the Yamame Corps vanish into thin air? the miffed Mediator immediately shot back.

Thereupon the two Corps members looked up from their plates, gazed straight at the inquirer, and then glanced at each other, smiles beaming from ear to ear. That was not enough; their smiles were superseded by an outburst of raucous laughter! The near-bored truckers' attention was immediately regained by that outburst, and the mood in the diner turned palpably dangerous—after all, laughter is insolent behavior.

Able Official cleared his throat and sat up in his chair, as though he was trying to *cut off* the hostile looks of the truckers. He turned his cold, beady eyes on the Mediator—no trace of laughter in those eyes.

——The Corps has not vanished. That's the reason we're unable to tell you, even now, anything specific about the March. . . . I think we've aroused enough interest around here; it's time to split. I've already told you how healthy our finances are; we'll pick up the tab.

——Nope, his comrade corrected, it doesn't look like we have to.

Sakurao Ōno was standing solemnly at the cash register, paying the bill. For the moment, she'd set aside her sorrow over the Righteous Man's death and begun to worry about the cost of the meals. True activist that she was, she had pulled herself together and gotten out of the van.

4

When we stood up to go, Able Official diplomatically thanked her on our behalf, and the scriptwriter-to-be politely nodded and listened. She suggested that the Mediator and I go wash our faces in the restroom. *This kind of place isn't for eating, but the restrooms are great,* she said inviting a potentially angry retort from the cashier.

The Mediator's voice was full of adoration for Ōno's thoughtfulness as he said, *She's even got a towel ready for you,* trying to elicit admiration from the man in the mirror. His comments weren't addressed to me, that's for sure. I heard his voice from outside the tiny chamber where I was sitting on the john. I bet his face in the mirror looked as bad as mine, and the expression it elicited would have been none too cheerful, either. Mori and Sayoko entered the restroom just as I was coming out. I wonder what sort of self-sacrificing assistance she gave him tidying up—she looked flushed when she returned to the van a half hour later. Boy, he must've been good, ha, ha.

She selected a spot in the van where she could observe the rest of us—we sat in random places—and with her butt on an armrest, her arm around the back of the seat, and a defiant tone in her voice, she challenged us all to a debate.

——Now, where do we go from here? Just a few of us know where we're headed, the rest are in the dark—that's not democratic! I've been a gofer up till now, but no one's told me anything about our plans. That's not only undemocratic, that's male chauvinism, right?. . . Has the Corps dispatched you two to keep a watch on Mori, the kid, and the Mediator? Well, don't you treat me like one of them! I'm from the Revs, you know. If you intend to keep me out of things because I've worked in the movement for fewer years, that's just bureaucratic b.s., isn't it?!

Thereupon, Able Official responded to the girl in an intrigued, good-natured, and genuinely confused voice as if he hadn't expected that kind of criticism at all.

——Did you say we're playing the bureaucrat? No, we're not. When we think about the bigger perspective of the revolution, *how long we've been in the movement* is not nearly as important as *how long we'll continue in it,* right? Because we respect you, we won't try to shoulder you out. . . . Besides, we're the minority here, so how can we be the watchdogs? We're just volunteers who've come along for some action in whatever the switched-over pair does next.

——Aren't we all going to fight the next battle together with Mori? You've fought by his side from the very beginning, so why do you feel you're being left out?

The Mediator also put in his two cents worth, forcing the girl to turn to Mori, as though asking for support. I also followed her gaze as I turned around, but the object of our mutual attention was already fast asleep, curled up in a blanket, his wounded head shielded with an elbow just the way he did with plastic sheets back in his pre-switchover days. As I watched him, I felt the need to get certain things straight—after all, although I was his junior in the chronological sense, I was still his father. I therefore focused my questions on the two Corps soldiers, beginning my inquiry in this manner,

——But, why volunteer to protect Mori? You're at an age where belief in our switchover story is less likely. What's the reason?

——There's a good reason! We were moved by the speech you two delivered at the meeting. Whether we believe the switchover or not is another matter. All six of the Corps members present at the meeting were greatly impressed by what you and Mori had to say and the way you said it, standing up there, shouting your message to the audience! We agreed with everything in the speech, and the next logical step was to join forces with you.

Wavering between belief and disbelief, I withheld judgment, but even Dog Face, normally quiescent, was hot in pursuit of Able Official's line of thought, trying very hard to make me understand the significance of what he was saying.

——You might wonder why we mingled among the young people, why we were the only people there who were moved by your speech, right? Frankly, we wholeheartedly concurred with your summary of Big Shot's grand scheme for world domination. From our experience, it was totally plausible; but for those kids, it was unthinkable. Toward the end of the war, the Big Shot was hauled out of Hong Kong on a military cargo plane with all his gold, silver, and diamonds. But the free ride was to Hiroshima, where he arrived just in time for the A-bombing. He and his assets survived but his own children were killed. This guy's gone through hell, tasted the vilest stuff humankind can dish out. A real survivor. It seems to me that something is driving him to get even, to create a superstructure that will match the evil forced on him by the bombing. I think that's why his takeover program is so gigantic, so all-encompassing. In other words, we don't think your overview on him is an elaborate fantasy at all.

Dog Face then chimed in, and detailed the facts about the radiation dosage Big Shot received, but in the manner typical of a leftist who knows you know all the information but still wants to review it to make sure you and he have common ground. I was stunned by his account. Sayoko took advantage of my silence to ask a very sensible question,

——If the Big Shot was a witness to evil at its ugliest, Hiroshima, why doesn't he try to counter it with something good?

——Logically, that's the way it should be, Able Official responded approvingly. And, the day may come when his actions could be reappraised as having been for the greater good of humankind. The scenario you and Mori described in your speech, if materialized, is nothing for anyone to snicker at, yet many people would consider it to be the ultimate good deed. Every detail of the scenario could be interpreted that way. He'd be a shoo-in for the Nobel Peace Prize. But to bring about the good requires the completion of his plan. There's no doubt that for the ruled, the Big Shot would become the creator and manager of a gigantic structure of goodness. But once he goes senile and dies a peaceful death, only the structure he created would remain behind. There'd be no more ruler of humankind. But—

——BUT! Dog Face took over in tag-team fashion. We mustn't jump to the conclusion that he tried to accomplish something terribly good from the very beginning. Who was it, Mephistopheles? Like him, the Big Shot didn't set out to make himself so utterly evil in order to create the ultimate good, either. There's no room for ethics in the structure of domination he's trying to materialize. When you consider his own A-bomb experience, I don't think he'd hold the potentially chaotic situation arising from a nuclear blackmail operation to be *evil.* Of course, he's not the type that would think it a good thing, either. He'd merely accept what the A-bomb touches off as a natural evolution of human enterprise. After all, he'd say to himself, others have already done this kind of barbaric thing on a grand scale. I can do something equivalent; we're all human—if they can do it, I surely can. In plain language, his A-bomb experience was a great eye-opener for him, vis-à-vis his fellow humans. Anyone else who reacted to the A-bombing the way he did would be equally capable of doing whatever comes to mind. In terms of scale, the explosion of a nuclear device corresponds in magnitude to whatever humans have done so far. But to go beyond the *bomb* you'd have to go into space—deal with the larger universe. And of course, the Big Shot has no further ambitions beyond Earth; he just aspires to total domination of every human being on this planet. Interest in phenomena on a cosmic scale hasn't even entered his head.

Just as Dog Face said this, out of the corner of my eye, I saw Mori writhing in sleep, in obvious pain. I took it to be some sign of his desire to express himself. Mori's blood, flesh, muscles, and bones, his entire physical being was trying to give voice to a spirit which possessed him and caused him to twitch. I heard a voiceless cry resonating inside my head. **IS THAT ALL HE DESIRES? BUT OUR SWITCHOVER ORIGINATES IN THE WILLPOWER OF COSMIC SPACE, SO OUR BODIES CONTAIN A SUPERPOWER THAT SURPASSES THE BIG SHOT'S AMBITION!**

Now I grasped the meaning of Mori's targeting of the Patron right after the switchover, and that knowledge, I knew, made me Mori's unshakable comrade. Fortified with a new self-confidence, I felt my suspicions of the seasoned Yamame Corps soldiers who had volunteered to protect the both of us vanish. I realized as well that we had met the first true comrades with whose help we were to make the switchover available to the whole of humankind, a switchover that until now shut out all but Mori and me. I no longer hesitated about talking with these new comrades and began to discuss our strategy and tactics.

——Submitting summaries on developments in the nuclear industry abroad was my main job, but in the course of establishing background for these summaries I did cover the Hiroshima-Nagasaki bombing material as well. He never, ever, spoke about his radiation exposure. Does that mean anything? Is it in any way significant for the struggle we are about to take up?

——He didn't tell me anything about his A-bomb experience, either, even after I began working for him, Dog Face replied. I've heard from different people that during the Occupation he did make an issue out of his being an A-bomb victim. In fact, I frequently ran into Americans who told me they remembered hearing about it. He made it known far and wide that he was an A-bomb victim at a time when the media was still under very strict American censorship. What's more, many Japanese businessmen lost out on important international concessions because he often used his connections to block these transactions. Later he got even bolder; it's said that he took the figures for his own radiation exposure and hyped them up as some sort of motion-energy quotient to indicate how superior he was. He then tried to form a global corporation. I heard something to that effect from an American who had dealings with him during the Occupation. The American later resumed business talks with him and in the course of those negotiations— I was present as the Big Shot's interpreter—I heard the two of them reminisce about his motion-energy theory and its relation to conducting business.

——Dog Face is one of the best English speakers in Japan, and went to the States many times as the Big Shot's interpreter, Able Official interrupted by way of a footnote to his story. The two Yamame Corps members exchanged contented smiles. While he was on the Long March as a Yamame Corps soldier, he slipped out and went abroad as an interpreter. Well, didn't the Big Shot know you were a Corps member? When you were in Atlanta with him, he made contact with the Black Panthers through you, right? Able Official said to his comrade.

——Unfortunately, they weren't any help, not really committed enough for us. . . . From what I could gather as his interpreter, his peace plan after the end of the war went like this: Open up Hiroshima and Nagasaki as free ports à la Hong Kong, and invite banks from all over the world to set up Swiss-style banks. Since A-bombs had already been dropped on those two cities, they're unlikely targets for another nuclear attack. In a nuclear age, wouldn't depositing one's money in Hiroshima-Nagasaki banks be much safer than in Swiss banks? It also appears that during the preliminary negotiations, he even threatened those involved; what would you do, he reportedly said, if an unidentified aircraft dropped an H-bomb on Switzerland? To which the American I mentioned earlier retorted, How can you even hint at using nuclear power in this manner when you yourself have been harmed by an A-bomb? Whereupon, so the story goes, the Big Shot replied, **THAT'S PRECISELY WHY I CAN!**

——His peace plan fell through, but it had some marked effects on the Swiss banks' super antinuclear defense system, Able Official commented. It would seem that whatever the Big Shot attempted, it just petered out for lack of interest, right? But, behind the visible disintegration of one project lay the completion of even larger covert transactions.

——What were the negotiations about between the Americans and the Patron when you served as his interpreter?

——Those negotiations eventually fizzled out—just camouflage for some behind-the-scenes deal; one such failed venture would have set up a plant in the States for manufacturing residential bomb shelters.

——It might have had something to do with one of the briefing papers I put together.

——That's true. Besides, whatever relationship might have existed between you and me was cut off by the Big Shot. To track down what each of us did independently for him, and what parts we all played in the greater scheme of things would be very difficult.

——One of my college friends who was the Patron's European contact, committed suicide right after the Cuban Missile Crisis. He was a lifelong friend, but I still don't know what he did for the Patron—not his real job, anyway. . . .

——We know about that guy too! He tried to build a base for the Yamame Corps in Europe.

We began to feel the shadow of the Patron hovering near us in the form of an ever larger threat. We all fell silent—nothing else to do but mull over what we'd just learned about him.

The scriptwriter-to-be, seemingly listening attentively at the wheel, called out to me.

——Mori-father, we've got to get some sleep if we want to keep up with Mori when he sets about his mission. . . . You may've played the all-suffering martyr in the past to protect Mori from the Yamame Corps, but now we know we're all in this together, all of us are his guardians, and we're all fighting the same struggle. There's no longer any need to keep a vigil.

——That's right, the usually stalwart Mediator chimed in. Let's get some shut-eye! But where? Can we get the van and all into a motel? His drowsiness was hastening a slide into incoherence.

——Why don't we just sleep in the van? Like Mori. We can keep warm with the blankets on the storage rack. Recline Mori's seat, gently—don't wake him—and put a blanket over him. . . . I'll keep driving so we can keep warm with the van's heater; if I get too sleepy to go on, we'll just park wherever we can and do without the heater.

When we began to get our bedding ready, the girl put a blanket over the sleeping Mori and returned to her seat next to the driver. She seemed prepared to give a helping hand in case Ōno nodded off. I was very impressed by this display of attentiveness to down-to-earth, practical matters. I drifted into a restless sleep, worried whether I was about to assume the role of salt of the earth, the way the girl was obviously doing. And whether I could possibly play the role myself. . . .

5

And I had a dream. A dream? Suspicious? How convenient! you say. But I really did have a dream. It gave full expression to a metaphor which truly described the relationship between the real world that the switch*ed*-over Mori and I lived in, and the Cosmic Will which existed beyond Earth and time. At this stage of the game, I shouldn't keep this important dream to myself, should I? Even though what I've been *talking about with such urgency all this time* seems to be a dream within a dream, ha, ha! I hope you don't misunderstand anymore what I've been trying to do, that I'm trying to make you laugh. I'm laughing because I don't know what to do with myself, because telling you about my dream is so hard, much harder than before, now that I'm burdened with the dual persona of a switchover. Mind you, although what I'm telling you is a dream within a dream, I hope you'll take it seriously and record it faithfully.

In the beginning was the dream; the world Mori and I lived in had a clear shape, so delineating the substance of our life with some accuracy is fairly easy. What I mean to say is that Mori and I were Yamame Corps soldiers in this dream world. And when the dream opened, we were at that very moment on the Long March in the mountain range bordering the Kuma River. All of us wore camouflage combat fatigues, with silver-colored diving goggles. Our fatigues didn't so much blend in with the surroundings as they delivered us out of the humdrum of everyday life.

The camouflage pattern consisted of a light milkish color covering dark gray patches, with speckles of scarlet oozing out of the milkiness. The dazzling coloration of the *yamame* jumping out over the clear rapids—that was the color of our fatigues. A large formation of camouflaged soldiers on the march as far as the eye could see (I was immediately reminded of an underwater photograph taken in a river on the Kansen Plain)—a school of *yamame* clustering in the water like cherry blossoms in full bloom.

The soldiers in their *yamame* fatigues were stretched in long lines along both banks of the river which ran into a sparse birch grove; the lines marched calmly and swiftly. The cadence of their **GO, GO, GO** was just discernible above the murmur of the river. **GO, GO, GO**, to gently stoke the fires of our comrades' own secret pride. But these **GO, GO, GO**s were somehow entirely different from what once assaulted me as a boy pining for a chance to show my stuff on first base, ready to run yet so strangely alone in the presence of the whole community! In our chanting of the new **GO, GO, GO**, Mori and I, the new raw recruits, clearly saw the Yamame Corps as an ideal human collective. We continued with the marchers, spontaneously taking up the chant **GO, GO, GO.** Meanwhile, in the columns of soldiers, we recognized the faces of long-time acquaintances! What a pleasant surprise, *You, too!* alternating with an even deeper recognition, *You must be a real good Yamame soldier!* The way the dream ranks moved, like three-dimensional images on panoramic projector screens, Mori and I were able to see our old friends over and over again.

And those people-soldiers we had missed seeing for so long left my dreaming soul fully charged, and with a true sense of security, ready for the onset of a total liberation. Every fragment of my past dwelling in the tiny corners of all those friends' existences cheered me along as I dreamed, *The way I've lived my life so far, not everything I did was so bad.* In my dream, Mori also shared this feeling. Mori and I walked on, not yet sufficiently toughened up but full-spirited and ready for action. I almost believed that as long as I tried to peer deeper and deeper into the depths of this multidimensional image, I might be able to make out a school of speckled fish among the soldiers, like the pale shadows of cherry blossoms, a future image of Mori and me bravely marching with the Yamame Corps.

In this dream panorama of the Corps, I also spied the friend who hanged himself in Paris, his neck wrapped in bandages elongated like that of a quiet horse. . . . When he stepped into some bushes in the river shallows, I saw purple sparks flying from his downcast eyes. His French wife stood right next to him, looking like some sort of volunteer nurse. My friend probably wanted to pick some of the wild berries for her. She seemed aware that he was already dead, but acted as it was all perfectly natural.

The Righteous Man was also in the march, his movements stiff and unnatural, like those of a wooden soldier on parade—the doctor must have bungled this repair job. But his hands were clasped tightly over his chest. Looking at him, you somehow got the impression that he was working out a math problem in his head while he continued the march. And there by his side was Sakurao Ōno, devotedly tending to him and trying very hard not to notice the purple fire in his eyes. Without her assistance, the meditative toy soldier would have fallen flat on his face. But the Righteous Man somehow also had the appearance of someone who would sneak behind a willow stump as soon as the word to halt for a short rest was passed down. There he'd make love to Ōno in the quiet manner befitting someone of his age, ha, ha.

I look back now on all that happened recently, armed with the clear insight that's granted anyone who's dreamed before; I see how the brawl at that meeting, lit by the flashing strobe as though a time-lapse slapstick comedy, was a free-for-all designed by the Yamame Corps to probe into and destroy the Patron's scheme as it unfolded on a large scale everywhere. Remember the valiant Righteous Man fighting people off with his denture-castanets!

For the Corps, this was no longer a symbolic battle but an actual combat offensive. Raising their voices in the chant *GO, GO, GO,* to strike down the strongest, the worst nemesis, the Patron.

But then I woke up screaming, **AHHH!** This dream, which seemed to be moving toward liberating Mori's and my souls, concluded with us trapped on a dead-end street, pressed up against a wall of feeling so oppressive that our hearts were almost crushed. The dream instantly transformed itself into the piercing thorn of a nightmare of thought lodged in my flesh and spirit. Brought to the surface now, what stayed with me were the horrible scars from that thorn piercing through the lovely dream, rending it and then reality asunder. *The Corps's Long March aims to attack the Patron. But isn't he the Cosmic Will and the originator of our switchover? If the Cosmic Will and the Patron are one and the same, what will happen to us?*

Eyes shut tight, body shaking from both the cold and the shock of the nightmare that had pierced the core of my being, I became conscious of something touching my cheek—a wet curtain moistened by the vapor condensing on the window glass. I realized that I was no longer suspended in a cosmic hell but was in a van with Mori. When I peeped through the curtain, Yokohama Port stretched below me—we were on a hillock lined with a decaying section of apartment complexes being demolished. It was just before daybreak. The sky, a gray blackness, merged with the thin milkish film which hung over the harbor, a tinge of scarlet suspended in the milkiness. The earth rumbled—I surmised a highway on the other side of the hillock. An image came to mind: a car driven by my wife/*ex*-wife, with her giant brother in the passenger seat, weaving in and out of lanes of long-distance trucks. I pushed the curtain back in place, and returned my attention to the cold darkness of the van as I listened to Mori's breathing, and the breathing of all the other sleepers, now my trusted comrades. . . . I forgot to tell you something: you and your son were also there in the dream Long March, bravely walking with the rest of us.

11

The Clowns Arrive in the Capital

1

Details, details. I can't keep on talking like this, hung up on the details of my experiences, although I'm sure every little bit of information is important. Let's say, while my tale slowly unfolds, with Mori and me burning the candle at both ends in our switched-over lives, if we suddenly fall silent, clam up, so to speak, you wouldn't feel too comfortable about that, now would you?

Well, I didn't think you would put down everything I said, word for word. Listen, you could thin out as you see fit this jungle of words running riot, and after a good airing, transform it into a forest with shape and style. I always assumed that was your job, and that was also how my words and your account of them were related. When you first started putting things down in writing, I was afraid you might delete significant details—so I let it all hang out. But I find that you weren't judicious at all in choosing what to take down; instead, you transcribed everything I *had to say*.

The way things are going, we'll need an additional 100,000 words or so before we arrive at a telling description of the future action highlighting the cosmic purpose of Mori's and my switchover. If our communication process bogs down, the future action itself would end up miscarrying, and never be realized. Only your account ensures the existence of the switched-over pair!

* * *

As I mentioned earlier, I, the ghostwriter, admit that by putting down Mori-father's *insistent* words, I am actually being influenced by him. But I also feel the influence of my account on Mori-father steadily deepening. For example, notice the keen interest he now has in words: it's the kind only a philologist who experientially acquires such a passion for words would show.

At any rate, it's quite beneficial for us that our relationship, which shares the *written word*, has been reconfirmed. The ghostwriter won't conclude this narrative until Mori-father indicates, through his *insistence*, that the true significance of the switchover has been realized. The ghostwriter hereby requests that Mori-father give his word not to stop talking until that moment of realization occurs. If he ever stops contacting me, I will leave no stone unturned to find him and demand, What happened to your mission, the mission entrusted exclusively to the switched-over pair? That will be my new task as ghostwriter.

* * *

I promise. Something just popped into my head, though; call it an alternate plan in case I'm no longer able to utter words! Now that you've voluntarily recognized our joint venture in the world of the written word, you should continue to heed the words coming from within yourself, and set them down as soon as they come to you. Right? Isn't that the way you should materialize the true meaning of the switchover? In the near future, if I become incapable of speech because I've been either incarcerated or murdered, that silence will be the result of Mori's and my action. The media will of course cover the whole thing, so it won't be too taxing for you to speak for me, to put it down, will it? Besides you're well trained for that, ha, ha.

* * *

When I woke up, raucous noise engulfed the van, *DONGAN, DONGAN, GUUURRRUUU,* a din so intense that it stunned me for a moment. How could I have slept through this?! A mobile power generator must have been set up next to the van and the jackhammer hooked up to it was probably tearing up the concrete around us.

It really wasn't the jackhammer that woke me up, though. Another kind of rumbling emanated from somewhere in the van, and I felt my own breathing became more and more labored. The source of that noise, a piteous, incessant mumbling, was none other than the Mediator, lost in prayer. Apparently, my young body had resisted the sound longer than any of the other passengers. They were almost catatonic, as though they were afraid to move a muscle as long as he continued his prayers.

Although the *DONGAN, DONGAN, GUUURRRUUU* made it difficult for me to hear what he was saying, once I got the drift, I was frightened a little by the fact that he'd kept so many worries to himself. Was this the same Mediator who was always shameless in his groaning and moaning when he'd been knocked down, kicked around, and punched in the face? He was earnestly imploring the Chief Justice of the Cosmic Court to carefully consider who he'd select as a witness for his ruling on humankind. The day when Earth will be moved to its assigned place in the ultimate structure is fast approaching, and evidently all that humankind can do is plead for the move to be postponed another four or five thousand years. As far as I could gather from the Mediator's entreaties, the final appeal hearing was already in session. The judges, who'd come from every corner of the universe had decided to hear the testimony of only one earthling witness. Under the circumstances, what else could he do but continue praying? **PLEASE DON'T MAKE THE WRONG CHOICE! AND DON'T EVER PICK A FEMALE TV PERSONALITY, EVEN BY MISTAKE!**

_____**PHEWW, AHAHAHAHA!** Ōno's burst of laughter broke the prayer vigil's spell over the van. . . . I support your purpose in praying. But your list of undesirable witnesses just moved into the realm of the weird, **PHEWW!** Sorry. I've appeared on a lot of women's talk shows and met quite a few people I'd refuse to let represent humankind! **PHEWW, HAHAHAHA!**

_____ . . . So noisy out there, I didn't think you could hear me, the Mediator said with an embarrassed look.

_____Anyway, sorry I laughed! . . . Let's get moving! There's a real strange article on the Big Shot in today's paper.

_____Don't open the curtains yet! Sayoko interjected from the passenger seat. Not until the van's out of here. . . .

Although puzzled by the request, we somehow agreed that the precaution was appropriate—even though still a bit uncertain as to why. The engine started, and the scriptwriter-to-be—who, practically speaking, was always prepared for anything—let it idle for a while, then told the girl to open the front window curtains as she stepped on the accelerator. The vehicle lurched and bumped forward, and the front window provided me with a panoramic view: a clear blue sky and the majestic, picture-perfect Mt. Fuji dead ahead. The combination of the breathtaking view ahead and the **DONGAN, DONGAN, GUUURRRUUU** be-hind us was too much for me. A meaningless chuckle escaped, Hheee! as if letting air out from my pent-up body. Ōno's broad shoulders swayed right, then left, as if she were turning the wheel of a storm-tossed ship, but as soon as the van was back on paved ground, she propelled the machine swiftly and smoothly down the highway. Once the van managed to get onto the paved road, away from the **DONGAN, DONGAN, GUUURRRUUU**, the workers began to chase us, jumping over the concrete debris. As Ōno steered the van, she glanced back for a second over her shoulder, a triumphant smile spreading across her face.

——Some of the road crew showed up early this morning, she shouted over the engine noise. They told me to move the van off the shoulder, so I gave them a line about a movie being shot here! I told them that after the actresses had taken a breather, we'd shoot a scene: naked women running all over the gravel and concrete! They were so sweet. Let me use the restroom at the construction camp, and lent me the morning paper. They increased the noise level of the jackhammer, though, I guess, to make the actresses wake up quicker.

——Two helmeted guys with a camera jumped from the bulldozer! the Mediator eagerly added, playing along with the driver.

The girl, typically cooperative but never ingratiating with Ōno, some-how managed to stick to her principles. She responded,

——I do give you credit for keeping the van stationary, but you didn't have to say we'd be shooting naked women. That was so bour-geois. Putting them on like that, using female nudity, caters to the worst male sexism.

——You said it. I was very depressed. I wanted desperately to do something entertaining, off the wall. And Ōno seemed a new person this morning, actually quite vulnerable.

——It's OK, water under the bridge. . . . Do you all want to see today's paper? Some real weird stuff!

The Yamame pair's response was enthusiastic and immediate, but without hesitation the girl handed the paper to Mori—perhaps a mani-festation of a tacit agreement that Mori had to read it first.

He wore an intent look on his face, along with what I'd say was a three-day beard. Actually, the growth adorning his jaw-line and cheeks framed the features of a much older man. The switchover couldn't have instantaneously produced that, I thought. To put it the way the German shrink Erikson* would, it was a face which expressed a calm sorrow, that

*Erik H. Erikson (b.: 1902) is the German-born American psychiatrist and social philoso-pher who links psychoanalysis with political science, ideology and theology, and history. His school of thought is called "psycho-history."

of a man who, having already experienced the vagaries of an adolescent identity crisis, grasped for the first time the quintessential meaning of his worldly existence, and was determined to carry out his assigned mission.

Soon Mori looked up and stared straight at me. Still not quite awake, my puffy, beardless teenaged face so naked, I flinched under his gaze—but his eyes seemed full of encouragement. Something cheerful danced behind those familiar eyes, lighting up the slightly melancholy brown of his pupils. They said: Trouble is brewing, but whatever it is, let's get something out of it, have some fun. Even before the switchover, his eyes sparkled and danced just like that when he fell into a hot bath, was bitten by a big dog, or fell out of a tree. In response to his message, I said to myself: *Mori will squeeze every bit of fun he can out of his premonition, while accepting the challenge of the adventure to come. This time I'll go with him!*

I reached for the paper Mori handed me, read the article, and re-capped its gist for the group.

——The Patron is hospitalized. A group of his constituents—peasants, forestry workers, etc.—fifty in all, went to pay a visit. The article says that now they've congregated for a sit-in right in front of the hospital, dressed as clowns. The reporter is obviously making fun of them, though. He says some are in folk costumes, some in Yakuza outfits, and others are dressed like the comedians Chaplin and Takase. Everyone is grouped in pairs. However, the article says, the clowns' gathering is about to turn into a refugee camp. The hospital administration wants to get rid of them, but the Patron insists that they're a "good omen" from home, and they should be allowed to continue their sit-in. Looks chaotic from this tiny wirephoto. But the call to action I read in Mori's eyes was gradually taking hold of me.

2

After the paper had made the rounds, the girl let out a long sigh as she pored over the picture.

——Why is the Japanese peasant's political consciousness so low, so crude? They look so depressed, uptight, so squirmy—I detest it! They're far from the image I have of revolutionary peasants.

——**HUNH?** The rest of us lacked words to respond.

——And what's the use of putting on costumes at a time like this?

——Now's exactly the time for them to dare to disguise themselves, Able Official said, trying to enlighten us. The cruder, the better for a peasant masquerade, don't you think? Still, as far as I can tell from this picture, there is a distinctly depressed mood at the gathering. But once they get going so that the spirit of merriment can start percolating, they'll crack the audience up, and soon even join in the laughter themselves. This is an authentic grassroots confab of clowns. In the Big Shot's home territory, you know, they dress up in costumes for local festivals and Shinto purification rituals. That's all mentioned in the article. Their illustrious guardian's in a bad way, as they see it, and they've come to exorcise the evil spirits.

——But the report says they're just sitting around like refugees, there's nothing about dancing or exorcising anything. . . . And if they're going to conduct a ritual exorcism, why don't they dress for that occasion? The article says they were already decked out in their crazy outfits when they arrived on the Bullet Train, ahaha—a group of fifty! Why? What sort of logic is that?

——Simple. They were basically scared. They can't approach a man as terrifying as the Big Shot without the costumes, without painted faces. Besides, wouldn't they also be frightened of going to Tokyo, of getting on the Bullet Train? So, to rally their courage, they summoned the power of a world far different from the real one through the medium of masquerade.

——I'm also from the provinces, but my area wasn't as underdeveloped as theirs, and we didn't have any customs like that.

——Can you determine if something's developed or underdeveloped just by taking a superficial look at it? Able Official turned to Dog Face and they both burst out laughing. Doesn't this remind you a lot of what we called the *iwana* method?

——We learned it from the *Mountain Fishing Places* book the Corps used for their Long March. The fisherman-author wrote in a strikingly unique style that matched the originality of his concept. He held that a subterranean river lies concealed below every little mountain stream. A passage, called a *goro*, connects two rivers. *Iwana* spawn and develop in one of these subterranean rivers, where they also die. Only a small number of all the *iwana*—the number is fixed by the whole *iwana* society—come up to the surface river. Proof of this comes when a storm sweeps over a mountain range, burying its mountain river in mud and silt; once the water begins to flow again, you can easily catch *iwana*. The writer says this means that the surviving fish in the subterranean river have surfaced.

——We once tried to define the Yamame Corps as guerrillas who create an alternate society underneath the real society, and continually pass through the *goro* out into the world. . . . But, you know, revolution actually always occurs from within society; guerrillas only function as a catalyst for the revolution, right? Wasn't that how we got around the *iwana* theory?

——If we apply that way of thinking here, we see that this party of clowns is adopting the very same method. Don't they have a subterranean society below the local society? Didn't they just happen to come out of the *goro* en masse because of the Big Shot's injury? Probably they came out one or two at a time, until they arrived at the necessary number of clowns—something like one from each village community would do it. At the very moment when the "surface society" seems to have been buried in a landslide of modernization—just look at Tokyo—and when buffoonery seems on the verge of extinction, isn't there a place in the subterranean society for birth and death à la the *iwana*/buffoon method? The Big Shot knew of it, he probably invited them himself. It's costing them a lot to come here.

——For what reason?! the girl shouted irritably.

——**MORI AND I SAY THE YAMAME CORPS IS RIGHT!** I couldn't help cutting her short. Didn't he also hold the party to give Mori and me a silent invitation? We'd fit in, we'd feel more comfortable at a party for buffoons. As long as the Patron is communicating with us, we must watch for a chance to join the group and approach him.

With the greatest of ease and the slightest of gestures, Mori restrained the girl. She was just about to strike out at me. Didn't that gesture mean that he wanted me to tell everyone about what had just popped into my head? Armed with that sort of moral support, I began to explain.

——The Patron is a very powerful figure. He subsidizes the hospital he's staying in, so it's very easy for him to keep the media in the dark as far as the true nature of his condition is concerned. Of course, it hasn't been reported anywhere, but I can't help thinking that he's dying from wounds suffered in Mori and Sayoko's assault. Don't you think he knows it? If he's to pull off the ultimate gamble, doesn't he need to capitalize on the power of our switchover? I can't believe a seasoned gambler like him didn't pick up on Mori's supernatural power. If he compared his hunches with my wife/*ex*-wife's ranting and raving, he'd put two and two together. So he's made an educated guess: what's happening to Mori and me is so cataclysmic, that the whole world might be turned upside down. Or it may have just been his hunch that he could capitalize on our bizarre state. At any rate, I think he's lying in wait for us.

——Maybe, Ōno remarked coolly. But it might be a trap for just you and Mori.

——Why would he have to put together such an elaborate trap to do the police's dirty work? I don't think he operates that way. But whether it's a trap or not, Mori and I have to go ahead with this. I now feel driven to it. It's the will of the switchover. . . . If the Patron is going to make use of it in his takeover plan, then we've got to turn the tables on him, use his own weapon against him, and defeat his plan for world domination. At this early stage in the struggle, we've got the upper hand. We know more about the switchover than he does.

——That's right, Dog Face said with a sharp look and decisive tone of voice. Even if you're cornered, you can self-destruct and nullify the power when he tries to use it! You can deny him an easy victory!

—— . . . I've given this a lot of thought. Those Revs are hardliners. Once they come to believe in the switchover, they and the Counterrevs will both vie with one another for control of the pair. If neither party comes out on top, they'll both try to snuff you out rather than hand you over to anyone else. My opinion is that Mori and Mori-father had better begin their job, their switchover mission, as soon as possible. You don't have much of a head start. I'm all for you two slipping in with that gang of buffoons to have a showdown with the Big Shot.

Mori smiled broadly in silence. The eagerness he had gradually built up was now obvious in a smile that said, **FINALLY, OUR ACTION AGAINST THE PATRON HAS BEEN RECOGNIZED!**

——Well, if that's the case, then there won't be much use for a rescue operation, Able Official commented forlornly, in sharp contrast with the unsentimental Dog Face, who'd predicted Mori's and my self-destruction.

——Nope, but we do want you to get rid of my wife/*ex*-wife when she pursues us to the hospital. That'll be a great help. Who knows. That getup of hers—you know, the black helmet—might get her into the costume ball.

Everyone except Mori laughed. I hadn't meant to be funny—I was really worried. . . .

——You two don't quite look like clowns. You've got to dress the part! I'll pick up some costumes from a TV studio while you rest a bit and have a bite before you go. Now this is my plan: Why not put a spotlight on the direction in which the switchover has taken each of you guys, and go for costumes which emphasize the fact that one of you has gotten older, the other younger?!

3

Three hours later, Mori and I set out for the hospital where the gang of buffoons had assembled, in costumes perfect for the occasion, the result of the scriptwriter-to-be's brilliant imagination.

Mori was dressed up as a decrepit old man, escalating the effect of his switchover by one hundred years. Dirty caramel-colored hair down to his ankles, with a similarly colored beard and two rabbit tails for eyebrows. A floor-length robe made out of a grayish blanket, a metal staff twisted and gnarled to look like a banyan root. Wood slabs tied around canvas shoes: instant wooden shoes! The only vestige of Mori I found was in the subdued brown of his irises and the cheerful luster of his pupils.

Me, a kangaroo-baby! I was outfitted in a one-piece baby costume—its former pink color now a soiled gray. To top off the effect, a pink frilly hat. Too bad I had to bare my teenaged face, ha, ha.

The gang of sit-in clowns in front of the hospital compound—each in his own outlandish costume—were obviously startled by the sight of Mori and me as we got off the bus opposite the hospital and started across the street. You can picture our cleverly consummate disguises, can't you?

The first looks they gave us as they huddled closer together, told me that hostile external social pressure had forged this group. In response to our appearance, two security guards immediately leapt out of the crowd. They wore black rubber suits and gas masks. The "weapons" they carried looked something like flame throwers. The face plates on the gas masks were fogging up, apparently because they were constantly twisting and craning their necks to get a better look at us, ha, ha.

We tried to weave our way through the traffic but got stuck mid-street, forced into the role of onlookers at a distance. There we stood: a superannuated oldster in makeshift wooden shoes who had difficulty walking, and a grown-up dressed as a baby. It was an early spring afternoon. Mori and I were soaking in our own sweat. Our breathing grew more rapid and labored as we waited for the heavy traffic flow to subside. Passing drivers and passengers goggled at us, with a look of mixed embarrassment and indignation as though they'd seen a pair of eccentric cripples, and then relaxed into a faint smile, though they still continued to gape. I guess they *figured* a "Candid Camera" show was being shot somewhere!

When we somehow made our way down the street and trotted toward the gang of clowns, scooting past those two rubber suits—on closer inspection I saw they were dressed as a pesticide spray team—before they could bar our way, the gang's public relations people stepped forward: a dour-looking man—I first mistook him for a young boy with an oversized head—and a hugely corpulent woman munching on something in a plastic cup. One a dwarf, the other certifiably obese, no fancy costumes, yet people most probably regarded them as authentic clowns. I'm sure their physical handicaps suffice for normal folks to say, no disguises or slapstick needed: they can play PR front men because they embody the essence of buffoonery. Isn't perversion of physical standards the requirement for being a buffoon?

——Hey, hey, you! The dwarf displayed all the dignity appropriate to his PR role. True, he waddled a bit, but was otherwise perfectly composed. He called out to us again. **HEY, HEY, YOU! WHAT'RE YOU DOING IN COSTUMES LIKE THAT?**

I roared! I laughed so hard that my constricting baby outfit began to choke me. Mori also started laughing, waggling all the hair that hung over his entire body. The opening he had for a mouth gave out a prolonged **HAAAAAN, HAAAAAN!** Before the switchover, Mori and I used to laugh together like that. . . .

The brown-suited PR dwarf, straightening his tie with tiny fat fingers, kept a wary eye on the two of us as we shook, speechless with laughter. Suddenly wrinkling up his face, he let out an approximation of a sneeze. And that sound was the start of his own vigorous laughter! Dumbfounded, it was our turn to turn serious; the dwarf spokesman, turning red and black from laughter, disappeared into the sit-in. He'd realized the ridiculousness of his own question. Wouldn't you say that's a pretty smart clown?!

The obese woman, who still remained behind, pressed the plastic cup against her mountainous chest, popped its lid, poked her fingers in, kneaded something and then shot it into her mouth. I surmised she'd earlier poured some tap water into a cup of instant noodles, and now wrapped the glutinous contents around her fingers and scarfed them down in one gulp. With crocodile eyes, she looked at the now composed Mori and me accusingly. We became aware of the deadly silence that had swept over the gang, curious for the moment yet feigning indifference.

In the meantime, the fat woman used her shoulders to wipe off the three greasy fingers she'd used for the food, leaving smooth shiny marks that looked oil-brushed. Pushing the lid of the cup back in place, she put it inside her voluminous dress!

——**WELL, FOR NOW, YOU SHOULD SIT DOWN!** she yelled, arrogantly indicating with her triple, no, quadruple chins the spot where we were to sit!

We'd gotten into the gang of buffoons without a hitch. We squeezed ourselves past a group which I noticed included Kunisada Chuji and his boys—when sandlot baseball was all the rage, every night the young demobilized soldiers laughed themselves silly over his play about yakuza, harlots, and an evil local magistrate. But when Mori's makeshift wooden shoes trampled a man's straw-sandaled foot, all that ensued was a shake of his dyed topknot. His head hung low; he looked utterly depressed. In fact, the whole group appeared down in the dumps.

We finally found a spot to sit, covered with a styrofoam sheet—probably the Patron's secretary had furnished it. I then discovered we were rubbing elbows with a man and woman whose bodies were swathed in bandages. Loose yarn threads hung between the cracks. That reminded me. A conscript worker, an A-bomb victim at a shipyard in Kure, came back to our village with bandages covering his entire body. When my mother removed them for him, clumps of fat maggots fell out of his wounds, filling a large bottle. . . . Were this man and woman depicting a new strain of plague or pestilence from a local festival for the dead, like the one that killed that poor guy in my village? Were they a pair of avenging spirits for those who died in the A-bomb attacks?

I took a closer look around. A Charlie Chaplin, the Marx Brothers, were rubbing shoulders with an infantryman who died on a South Pacific atoll, a sweat-banded suicide commando, and a drowned sailor. An air raid victim covered in soot, wearing a split soccer ball on his close-cropped head, was also present. . . . I was so intrigued by each costume that my hand unconsciously began to pull the bandaged man's yarn maggots, but he feebly shook me off. The gesture indicated how angry he was, but he was hardly the exception. The silent gang was obviously exhausted and irritated, up to its neck in ill humor. Still, no one seemed ready to drop out. They were sitting around with an air of necessity about them that said, So long as we put on these costumes, we've got to have a festival before we do anything else.

The tense atmosphere was almost overwhelming to me, but Mori seemed relaxed. He held the white hair which had been swinging in the breeze against his chest so that it wouldn't get in the way; he quietly raised his bearded face to the sky. His presence gave me renewed confidence, reassuring me again of his total reliability. I was now convinced that as long as I stuck by him, in due course we'd succeed in our goal!

The buffoons—who now included Mori and me—were sitting at the corner of the left side of the T-shaped hospital complex: the main building stretched out horizontally and merged on the left with a high-rise annex sheathed in glass. Beyond the glass wall we could see, in sharp contrast with our group's eccentric and seedy appearance, hordes of neatly turned out children who'd evidently tired of waiting in line and had gathered there to watch. Then I caught a glimpse of an interesting development among the crowd of kids. Using them as a cover, two men—one with a large Polaroid camera—were taking pictures of our gang, impatiently pulling out the film after each shot! There was no doubt: they were the Patron's secretaries. Nor was there any doubt that they could very easily compare pictures taken at various times of the day. In the fresh batch of photos they'd just taken, they should find a noteworthy change. And they would circle Mori and me with a red embossed grease pencil bearing the name of the Patron's company. No wonder Mori was standing so confidently among the clowns!

4

In the meantime a substantive change was occurring in the gang. Their consciousness, coalescing but still fragmented till now, was finally gathered into a collective whole. And this unified consciousness had physically turned in a direction totally opposite to what I assumed it would—even Mori turned to look in that direction.

What was happening in front? Two of the gang, not outsiders like us, who'd gone out on an errand had returned; the two had donned demon masks and now brought back a festival float with them. Mounted on a three-wheeler—you don't see them in Tokyo anymore— was an altar, secured by a wooden frame twice the size of the cart, and on top of that sat the huge head of a lion. Sandwiching the cart were two demon escorts on one side and a clown in fireman's gear arguing with a rather bureaucratic-looking colleague on the other. I was impressed by the authenticity of their costumes until I looked closer and realized they actually were from the Fire Department, ha, ha. Flanked by the rubber-suited security guards, the dwarf and the fat woman joined in the argument. With the undisguised curiosity typical of a teenager, I pushed my way through the gang but reached the cart right in the middle of a heated discussion, so I couldn't get the full gist of what was going on. While trying to pick up the thread of their argument, I carefully studied the structure of the cart in question. The lion's head itself had a certain aura of dignity about it; but its lower jaw was missing and that forced the entire head into a backward tilt, which actually made it look rather foolish. Despite this, the head—with its blood-red and gold lacquer peeling off—was securely fixed in that position by a bunch of stuffed toys stripped of all clothing. A chalk-white bellied Kintaro, a Girl's Festival doll* with its straw stuffings exposed. Strange? Well, Cupid doesn't wear any clothes, ha, ha. Besides the

*Two traditional holidays in Japan celebrate children: the Festival of Boys (May 5), and the Festival of Girls (March 3). On these occasions the children are wished the best of health and every future success appropriate to their gender. The tradition grew out of the terribly high infant and child mortality rates of ancient times. The boys' festival revolves around military paraphernalia—armor, armaments, ceremonial battle dress—and is epitomized by the figure of Kintaro, a folk hero represented by a doll on the holiday. Kintaro was a legendary mountain warrior, and a sumo champion who successfully wrestled bears and other wild beasts. He symbolizes the heroic strength, the bravery, the invincibility in battle wished upon the boy-child. The girls' festival celebrates the courtier life. In each

traditional folk dolls, futuristic toy robots, and various other figurines were crammed into the lion's mouth, giving the impression that they were spewing out of its lower jaw. Tattered banners—the kind you see hanging at the Jizo Temple—were heaped around the head; multicolored flags, dolls' clothes, and piles of futons were strewn helter-skelter.

Meanwhile, it appeared that the disputants could no longer communicate with each other; the situation was deteriorating. The two demons pushed their wooden masks up over their hempen hair, revealing dark peasant faces, drenched in sweat. At least their voices were now more audible, even though their argument still made little sense.

——This is a national scandal, you hear, and we've got to inform our *sensei*! We hate to bother him in his serious condition with such a trivial matter!?

——**IMBECILE!** Don't mention the patient's name, Master, Master Nine-Eleven!

——A scandal is a scandal, isn't it? Are we duly elected town councilmen or just errand boys?

——Don't say that! In those ridiculous costumes, coming all this way to Tokyo, councilmen my ass! **IMBECILE!** Just get to the point. Don't digress!

——We've had these ceremonial bonfires for generations, for hundreds of years, got it!? We could've done it without informing anyone! The authorities were kind enough to tell us to register at the local Fire Department for a permit, so we dragged this cart all the way down here just to be told, No permit! That's a scandal. If they can't issue a permit, then why did they tell us to apply for one?

——You know you're an **IMBECILE!?** Sure you can be denied a permit. If anything and everything's permitted, why get a permit in the first place? You're in Tokyo now, don't act like a hick from the sticks!

——That's the way it has to be, got it? The Fire Department bureaucrat edged closer to the seemingly sensible demon. But the demon shot back a declaration!

——If we can't get a permit, we can't get one! So we'll burn the cart the way we damn please!

——**WHAT THE HELL ARE YOU TALKING ABOUT!** Didn't you hear what I just said! The bureaucrat was once again hopping mad, ha, ha.

——If you ask me, the dwarf spokesman interrupted, **YOU'RE** the know-nothing! **WHAT THE HELL ARE YOU TALKING ABOUT?**

——**WE**, the fat woman added, **ARE ALL IN THIS TOGETHER!**

---

home with a girl-child, an extraordinary display of beautiful and elaborately dressed dolls is set up, featuring especially those dolls in costumes depicting attendants of the imperial family.

——There are ten million people in Tokyo besides you, got it. You've also got to think about them. Everyone in Tokyo can easily see you guys have no common sense. You swarm all over the hospital lawn, in getups like that, and then want to torch a cart. The public wouldn't stand for something so preposterous. You accept the fact that it's our job to protect Tokyo, don't you?

——We've got a job to protect the ten million people in this town, too! That's exactly why we're doing this!

——Aren't you just offering prayers for Mr. A's complete recovery?

——Whoever he is. Do you think we'd come out in such a big way, in these outfits, disgracing our community, just to pray for the recovery of one sick person? Think about it. Use your common sense!

——You sure talk big, but I've got to point out that compared with the welfare of ten million Tokyoites, you're nothing.

——**ARE YOU SURE YOU WANT TO SAY THAT?** The dwarf spokesman hastily made threatening noises. We've brought a lion's head here with its mouth open wide to the gates of hell. We've got to burn it, in Tokyo! In the midst of ten million people!

——**I TOLD YOU, YOU CAN'T SET FIRE TO A CART IN THE MIDDLE OF THE CITY!**

——**ARE YOU OUT OF YOUR MIND?** The fireman who'd kept his mouth shut up till now pushed his big helmet up over his forehead and chimed in with the angry bureaucrat.

The more incensed the two from the Fire Department became, the more the PR dwarf treated them as he would a pair of winos, projecting an air of studied indifference. The clown with the demon mask, a man with a modicum of good sense, then took over from the spokesman.

——We just want to burn a little altar! You mean that'll frighten ten million people? he said accusingly.

The other demon, who'd been continually put down by the sensible demon—was he pushing a good thing too far, or, just giving up in despair?—lifted his hempen straw coat to reveal a red jerry-can underneath, marked ESSO!

——We'll souse everything in kerosene and burn it. It'll be over in ten minutes!

——**WHAT, WHAT, WHAT THE HELL ARE YOU TALKING ABOUT? WE'LL CONFISCATE THE KEROSENE!**

In response to the bureaucrat's shouting, the fireman leapt at the kerosene demon, who dodged him with ease. His demon mask back over his face, the pyromaniac started beating on the kerosene can tied to his belt with a wooden pestle as he continued to outrun his pursuer!.... A small riot squad—God knows where they'd been hiding all this time—stormed in, one of the riot shields glancing off the demon with enough force to knock him to the pavement. They seized the container and stripped off the man's demon mask and straw raincoat, leaving him exposed in his underwear. Lying on his right side, he cradled his head in both arms; the sunburnt face visible between the elbows looked a dull black.

Whereupon, the entire gang of clowns stirred, crying out in one voice **WOOWW!** I first thought the cry was one of anger, a sign of protest, but when I turned around, the gang was hooting with laughter! Stunned by this, I frantically searched for Mori; the masquerading old man was standing away from the group in front of the glass wall, the Patron's secretary right next to him.

12

The Switchover Pair's
Sparring Match

1

The Patron's secretary, as he saw me—or rather, an infant—trotting
toward him, quickly averted his eyes.

——We caught on soon enough that you'd joined this loony bunch.
He displayed the same capable air he always did whenever I presented
my briefing papers. The Patron told me to bring you to his room. The
police have staked out this building, but we'll work something out. He's
already managed to admit a representative of these loonies to do a
ritual *Shinto* dance. If I escort you in, the police will figure you've been
invited for another *Shinto* dance.

Without bothering to wait for our reply, the secretary started to walk
away from the hospital entrance. Mori and I reluctantly followed him—
of course my switched-over soul leapt in anticipation!

——Putting one over on the police might get you in hot water later.
I found myself trying to play up to him.

——I'm just faithfully carrying out the Patron's orders. . . . Fact is, I
don't care what happens to him! He's finished. He's apparently hanging
on to a wild fantasy, you know. The tough, globe-trotting realist Patron's
gone! He's making sure that those crazy peasants of his are well taken care
of. . . . No matter how you look at it, he's out of it, psychologically.

——Then why keep hanging around the old fruitcake?

——*Curiosity!* the secretary replied, with a quick glance at me. And to think I'd tried to curry favor with this little puke, I thought to myself.

We turned the corner at the end of the glass wall and walked along a row of hospital rooms. A fence and passageway began at the other side of those rooms, with another row of rooms, a fence and passageway beyond. The patients hadn't seen anything of the gathering of clowns outside the hospital entrance. Their caustic gazes took us by surprise; they seemed to be rebuking us for our costumes, *When we're suffering, how can you cut up like that right under our noses?* We breathed a little easier when we finally reached the service entrance. But it was a do-or-die situation for us the moment we saw three policemen standing guard in the corridor leading to the Patron's room.

Inside the large room—five meters from where we stood—lay an old man, his head swathed in bandages. He looked straight toward us, his unfocused pupils straining to make out what we were wearing. The Patron, once suave and handsome in a Western sort of way, now looked like an aged nineteenth-century woman! I immediately sent a telepathic message to Mori: **THIS IS A PREGNANT OLD WOMAN, WHAT THE HELL'S HAPPENED?!**

All we could do was wait and watch while the immobile Patron rolled his eyeballs as far as they'd go from left to right. Apparently there was nothing for the two secretaries to do, either the one who led us in or the other one posted at the sickbed, until the Patron requested something. Then I noticed someone else inside the room, whimpering, **BURRRRUUU**, like a dog. The whining came from a man with a huge bald head; he squatted on the floor, right next to, almost on top of, the Patron's enormous swollen belly. He seemed to be taking note of the patient's vital signs, the condition of his phlegm, and any other bodily changes. The big head looked familiar. Yes. He was number one or two in oil tankers in Japan, and often regarded in the political and financial communities as the champion of the postwar nouveau riche. Particularly adept, I recall, in the arts of bribery and corruption. He twisted his thick, sinewy lips and whined as he raised his head toward Mori and me.

The whining was perhaps a silent signal, because the Patron formally recognized our arrival, first by a barely audible laugh, then by what he said in a very hoarse voice, which I didn't anticipate from one who'd always had a deep, resonant voice,

——Phha, phha, phha, you sure love doing unexpected things, . . . and after all of that serious philosophizing, phha, phha, phaa, how unusual! I assumed you in that getup were the one who assaulted me, phha, phha, phha. You look pretty convincing. As a pair I can almost believe that something really extraordinary has happened, that you're part of something supernatural. Was it you, or the other one there, who paid me the visit at my office? I can't tell anymore. Phha, phha, phha. Don't just stand there gawking, come over here. It tires my eyes if I've got to strain from this angle to make out what kind of weird outfits you're wearing. But leave that long staff there, the sight of it makes me uneasy—you might attack me again, phha, phha, phha.

The Patron's voice had been feeble throughout, and the mottled reddish black skin at the collar of his nightshirt betrayed his weakened condition. Taking his cue from the Patron, the tanker dealer strode around to where we stood at the foot of the bed. The muscles in his neck and shoulders bulged, and with his rosy complexion, I'd never seen a man in his early fifties looking as fit and robust as this one did. Mori's metal staff was taken from him. The dealer carefully scrutinized it, his thick lips pressed together in concentration. From head to toe, he looked to be a thoroughly dynamic individual; even his bald head added something to that powerful aura. But the expansive, melancholic cast of his face threw one's impression of him totally out of sync. During this inspection, the two secretaries had been tiptoeing around the room, trying to decide where to set two chairs, before they were put beside the bed, *No, this is too close, and that'd be too far, wouldn't it be a mistake to let them sit too close?* Compared with the calculated gestures of the businessman, the two were quite inefficient.

——Have a seat, the Patron said, waiting till we took our places before he closed his eyes and put the tip of his whitish tongue against the upper plate of his false teeth. You get the picture. I was sitting very close to the Patron, close enough to see the inside of his mouth. Phha, phha, phha, just talking hurts, you know. I might as well forget about talking, keep my mouth shut till I die, but I guess I need to say something to wrap things up in my life. Now, what words have I chosen in my life? Phha, phha, phha. What were my first really meaningful words? It's been a long time, my parents and brothers should know but I've got no way to find out. Phha, phha, phha.

Steam appeared to rise from the moist eyelids above his closed bloodshot eyes, even as tears streamed down the crevices and cracks around his turtle-like eyes. Almost instantly, a large, shiny, hairless hand shot out with a piece of gauze and wiped away the tears. Fresh gauze appeared almost as quickly to remove the spider web of phlegm which hung over the gaping mouth. Wasn't it strange? This same proficient nurse was the bigwig whose imprint could be found on every kind of real and implicit scandal. I also couldn't shake the impression that those unusually large pink hands of his belonged to a sumo wrestler, a eunuch wrestler at that. In any case, the hands moved with great speed and accuracy. If we'd shown any sign of harming the Patron, I'm sure those same hands would immediately reach from behind us and break our necks. The thought of this potential threat to my life set an immediate tremor in motion from my throat all the way to my testicles, ha, ha.

——I'm dying, but it's nothing to do with your companion hitting me in the head. They found a cancer in me when they were fixing me up. If they got the cancer before it's spread too far, you might even say I benefited from that incident, phaa, phaa, phaa, the Patron said in a slightly more audible voice. And while he gave Mori and me the once-over with his single open eye, its cloudy center began to sparkle with a triumphant glea. . . . They say the incidence of cancer is very high among people who've been exposed to A-bombs. In my case, lung cancer developed quite rapidly, then moved into the spinal cord. At this stage morphine is the only thing that can ease the pain. I've had it for such a long time, though. . . , the Patron trailed off. Tears oozed again from his eyes, and again the whimpering nurse-cum-wheeler-dealer nimbly stretched out his hand and wiped them away, together with the accumulating phlegm. . . . I'm a dying old man, and I often look at myself and everything around me and see there's nothing, only ugliness and misery. . . . I really hate it. No hope, nothing wholesome to cling to. . . . After all these years, what an awful way to end! Phaa, phaa, phaa— the Patron was really sobbing!

Mori and I kept our silence, as the tanker trader's arm once more zoomed into action; the two secretaries—even the one who'd sounded so cynical—began to cry aloud.

——Phaa, phaa, phaa. . . this is awful. I want somehow to turn my horrible, despicable death into something good, turn things topsy-turvy. . . . The cancer's in its last stages, no way I'll make it. I was just thinking. Maybe there's a way to turn this ugly death upside down, convert it to something eye-opening, spectacular—like a huge fireworks display. Then I thought about you. Besides, I'm really convinced that your attack in that clever disguise led to the discovery of my cancer. . . . Phaa, phaa, phaa, now that you're here with your companion, I'm even more convinced that I can count on your ingenuity. . . . What're you supposed to be in that getup? What in the world happened to you? Phaa, phaa, phaa. . . . You—or was it your companion pretending to be you— came into my office and whacked me in the head. What was that all about? So I'd know about the cancer? Phaa, phaa, phaa. . . . Come on, what's up? What convinced you to pull off something as daring as a daylight raid? . . . Compared to those yokels of mine sitting out front, you're a pro, the real exorcist. Phaa, phaa, phaa, What're you doing here? Whatever it is, it's a lot more interesting than those briefs you used to submit. Phaa, phaa, phaa. . . . What's this all about? What do you intend to do?

Fear, searing like acid through my spine and nerve endings, overwhelmed me the minute the Patron's raspy voice broke off. Mori might declare, *Well, this is what we came for* and then attack the Patron. Those gigantic hands behind us could easily snap off our heads. In panic I began a nonstop monologue.

——My son Mori and I have been switched over. When the sun rose one morning, after a very difficult night, we were switched over. If you remember, I was thirty-eight. But somehow during that night I lost twenty years and was transformed into an eighteen-year-old! It's obvious in the mirror, my own body proves it. I feel it's taken over everything in my life. You see, I've already been an eighteen-year-old. I know that in my head, but once your body's transformed, your senses, your soul, everything, gets changed! A sort of memory inertia is at work against the rest of me, so there are uncertain moments where the switchover and my spirit jostle backward and forward. . . . But what's important is that my son's been switch*ed* over in the opposite direction! He was a retarded eight-year-old, and now overnight he's turned into a twenty-eight-year old, in both body and spirit! Also, we've both experienced a kind of switchover that taps our strong parent-child bond as a lever for the transformation.

(The Patron moved his head toward us almost imperceptibly; his bleary half-closed eyes continued studying me. He seemed to be struggling to say something but his overheated brain, probably at the melting point from the fever and drugs, wouldn't cooperate. Apparently he was not winning the struggle because his eyebrows twitched impatiently. Suppose the words had come. Just imagine those desiccated purple lips moving. Interrupted occasionally by a feeble laugh, they'd have said something like this: *Your wife, you see—well, you said you're separated, so I should say ex-wife, right? According to what she's passed on to my secretary, you were just disguised as a young man, and your son as an older man. And then you attacked me. The way you guys're dressed, it's hard for me to verify what you're telling me. Your wife/ex-wife said that because you were afraid her brother might harm you and your son, you made him disguise himself as your companion, and ever since, the both of you've been on the run. I was told she couldn't quite explain your motive for attacking me in disguise.*)

——The switchover has placed us under an ominous cloud, forcing us to keep on the run. . . . No, on second thought, the dark clouds apply only to me, the eighteen-year old! I'm sure the older, switched-over

Mori must know not only the Cosmic Will's whereabouts but also the kind of mission it has preordained for us. Mori attacked you right after the switchover. Clearly he did as instructed by the Cosmic Will. Although my wife/*ex*-wife insists that I disguised myself and struck—you must half-believe her—that's not what happened. Mori attacked you without telling me about his orders. If my wife/*ex*-wife had learned of this, she'd say that I was hiding with the retarded child, both of us in disguise, so I could somehow transfer my own violent crime to the boy! She really believes that, has organized a vigilante group, and has been chasing me ever since. But it wasn't me who attacked you. If Mori had told me about the Cosmic Will's instructions right after our switchover, I'd have joined him in the assault. . . . But I think Mori wanted to protect me, the teenager, from harm; he removed me from the attack plan. The father being protected was a teenager, so wasn't that his parental concern showing through? . . .

(Phaa, phaa, phaa, the Patron laughed feebly, the bloodshot eyes smiling. Perhaps the drugs he was on were subjecting him to some sort of manic-depressive roller coaster ride, from depression to elation. He'd recovered a little of his former bellicosity and appeared to want to speak again; it sounded like he said, *Phaa, phaa, phaa. You say the Cosmic Will caused this switchover. But all you've told me about so far are your domestic squabbles, nothing about this Cosmic Will. What is this Cosmic Will? Why did it order you to clobber me? Don't you think I've at least got the right to ask that question? Phaa, Phaa, phaa.*)

——This is what I think's going on. The Cosmic Will continues to pass on instructions to Mori. And he knows that the Cosmic Will's the source of those orders. All I need to do is give him a helping hand when he takes action. Rather than chance the directives being misinterpreted by a overzealous teenager, it's best that I know nothing specific, just believe in the Cosmic Will's existence and follow Mori's lead. A prime example: I'm here without the foggiest notion of what's next in the plan!

I still follow Mori because he communes with the Cosmic Will. Don't get me wrong. It's not that we're being dragged around by our noses. Mori's completely free, and so am I. The mission is one thing, but the switchover is another kettle of fish. The Cosmic Will did it to us without so much as asking whether we wanted it or were available. Don't you think it's impudent to dictate such an important change? From now on, I won't let the Cosmic Will behave so arrogantly toward Mori or me! . . . If you ask me if there is a way to object to the Cosmic Will, I say, Yes. We can still outsmart the Cosmic Will; the computer that was responsible for our switchover could be put out of action! Mori and I could commit suicide and all the investments made on us would be down the tubes!

(I made this comment in what I thought was an encouraging tone, and suddenly I felt a tremendous pressure on my left wrist! I nearly let out a loud groan as I asked myself where the pain was coming from. Mori. The enormous power of his right hand. The vise-like grip on my left wrist became tighter just as I was saying that it was impudent of the Cosmic Will to cram its orders down our throats. Initially I only felt something on my wrist, and even felt an embarrassing sort of pleasure as Mori's hand continued to apply extra pressure to my wrist, lying motionless on his powerful muscular thigh. So I kept up the monologue. But the pain of the pressure continually escalated, **WOO!** I tried to shake free of the vise. No use. By the time I was telling the Patron that we could outsmart the Cosmic Will by committing suicide, the pain was unbearable; sweat began to pop out on my face. In frustration I fell silent, waiting for Mori's reaction. His face was hidden in a mass of caramel-colored beard; with no visible expression, I couldn't tell if I'd gotten through to him. But as soon as I stopped talking, the superman grip on me was withdrawn. And Mori ever so gently caressed the injured spot. His right hand had eloquently formed his critique of what I said.)

——There must've been some cosmic significance in the fact that Mori attacked you right after the switchover, I said to the Patron, because he took the enormous risk of endangering the mission! Your guards could have beaten him to death or shot him. Also, there was the danger of being arrested.

An arrest for Mori'd be a terrifying situation! He might remain silent under interrogation; that could be misinterpreted as taking the Fifth, a near-admission of guilt. But once the authorities began a routine background check, and the more logical and rational their speculation on his life and actual biological age became, the more difficult it would be to pin him! After all, he's a new being, a switchover! A global background check would be impossible. Even if I say I'm his father, and offer to take him off their hands, how could an obvious eighteen-year-old convince them he's the twenty-eight-year-old criminal's father?

Worse, our communication would be cut off if he got killed or arrested. What would happen to the switchover mission? Mori's the sole communication link with the Cosmic Will. I'd end up a cosmic foundling! I might have to wander the ends of the universe as an eighteen-year-old orphan, at precisely the moment when the destiny of all humankind might depend on the switched-over pair!

(When I'd said this, I felt tongue-tied, a pitiful anxious feeling stabbing my insides. The Patron was laughing, Phaa, phaa, phaa, the discontented tanker trader was still whimpering, and the secretaries who'd stopped their weeping chorus merely smiled at my loquacity. The expression in Mori's right hand was very simple, gently reassuring. It transmitted to my body and spirit the benevolent voices in that chorus of long ago, *GO, GO, GO!* I had resolved to insist with renewed conviction that the switch*ed*-over pair had been picked as a pinch runner for humankind. If I had to respond to strangers who smiled or whimpered at us, I'd just say, I never ask myself what qualifications made the Cosmic Will designate us as the pinch runner. Besides, if we were really a superior player we would've already been a regular in the rescue game for humankind. But we can't hesitate now, or lose our confidence. We've already been picked. We're on base, where we've always wanted to be; the Cosmic Coach has given us the sign, concentrate, be alert for the chance to run. What's more, we've got to rely on our own sixth sense to make that decision! *GO, GO, GO, GO, GO, GO, GO, GO, GO.)*

——I was one of many collaborators all of whom did the same work and none of whom ever got to know the others, slaving for you for such a long time! I never gave a thought to how my task fit into the grander scheme. You made sure the rest of them wouldn't think about it either, didn't you? But my seemingly insignificant assignment, as part of the greater aggregate of work done by other workers, achieved a specific result! It ran contrary to the direction that I as a collaborator hoped it would take. . . . You used us as you liked all along to create a structure with which to dominate the whole world. Clever. You had it all figured out. Egged the radical student parties on, Go nuclear, you said. Then you funded them. Besides, you knew all along that even if word got out, nobody would take the rumor seriously, *Some group's going to make an A-bomb? What a joke, another leftist infantile disease!* Once the A-bomb's made, everybody would be too stunned to try and figure out the sudden turn of events. And now I've found that I had a hand in this! You meant to create the ultimate domination of man by man. The Cosmic Will just had to move against such an abomination; and since no power on earth could thwart your scheme, the Cosmic Will had no choice but to resort to direct intervention. . . . But there's something I don't quite understand. You say you're terminally ill, with cancer. Why bother to attack someone who's dying anyway? The Cosmic Will really doesn't have to do anything about your plans for the world, just sit tight and wait! Why switch us over and dispatch us as protesters? Isn't it meaningless to give us such a responsibility if you're going to die?

——**NO, IT ISN'T MEANINGLESS**, the Patron, said after he'd coughed up all the phlegm stuck in his throat. His spirited reply was clear, as clear as could be expected from a dying man. At this stage of the game, phaa, phaa, phaa, it's absurd for a wretched, dying man to expound on the global aspects of the issue at hand. What I can say is this: The Cosmic Will has engineered a switchover, and it's directed at me. How should I deal with it? For argument's sake, let's say there's a Cosmic Will. Asking, Why me? will get me nowhere. When you start asking questions like, Why was I born in this particular galaxy, out of all the millions of other galaxies, and on this particular planet Earth? you'll never find an answer, will you? Phaa, phaa, phaa. We're born on this planet, and all we can say is, Where do we go from here? So, if, as you said, I've been targeted by the Cosmic Will, then all I can really ask is, Where do I go from here? Phaa, phaa, phaa. You or your son actually came to attack me after the so-called switchover. Honestly, I first thought you'd gone bonkers, and just disguised yourself. Phaa, phaa, phaa.

. . . I passed out after you hit me in the head. The doctors who examined me found I had terminal cancer. Those same doctors were not allowed to touch me at all other than give me painkillers whenever I couldn't take the pain! Phaa, phaa, phaa (the Patron was sobbing again). . . . Well, assuming the Cosmic Will exists, and has chosen to work on me, then I regard my treatment here—or lack of it—as a sign that the moment to wrap up my life has come. *Phaa, phaa, phaa* (this time the Patron was laughing). And you and your son are here to help me with the finishing touches. Take your costume for example; that wouldn't have occurred to a mere earthling without some inspiration from the Cosmic Will, *phaa, phaa, phaa.*

When you look at it from that perspective, it's very difficult to say that what's happening is all meaningless. At the very moment I was beginning to think about how I should put the finishing touches on my life and to whom I could entrust the preparations, behold, you arrived—you and your son. **NO, NONE OF THIS IS MEANINGLESS, NOT AT ALL!**

A nurse entered the room to give the Patron an enema; I stood up to leave when something that felt like a hard rock smashed against my upper body. It was the hulk behind me grabbing my shoulder. Was it a reminder that I shouldn't even think of attacking the Patron? Glancing at Mori and me, the nurse relaxed a bit, but when she saw what sat behind us, she almost cried out in fright. She busied herself with her task and never again looked at us or the tanker trader.

——Have you let the hospital people know that after I defecate, my anal lining needs to be pushed back into my rectum with wet fingers? The tanker trader's huge head moved ever so slightly, a signal to the secretaries, one of whom immediately tiptoed out of the room, visibly shaken. You can be sure that in less than three minutes, all the floor nurses must have wet a couple of fingers, ha, ha.

For some time now we'd been hearing the sound of a great many people moving in the passageway next to the glass annex; it still continued. But the crowd seemed to stop at the end of the passageway, as if they'd come to a dead end. It wasn't that a great deal of shouting or noise issued from the passage, but the sound of a muffled mass of people moving about in a narrow cramped space was quite noticeable. I imagined they were trying to lower their voices so they wouldn't be heard, achieving the exact opposite effect: their low murmuring was increasingly audible. The muffled sound reached the bed. The fine features of the Patron's womanly face, which seemed impervious until now to the noise outside, instantaneously evinced the first signs of a hot temper building like a tidal wave beneath the calm exterior. But exhausted by his long illness, he now looked frightened in addition. The sound registered on the tanker dealer at about the same time, but he was trapped at his guard post, keeping an eye on Mori and me. His huge head rotated, this time more forcefully, and the remaining secretary in the room rushed to the window to scout out the situation.

——Those locals of yours have moved to the walkway between the main building and the new annex. They might start something. . . . They seem to have settled there, surrounded by spectators. Do you want me to clear them out? . . . We've been doing as instructed, letting them indulge in whatever they wanted; it must have gone to their heads, the way they're carrying on now. . . .

The Patron abandoned his usual tactic of diverting responsibility for his foul-ups by blasting out some choice insults at his underlings. His reply this time was phrased instead as though I were the key to the resolution of his problem. And actually I did feel a little better to be relieved of my own inactive moping around. This switched-over teenager is really quite naive, ha, ha.

——Would you mind finding out for me the specifics of what it is, exactly, those people intend to do, or what they're actually doing now? After all, you're disguised as they are; you must be able to figure out what's going on, phaa, phaa, phaa.

I walked by the tanker dealer, who gave me a guarded sidelong glance, and, looking down at the huge, shiny head that'd broken out in beads of oily sweat, I approached the secretary. He glared at me. When I saw the scene below, I couldn't restrain myself from sending a silent telepathic cry to Mori. *Boy, I have seen this scene before! It was the mural in the dining hall at the research center in California! The gigantic mural drawn by a Mexican painter, Diego Rivera!** It was *a pictorial history, with all the events*

---

*The three great mural painters of Mexico, Diego Rivera (1886–1957), José Clemente Orozco (1833–1949), and David Alfaro Siqueiros (1896–1974), each painted frescoes in

drawn as if they'd occurred simultaneously: the life of California Indians; con-
quistadors in search of El Dorado; and the conquest of the West by white Ameri-
cans. The emotions the mural evoked were transcended by an even more profound
feeling of nostalgia! If I'd had more time, I could have let Mori feel the
fullness of that nostalgia. . . .

In my mind's eye the style that the Mexican Mural Movement pio-
neered was now directly linked with the visual composition of the view I
had of the people down below. A low concrete barrier outside the
Patron's room afforded privacy but it also provided a frame for my
picture-perfect view of the swarming masses I beheld. On the walkway
cutting across my field of vision were clusters of clowns standing around
the cart, sandwiched between droves of spectators in a festive mood and
ready for any action. Patients' and nurses' heads peeped out from every
window of the other building. The riot squad stood ready with their
backs to us on the lawn next to the fence. It's no exaggeration to say
that, as far as I could see, throngs of human beings were packed into
this one view, exactly as in a Rivera mural.

The dwarf spokesman and his obese companion stood right in front
of the cart once again issuing a sort of solemn dignity, flanked by the
two ever-present guardsmen in black. These two appeared again to be
on edge. Now that the authority of the dwarf spokesman and the obese
woman was incontestable, the pair was trying to communicate with the
milling crowd about the opening of the festivities. Those in costume
were standing tall, obviously in an exuberant mood that sharply contrasted with their previous hunkered-down depression and ill-humor.
From my observation post I scanned the party with the encompassing
perspective offered by distance; when I'd been in their midst, what
appeared to be a hodgepodge of loitering buffoons now actually
seemed to have a certain structure, drawn out of the chaos. An entire
regional history was represented in their various costumes. It was local
history all right, but also a history of all humankind, in other words,
history being directly channeled into what I'd call a profound sense of
nostalgia.

——Dressed up peasants, forestry workers are all gathered around a
huge cart-shrine they've brought with them, I reported to the Patron,

---

California, some of which are still extant. There actually is an Orozco mural in a student
dining hall in a California college: "Prometheus" at Pomona College in Claremont. However, the description offered in the novel, and subsequent passages and events in the
novel, imply that what Mori-father is conveying here is actually a composite, almost a
generic overview, of the essential spirit and impact of the work of these artists taken
together. Each of the three, using his own very distinctive personal style, presents vast
tracts of history in a single time-plane, and each would use the spatial plane (a flat wall) in
such a way that the viewer is deceived, and sees vibrant, three-dimensional motion. The

who coughed up a glob of phlegm as if prompting me for more information. When we were down there with them a little while ago, we noticed costumes that said something about the calamities during and after the war. We stood shoulder to shoulder with that hero of the underdog, Kunisada Chuji, with Chaplin, and now I see the god Sarudahiko and his wife, the goddess Amenouzu-no-mikoto. I imagine all the participants are wearing costumes that express the uniqueness of their locale; it looks to me as if a panoply of human history is being reenacted right before our very eyes. Some of the characters remind me of descriptions of people in those local gazetteers. I also see an Emperor Meiji, and an Einstein. . . .

——An exorcism, isn't it? Is Sanemori the grain insect there to drive out the evil spirits? Phaa, phaa, phaa. These local-yokels are a thorough bunch. I bet they'll make sure the effect of the festival will be spread far and wide, phaa, phaa, phaa.

Despite his interruption of my commentary, something came to light in the crowd that suddenly grabbed my attention. Down among the hordes of spectators hemming in the clowns, I saw the bird-like face of my wife/*ex*-wife dressed all in black but with a red scarf wrapped around her neck, and her giant brother, looking quite haggard after the long chase. And there was Sakurao Ōno, maintaining an air of superiority as she held her ground against the jostling crowd at a spot where she could keep watch on the two. Sayoko, joined by the pair from the Yamame Corps, was closely scanning the windows of the hospital, probably in search of Mori. As soon as I'd spied them, I had a sneaking suspicion that the other spectators consisted of those two rival revolutionary parties—the participants of that chaotic antinuke meeting—reassembled here. If that was the case, no wonder the riot squad had rushed in like a house afire, ha, ha.

The only person I hadn't spotted yet was the Mediator. He should be standing around, slightly aloof from the group, waiting to be a witness to anything that could happen. My eyes continued to rove the crowd of spectators until they suddenly caught a familiar face, the tiny face of an overly conscientious individual, the Righteous Man, dressed in the same khaki tunic jacket I'd last seen him in! I was ecstatic! *Mori, there's been a*

---

details of the scene Mori-father mentions seem actually to come from a Rivera mural, "Allegory of California," which looms over a different dining hall—a private dining room in the San Francisco Stock Exchange. The fiery and tortured "Prometheus" scene of the Orozco mural also has pertinence to the novel, but so do Orozco's lesser known works "Clowning" and "Meeting of Buffoons." There are several relevant Siqueiros murals, though these would not be found in California; yet it is Siqueiros' artistic style—ferocious brush strokes, heavily overlaid paint—that most closely matches Mori-father's narrative voice and projected outlook.

mistake, the Righteous Man didn't die. If a fight breaks out here between those rival groups, he'll chomp into his opponent with dentures; I know he'll give them everything he's got. Look, there he is! A telepathic message to Mori. But I soon lost sight of the Righteous Man in the confusion of the milling crowd of onlookers. I knew for sure I'd seen him, but now he was nowhere visible.

——How's the festival going? Do you think they're powerful enough to control the cancer virus? Phaa, phaa, phaa. What do you think they're praying for? You don't think they've targeted me as a scourge to be rooted out, do you? Phaa, phaa, phaa.

——I don't know what they're praying for; they may not know, either. They did say something about protecting ten million people. One thing's clear about this ritual: those around the cart constitute a tiny cosmos. . . . I'm tempted to say that if we switchovers join the group, their cosmic structure would be more cohesive. Why don't you join, too? That slipped out before I had time to think. I had to restrain myself from saying, You'd be just perfect in that **OLD PREGNANT WOMAN** outfit.

——What do you mean this ritual's clear? Ridiculous! Me dying of cancer, in a clown suit? Forget it, the Patron said in irritation, ha, ha.

I had to return to my chair without being able to ascertain whether there was a real Righteous Man out there. The Patron's foul humor didn't last long, though. Once he'd seen it was useless to carry on a conversation with an audacious fantasizer like me, he decided it was high time for him to make a proposition to the switchover pair. He broached the subject as soon as I'd settled into my chair under the watchful eye of the tanker dealer.

——Are you and your son willing to listen to what I want to do in the final phase of my plan? If you leave without hearing me out, you'll get into trouble about that attack on me. Of course, I'm assuming the switchover is for real, phaa, phaa, phaa.

——Why yes, we'll listen, I replied, feeling Mori's strong approval on my wrist, **OF COURSE WE WILL!**

——The final stage of my plan concerns the student groups' nuclear option. I think you're already aware of the specifics, phaa, phaa, phaa. I've got a final card to play in this hand. **THIS IS WHAT I'VE GOT!**

Like a football player panting for breath beneath bulky protective padding, he removed the sheet that covered his bulging chest. He was straining his whole body, using his chin to indicate something on his swollen belly. For a moment, I wondered, *Is that where they've hidden the completed A-bomb?!* and then panic seized my mind: perhaps at any minute an uncontainable amount of poison gas might spew out, enveloping all of Tokyo! . . . The tanker trader in the meantime had evidently decoded the Patron's mysterious and belabored chin signals; he rose from his position, and began swaggering around the bed. The metal rod in his hand accidently smacked the wall near the bed, and he let out a sound of contrition and placed it on the floor. He leaned his knees against the bed and slipped his arms under the sheet, working them as though operating the plates of an old-fashioned draped studio camera. The eyebrows on his sour face worked feverishly, his lips puckering like hardened cysts. And from the abdomen of the dying Patron, as if delivering a baby from an **OLD PREGNANT WOMAN,** he pulled out a stuffed round deerskin Boston bag!

—— . . . **HERE'S FIVE HUNDRED MILLION IN CASH.** I want you to take this and work out some sort of deal with the student groups, a merger of their A-bomb factories. Buy off one of the parties and force them to merge with the other party. Or, strengthen one group and force the other to dismantle its operations. Do it. I don't care how. If they pool resources and become one party, with their combined facilities and fissionables, they could turn out an A-bomb in four to five weeks. . . . And at that point, the National Security Chief and I **WILL ROUND UP THOSE NUCLEAR BOOTLEGGERS IN ONE BIG RAID!**

I was stunned, but my eyes were still fixed on the Patron's flat belly. I began to laugh. I laughed and laughed, so hard I almost fell out of the chair. Given what'd happened, how could I contain myself? After such a long, hard struggle, we'd finally caught up with the enemy, an **OLD PREGNANT WOMAN.** Had a demon been delivered into the world? Would it bring disaster to humankind? What'd come out was a five hundred million yen payoff. **HOW COULD I CONTAIN MY LAUGHTER?!**

2

——The reason I'm appointing you to carry out this plan is because you laughed, not caring who you were with, or where you were; and because you're basically a buffoon. The Patron's mockery was very evident as he peered into my face, dull red eyes gleaming. Your case was different from mine. Your exposure to radiation sounds like farce whereas I was exposed to the real thing in Hiroshima. . . . This isn't the time or place for a lecture, but you're laughing your head off in front of an old man who's just found out he's going to die of cancer.

——I'm sorry, I apologized, but again burst out laughing at the sight of the Patron's belly, flat as a pancake.

——How's this for a plan: A clown like you, . . . a *former* thirty-eighty-year-old who's been switched over to eighteen, along with his twenty-eight-year-old son, a *former* eight-year-old; a clown who says he's working for the good of humankind. . . . Even if the police find out about the money, they won't connect me with it. The Patron began to elaborate on his scheme, not to me, but to the tanker dealer, who no doubt had furnished the five hundred million. Once again, I sensed his hulking presence behind Mori and me. Here you are, at this very important moment, to carry out your job; what a sight in that weird costume, phaa, phaa, phaa.

When I finally got myself under control, the Patron seemed to take up where I'd left off, his laughter drowning in the foamy spittle spewing from his mouth. I noticed his wrinkled eyelids had closed, and the palms of his hands, those large-boned hands with long slender fingers pressed together in prayer, lay quietly on his flat belly. Unsure of what he was doing, I continued to watch the Patron's inflamed nostrils, the dentures gleaming through his half-open mouth, and the soundless laughter endlessly bubbling up from around his large ears. In this foamy laughter I saw something utterly detestable: he was making fun not only of Mori's and my costumes but also everything he'd ever experienced, every person or thing he'd ever encountered in his life. Laughing was now the furthest thing from my mind.

——You're about to provide the police's vast search network with information which should enable them to confiscate two fully equipped plants and the necessary nuclear material for the manufacture of A-bombs; a group of top-notch physicists who went underground during the days of the student demonstrations, and five hundred million in cash. The mass media will call it the **BIGGEST NATIONAL CONSPIRACY IN POSTWAR HISTORY,** and the entire nation will be united in their hatred of underground subversive groups. And with all the hoopla, you'll be the public's savior! You have just crushed a conspiracy which would've given the country only two choices: a revolution by nuclear blackmail or the destruction of all Tokyo's inhabitants, including the Imperial *Family*. You'll enjoy a glorious death as a national hero, unrivaled in modern history, instead of the ugly, painful, and lonely death of cancer. . . . They'll give you a state funeral, the anniversary of your death will become a national holiday, pretty, innocent children will honor your memory with a song at the commemoration ceremony, and the Crown Princess will place a bouquet of chrysanthemums at the foot of your memorial. You'll become the **PATRON OF ALL THE JAPANESE PEOPLE**. The image of you as a resolute hero for the nuclear age will spread among all the peoples of the world. . . .

It was all in vain; my words were sucked into the bubbling vortex of the Patron's foamy laughter. Below the window, the party of clowns finally began their celebration in honor of the departed spirit—or was it an exorcism to chase out a spirit?—At any rate a truly rowdy shindig was in the making. Even after I fell silent, the Patron's praying hands—which he'd moved from his belly to his chest—remained so absolutely still that I thought he'd fallen asleep despite all the merry-making outside. However, he pushed out a fleck of foam from the corner of his mouth, and said in the same almost inaudible voice he'd used when he touched his white tongue against the back of his denture,

——Well, will you do it? I don't think the party's fundraisers would object to you taking a fifty-million-yen fee, phaa, phaa, phaa. That's the usual practice in our circles, phaa, phaa, phaa.

This last strangled bit of laughter really provoked me; I thought to myself. *Okay, we'll take the job! If he'd remained an* **OLD PREGNANT WOMAN,** *I'd have shied away from anything to do with his scheme; I'd have felt extremely guilty about lending him a hand in fulfilling his ambition. But what had come out of that swollen belly was after all, despite its staggering amount, nothing but money. What a joke. We'll accept the challenge and find out what's to happen in the afterlife. Because in the end, the switchover pair's time is at hand anyway. This old man here, dying of cancer, will see to it that his private nuclear development plan is destroyed, and he will die in glory. But that's not the end of it. Now, in addition to my great expertise as an engineer the switchover pair has access to vast funds! Since our switchover took place through the power of the Cosmic Will, doesn't it make perfect sense for us to use these resources to develop the power of a nuclear explosion, humankind's only comparable power source on a cosmic scale?*

... These thoughts were interrupted when Mori's right hand once again began to apply tremendous pressure to my wrist. The pain was unbearable; I tried to twist my hand free, but the power of his steely arm wouldn't allow it. I began to groan from the pain, *Wooo,* and Mori in turn replied with his own *wooo, wooo* as the pressure on my wrist gradually increased.

The pain was driving me mad, propelling me all the way back to the memory of my very first pain. As a toddler, after I realized I could do anything with my right hand—I also realized I could do anything with my left hand as well—I accordingly let the two hands fight it out for control of my body. My mother found me with bloodied hands, so she tied each hand separately to a wooden pillar in the kitchen. *Has my whole life been left up in the air, suspended in space and time, because I wasn't given the chance to let my hands have it out?* I let out a loud moan at this discovery.

The Patron's eyes were slightly open, crimson red with an excitement born of impatience; a look of ridicule replaced the red gleam as he awaited my answer, it said: Knuckle under. What other life do you have other than one as my errand boy? At any rate I shouted my reply—to the Cosmic Will or to the Patron, I wasn't sure,

——**I'LL DO IT!** Throwing my head back, I kicked off from the side of the bed, and backdived to the rear of the room! Struggling to free myself from the tanker dealer's crotch where my head had scored a direct hit, I was about to execute another head-on attack on his crotch. That was when I saw Mori arouse himself to a beautiful fight. He stood up and let go of my wrist in one fluid motion, grabbed his metal staff off the floor, and began blindly striking at the Patron. In the next instant the courageous superman Mori smashed out the window with the now bloodied staff, snatched at the Boston bag with five hundred million yen in it, and, with the two secretaries hot on his tail, leapt out the shattered window! I plastered myself to the tanker dealer, my awesome wrestling opponent, in a feeble effort to prevent him from rescuing the Patron. I was trembling with pride and excitement. I'd raised Mori and kept him alive just to witness this one brief moment of gallantry! I was proud of Mori, as only a father would be. I began to scream till my chest and throat felt they'd burst, *GO, GO, GO, GO, GO, GO, GO, GO!* On and on, I screamed, *GO, GO, GO, GO, GO, GO, GO, GO!*

The next thing I knew, the tanker dealer had kicked me with such force that I keeled over onto a pile of glass shards near the window. I tried to get to my feet. I saw the cart burst into flames in the center of the space opened up by the exuberant crowd. The clowns, every one of them, were sloshing kerosene on the fire from bottles they'd hidden under their costumes. There was Mori running toward the raging fireball, the riot squad in pursuit. In the midst of the shouting crowd I saw his steely arm swinging the half-open Boston bag in a wide arc. With streams of his caramel-colored hair dancing in the wind, he vaulted over the fence around the cart and right into the blaze! For a second the diving body floated in midair while the scattered paper money and strands of hair ignited in the heat of the conflagration. Leaning against the shoulder of the tanker dealer stood the Patron, dead, mouth wide open in a silent scream, his ultimate ambition reduced to ashes. And my Mori burned on. Knocked down again onto the pile of glass shards, and pinned to the floor by the police, I bawled my head off like a bloodied newborn babe, *GO, GO, GO, GO, GO, GO, GO, GO!*

Michiko Niikuni Wilson was born and raised in Japan, and studied in the United States for her B.A. in English, and received her M.A. and Ph.D. in Comparative Literature from the University of Texas at Austin. She teaches Japanese language, literature, and culture at the University of Virginia. Her interests cover a wide range of topics, including feminist literary criticism and cross-cultural communications. She has written many articles on modern Japanese literature, and is the author of *The Marginal World of Ōe Kenzaburo: A Study in Themes and Techniques* (M.E. Sharpe, 1986).

Michael K. Wilson graduated from the University of Texas at Austin where he majored in Asian Studies with an area concentration on Japan and China and also pursued graduate study in Comparative Literature and Education. Besides modern Japanese and Chinese literatures and cultures, his interests range from Latin American literature to environmental issues. He is an information specialist at the University of Virginia Health Sciences Center, and a freelance editor and translator.